SEX ROLE
RESEARCH

SEX ROLE RESEARCH

Measuring Social Change

edited by

Barbara L. Richardson **Jeana Wirtenberg**

PRAEGER

PRAEGER SPECIAL STUDIES • PRAEGER SCIENTIFIC

Library of Congress Cataloging in Publication Data

Main entry under title:

Sex role research.

Bibliography: p.
Includes index.
1. Sex role—Research.   2. Social change—Research.
3. Sociology—Research.   I. Richardson, Barbara L.
II. Wirtenberg, Jeana.
HQ1075.S488 1983   305.3'07'2   83-2426
ISBN 0-03-063149-1

This book is dedicated to current and future generations of research scholars.

Published in 1983 by Praeger Publishers
CBS Educational and Professional Publishing
A Division of CBS, Inc.
521 Fifth Avenue, New York, New York 10175 U.S.A.

© 1983 by Praeger Publishers

All rights reserved

3456789   052   987654321
Printed in the United States of America
on acid-free paper.

List of Contributors

Dr. Naida Tushnet Bagenstos
Senior Research Associate
National Institute of Education
Washington, D.C.

Dr. Carole Beere
Department of Psychology
Central Michigan University
Mount Pleasant, Michigan

Dr. Robert Boruch
Psychology Department
Northwestern University
Illinois

Dr. Patricia Campbell
Campbell-Kibler Associates
Groton, Massachusetts

Dr. David Gardner
Department of Educational
 Administration
School of Education
Hofstra University
Hempstead, New York

Dr. Carol Gilligan
Center for Moral Education
Harvard University
Cambridge, Massachusetts

Dr. Carol Nagy Jacklin
Psychology Department
Stanford University
Stanford, California

Dr. Gregg B. Jackson
721 Upshur Street NW
Washington, D.C.

Dr. Debra R. Kaufman
Sociology Department
Northeastern University
Boston, Massachusetts

Mary Ann Millsap
Research Associate
National Institute of Education
Washington, D.C.

Dr. Barbara L. Richardson
Research Associate
National Institute of Education
Washington, D.C.

Dr. Evelyn R. Rosenthal
Sociology Department
State University of New York
 at Binghamton
New York

Dr. Charol Shakeshaft
Department of Educational
    Administration
School of Education
Hofstra University
Hempstead, New York

Dr. Reesa M. Vaughter
Department of Psychology
Fordham University
Bronx, New York

Dr. Barbara Strudler Wallston
Vanderbilt University
Nashville, Tennessee

Dr. Jeana Wirtenberg
Research Associate
National Institute of Education
Washington, D.C.

Preface

For many decades research scholars have been studying, analyzing, and theorizing about important issues of social concern. The 70s saw a burgeoning of attempts to transform rhetoric about sex roles and related social changes into science, by systematically addressing controversial questions of great social import. Not surprisingly, many of those who sought the opportunity to undertake research in this area were motivated by their personal commitment to the issues. Many were not professionally trained in social science research disciplines. Too often, therefore, the methods they used in their research were inadequate to provide sound answers to their questions or strong empirical backing for their hypotheses and claims. Since the complexity of genuine social issues usually challenges the outer limits of technical research capability, it is particularly important that researchers be equipped to use the most sophisticated techniques. Where well-developed models from social science have been applied to these problems, the difference in the power of the analysis has been striking.

The establishment and maintenance of high technical standards is all the more important for research intended to form a basis for social policy decisions. For in that case, errors and misinterpretations can have real consequences that go far beyond the boundaries of scholarly journals and academic communities. Technical inadequacies devalue our investments in research, leave issues uncertain that could have been decided, and open the research to charges of biased interpretation from either side of a controversy. Clearly, the importance and significance of research questions should not become an excuse for lowering technical standards; quite the contrary.

Yet, even the most technically sophisticated researchers also may have shortcomings in addressing significant social research questions. While they may have the technical expertise to answer the questions, they may not know what the questions are, or what the relevant variables are, as they are perceived by the persons most concerned. Obviously, research must ask the right questions and attend to the right possible explanatory variables if it is to be accepted as meaningful. Technical experts, too, are often tempted to research technically tractable questions and to avoid the awkward complexity of socially significant questions.

Then, too, there is no such thing as a neutral, uninvolved technical expert in researching socially significant issues. Involvement and "bias" may be more or less obvious, more or less overt, and more or less acknowledged. It is always there. If research is to be accepted by and useful to the persons most directly concerned, it is vital that the researchers be perceived as having the best interest of those people at heart. Thus, the personal involvement of researchers in social issues is not the problem; the problem is their access to the most effective research tools and to guidance in applying those tools effectively.

We realized these general points about research on social issues during our experience at the National Institute of Education with a number of grants competitions focused on understanding women's entry into nontraditional fields of study and occupations. The researchers seeking funding for research on women's involvement in mathematics, science, and technology brought a wide variety of backgrounds, training and priorities to their proposed investigations. A typical researcher might be, for example, a woman chemist actively involved in encouraging young women to enter her field or a biological scientist concerned about his daughter's future opportunities. For many investigators the measurement of attitudes, interests, and motivations is a novel problem. The complex web of interwoven putative "causal" variables common to the social sciences would not yield to the familiar experimental scientific methods. While many investigators were knowledgeable experts in their respective fields, it was also clear that they could benefit from familiarity with the technical advances achieved in the social science research disciplines. Because the methods that would be helpful in research on sex roles most often were developed and used to investigate very different topics, they could be difficult for the novice investigator to identify and learn about.

This book is the result of our efforts to make outstanding research efforts a more common occurrence, to enhance the return on society's investment in research, and to increase the benefits of social research for the persons most directly affected by hastening the development of improved understanding. At my request, Jeana Wirtenberg and Barbara L. Richardson undertook a two-year effort to improve the quality of research methods in the social-processes/women's research area. Several strategies were employed.

The editors and other NIE staff gave very careful consideration to methodological problems that had been noted in previous projects and proposals. They pooled their own considerable knowledge and conducted computer and library searches toward this goal. In December 1980 the institute held a conference on "Attitudinal and Behavioral Measurement in Social Processes/Women's Research" at which twelve leading scholars were invited to present papers on various aspects of the topic. Several of these papers appear in this volume. Combining the insights provided by this conference with their own background research efforts, the editors commissioned six papers on specific methodological issues in sex roles and social change research that had been identified as serious problem areas in NIE funded research. The selected authors have outstanding reputations as scholars who have contributed to the integration of sex role research and research methods. In July 1981 these authors met to present the highlights of their reviews to the institute and to critique each other's analyses. These papers were prepared to bring relevant methods to the attention of persons interested in research on women's issues; at the same time they helped identify the relevant research communities that could help with the methodological problems of the research. Obviously, collaboration among persons with different expertise is often the best answer to the complex demands of research on social issues.

Our intention is that persons interested in research on other, comparable social issues will profit from these papers also. For example, research on minorities and mathematics education presents many of the same methodological problems as research on women and mathematics, even though the causes of the problem—and thus the outcome of the research—may be quite different. One of the key lessons to be taken from these papers is that research does not have to be on your own topic to be relevant and useful to you in your research endeavors.

Sex Role Research: Measuring Social Change should be welcomed by teachers and researchers working in the field of social measurement and sex roles research. It was intended to be an appropriate textbook for use in advanced graduate-level courses in education, psychology, sociology, social work, business school courses in marketing behavior, women's studies, measurement and statistics, research methods, evaluation, as well as for all researchers in the social and behavioral sciences. It is designed to familiarize researchers, from an array of backgrounds, with a wide range of research methods and to guide their selection and application of the best analytical tools and techniques for their research purposes.

Susan Chipman

Assistant Director for
Learning and Development,
National Institute of Education,
Washington, D.C.

Acknowledgments

This book was developed under difficult and changing circumstances for research related to women. Started at a time when sex equity was a high priority, it was completed in a far less certain climate, by two of the members of the former Social Processes/Women's Research team—Jeana Wirtenberg, Team Leader, and Barbara Richardson. When the project started, two people at NIE were instrumental in identifying the need for work in this area and helped to provide the resources necessary to bring it together: Dr. Susan Chipman, Assistant Director for Learning and Development, who wrote the preface, and Dr. Lois-ellin Datta, former Associate Director of the Teaching and Learning Program. We also appreciate the support and encouragement we received from our other colleagues on the Social Process/Women's Research Team. Dr. Sue Klein helped us keep abreast of ongoing developments and networks of individuals throughout the sex equity field. Dr. Veronica Thomas assisted us in conducting our background research on current methodological issues. We also were fortunate to have reviewers both within and outside NIE who were willing to give generously of their time and technical assistance. We have learned a great deal from our authors and each other throughout this collaboration. We look forward to a climate in which our research will continue to flourish, and make a difference in the quality of our lives.

Barbara L. Richardson, Ph.D. and Jeana Wirtenberg, Ph.D.

Contents

List of Contributors v

Preface by Susan Chipman vii

Acknowledgments x

PART I: INTRODUCTION

1 Introduction 3
Jeana Wirtenberg and Barbara L. Richardson

PART II: CONTEXTUAL AND CONCEPTUAL ISSUES IN THE STUDY OF SEX ROLES AND SOCIAL CHANGE

2 New Maps of Development: New Visions of Maturity 17
Carol Gilligan

3 Social Science Inquiries into Female Achievement:
Recurrent Methodological Problems 33
Barbara L. Richardson and Debra R. Kaufman

PART III: OVERVIEW OF RESEARCH METHODS IN SEX ROLES AND SOCIAL CHANGE

4 Overview of Research Methods 51
Barbara Strudler Wallston

5 Evaluation Issues in Women's Studies 77
Naida Tushnet Bagenstos and Mary Ann Millsap

6 Methodological Issues in the Study of
Sex-Related Differences 93
Carol Nagy Jacklin

PART IV: SAMPLING AND MEASUREMENT

7 Sampling: Issues and Problems in Sex Role
and Social Change Research 103
Charol Shakeshaft and David W. Gardner

8 Instruments and Measures in a
Changing, Diverse Society 113
Carole A. Beere

9 All Things Being Equal, a Behavior Is Superior to an Attitude: Studies of Sex-Typed and Sex-Biased Attitudes and Behaviors 139
   Reesa M. Vaughter

PART V: ANALYSIS AND INFERENCE

10 Statistical Analysis in Sex Roles and Social Change 153
   Evelyn R. Rosenthal

11 Methods for Integrative Reviews 173
   Gregg B. Jackson

12 The Impact of Societal Biases on Research Methods 197
   Patricia B. Campbell

13 Causal Models: Their Import and Their Triviality 215
   Robert F. Boruch

PART VI: CONCLUSION

14 Conclusion 251
   Barbara L. Richardson and Jeana Wirtenberg

Index 265

About the Editors 273

PART I

INTRODUCTION

1

Introduction

*Jeana Wirtenberg
and
Barbara L. Richardson*

The 1970s were a period of rapid social change in general, and in the area of sex roles in particular. Dramatic changes were seen in many of our fundamental institutions—from education, to employment, to health care. In the area of sex roles, we saw shifts in patterns related to women's participation in the labor force, smaller family size, expanded rates of maternal employment, increased divorce rates, increased proportions of women who were heading households, and increases in dual wage-earner families. These demographic trends were accompanied by a reexamination of our laws, attitudes, and norms governing almost every aspect of women's lives. This transition in sex roles continues to foster profound changes in all aspects of our society, from child-care arrangements to flexible work hours and job sharing, to changes in patterns of automobile and public transit use (Tangri and Wirtenberg 1981). More recently, the rapidity of the developments of the last decade has occasioned a backlash, or an attempt to return society to a version of the status quo ante.

The rate of social change and the associated complexities of understanding, measuring, and predicting relationships among variables during such times provided the impetus for this volume. The study of sex roles and social change is no different from the study of any other real-world phenomena involving sociohistorical-political and individual life changes. Although the methodological problems discussed in this volume are certainly

---

No official support or endorsement by the National Institute of Education or the Department of Education of the views expressed herein is intended or should be inferred.

not unique to the study of women or sex roles, they may be more acute. As Abigail Stewart and Marjorie Platt point out in their recent volume *Studying Women in a Changing World* (1982), the average rate of individual change is higher in women's lives than in men's lives. That is, over the life course, the average woman experiences more role changes (gains and losses, for example, of work and family roles) than does the average man, and the average woman also experiences more variability in the roles she takes on (e.g., part-time, full-time, no paid employment) than does the average man.

These rapid social changes have also created the desire on the part of researchers to keep pace, by being creative and flexible in their conceptualizations, theories, and methodologies. For example, in studying the prevalence of the construct of fear of success (FOS) in the population, researchers found that its nature and prevalence was changing even as it was being studied. Were people actually becoming less fearful of success, or were they merely becoming more familiar with the cues that were used to stimulate this fear-of-success construct? Studies which purported to find that this was primarily a female problem were quickly outdated by studies which showed a comparable proportion of males with this fear. As discussed further in this volume, it is a serious methodological challenge to separate genuine social change from possible artifacts of our limited measurement techniques.

The study of any changing phenomenon is difficult for a number of reasons. Stewart and Platt (1982) have identified some of the key issues. It is difficult to distinguish between personal life-cycle changes and simultaneously occurring social, political, and historical changes. Information that was gathered at a particular point in history cannot help but be affected by the intellectual sets, paradigms, and assumptions that were prevalent at that point in time. The same information, when gathered at another point in time may have very different meaning in a new sociocultural, political milieu. Information gathered from different age cohorts at the same point in time must take into account the ways in which their experiences have been affected by generational differences in demographics, economics, and related social and political realities. It is often difficult to determine the best time interval for studying a given change, or the strategy for sampling multiple observations (cf., Shakeshaft and Gardner, Chapter 7; Rosenthal, Chapter 10; Boruch, Chapter 13, in this volume). A related question is how far back we should go in data analysis for the findings to be useful to the present. As several of our authors point out, in sex role research there are often real limitations on how far you can go back—given the practice of excluding females in many early research samples (Campbell, Chapter 12; Richardson and Kaufman, Chapter 3, in this volume). This problem is particularly important in determinations of the utility of secondary analyses on data collected in earlier periods. Data collected at different points in time may not be comparable due to the influence of different researchers, coding changes, item changes, or semantic changes. This issue receives more detailed attention in several of the chapters in the book (e.g., Vaughter, Chapter 9; Beere, Chapter 8).

Research in the area of sex roles and social change is often seen as value-laden or politically motivated. This reinforces the importance of our being clear and deliberate in our choice of methods while understanding the biases we inevitably bring to the research process. We need to remain alert to the potential pitfalls in our accustomed research methods. This volume encourages researchers to bring fresh perspectives to the questions they ask and the methods they use to go about answering them.

We attempt here not only to raise new questions but to question the theories and models from which we derive our questions. We know that there is a tendency to continue to use old models long after the accumulation of anomalies has provided overwhelming evidence that it is time to move on to something new and different.

Building on this premise, we point to the perspective provided in the recent book *Einstein's Space and Van Gogh's Sky: Physical Reality and Beyond,* by Lawrence Leshan and Henry Margenau (1982). This collaborative effort between a psychologist and a physicist provides fresh insights into the inherent limitations of social science methods. They stress the need to continually raise fundamental questions in every domain: e.g., What are the observables here? What kinds of measurements can we make? What law or laws relating to observables can we hypothesize and test? And even more fundamentally, what do the terms "space," "time," "state," "observer," mean in the specified domain? They quote physicist Percy Bridgman who wrote:

> It is difficult to conceive of anything more scientifically bigoted than to postulate that all possible experiences conform to the same type as that with which we are already familiar and therefore to demand that explanation use only elements already familiar in everyday experience. (Leshan and Margenau 1982, p. 139)

Important advances in methodology can and do emanate from a more phenomenological tradition, in which the observer, rather than being "outside" and independent of the observed phenomenon, steps into the equation. That is, the perspective of the observer is intertwined with the phenomenon. Nor does our research have objective characteristics independent of the observer's values, biases, perspective, and methods. Thus, rather than seeking a "universal truth," we can start with the assumption that there are multiple truths, each of which can start with the assumption that there are multiple truths, each of which can be revealed by a shift in perspective, method, or purpose. "Since reality is knowable in an infinite number of ways, many equally valid descriptions are possible. The choice among them depends on the purposes of the investigator and the focus of the investigation" (Mishler

1979, p. 10). One common theme of this volume is the importance most authors place on articulating their own values and integrating multiple methods and perspectives.

A great deal has been written and attention focused of late on the importance of "context." In his article "Meaning in Context: Is there any other kind?", Elliot Mishler argues that the importance of context has been largely ignored by traditional research approaches in the social and behavioral sciences (Mishler 1979). As a result, Mishler asserts that in the social and psychological sciences there is a "crisis of confidence" among investigators, who continue to discover that research findings appear to be context-dependent. The problem seems to be that we continue to look for general, universal laws that are "context independent," even though we realize from our ordinary commonsense experience that human behavior is necessarily and intrinsically context-dependent.

Gergen (1973) has set off another continuing debate in social psychology by arguing that the laws found in both experimental and field studies are bound to their historical contexts. Similarly, Bronfenbrenner's (1977) critique of research in developmental psychology demonstrates that well-accepted findings on cognitive and social development are context-specific. For example, patterns of parent-child interaction are substantially different in the laboratory and in the home. Classroom research has also come under criticism for limiting the focus to short-run events and a limited range of meanings, while ignoring information on wider social and personal contexts (Mishler 1979).

These philosophical issues on the nature of social science inquiry form the backdrop for this volume on research methods and the measurement of social change. These broader concerns are reflected in our methodological analyses in various ways—in the controversy surrounding the use of quantitative versus qualitative measures, and the strengths and weaknesses of specific alternative approaches; in critiques of how to go about measuring hypothetical constructs; and in analyses of how to draw inferences from restricted samples. Useful resolutions of these, and related concerns, are suggested in several papers (cf. Wallston, Chapter 4; Beere, Chapter 8; Jackson, Chapter 11; Boruch, Chapter 13).

These broad issues are the frame for the specific concerns that provided the impetus for this volume—enhancing the quality of research methods in the study of sex roles and social change. We have organized the book into four parts. The first part presents the contextual and conceptual issues that are fundamental to the study of sex roles and social change. The second part presents an overview of the research methods that can be used in this research. The third section presents issues which are specific to sampling and measurement problems. The last section before the conclusion presents issues related to analysis and inference, and in particular raises questions related to causality and social change.

The remainder of this introduction and overview presents a description of each of the chapters of this volume. The conclusion is devoted to a review of the major issues which emerged from these chapters, and summarizes the major recommendations.

SUMMARY AND OVERVIEW OF CHAPTERS

In Part II we attempt to put the common methodological problems in sex role research into context. Each of the articles that we have included in this introductory set of chapters explores the relationship between the biases and assumptions of researchers and the resulting interpretation of their findings. They emphasize that human values, as well as scientific validity, contribute to the formulation and evaluation of what constitutes theoretically "interesting" or "powerful" research questions.

In the lead article in this section, Harvard psychologist Carol Gilligan addresses the difficulties in applying constructs derived from research on men to the interpretation of women's experience and thought. She argues that the failure to recognize the difference in men's and women's understanding of relationships poses a problem of measurement and interpretation. In particular, she seeks to understand more about the subjects of morality and the ways that women think. She shows that the lives of women call into question current thinking about human development, and can create the impetus for a new, more positive vision of human growth.

Gilligan's chapter illustrates the way in which the problem of interpretation arises when assessing female developmental stages. Girls' moral judgments could be considered a full stage lower in maturity than boys' when evaluated in traditional moral development theory. But seen in another light, Gilligan suggests that girls' views of morality contain the insights central to an ethic of care, and nonviolent conflict resolution.

Gilligan's research, it should be noted, uses a very small sample size, in a clinical research model, to draw conclusions about the differences between males' and females' constructions of reality. At the same time that Gilligan generates new insights from this clinical approach, her research methods raise familiar questions about the utility of small samples and the limits they create.

Barbara Richardson and Debra Kaufman make a parallel case for the reconceptualization and recontextualization of another important body of literature in sex roles and social change: in the area of achievement. Richardson and Kaufman point out once again that most contemporary achievement theories are predicated on the assumption that men's lives and experiences are the norm. In their paper they trace the impact of a growing awakening of consicousness about women in the disciplines, through the changing methodological approaches brought to the study of women's achievements. In chronicling the history of the gradual infusion of women into the research literature on achievement, Richardson and Kaufman show the resistance that researchers confront when they expose systematic biases which have shaped and maintained whole bodies of literature. They also demonstrate the reluctance of traditional disciplines to revise popular models even in the face of overwhelming empirical anomalies (Kaufman and Richardson 1982).

Another recurrent theoretical concern they raise is that constructs are best understood within a broad sociopolitical context, rather than through narrow definitions of statistical validity alone. Thus, while female achievement behavior can be studied in laboratory settings, it is better examined in relation to the daily structural realities of the educational and occupational institutions where women actually work and achieve.

In Richardson and Kaufman's discussion of the literature on the motive to avoid success, they point to several trends in the research on sex roles in general. One is a movement outward from individual explanations and interpretations toward more socially based variables and formulations. A related tendency is the move toward multilevel, interdisciplinary research designs, which is characteristic not only of sex roles research but of social-change research in general.

Finally, research designs have not taken into account the variability of achievement behavior over time; instead they are presumed to be in a stable steady state at all times. Richardson and Kaufman describe the need for an examination of achievement across age groups and life stages. The overall thrust is toward a research paradigm for female achievement that looks beyond experimental definitions to women's life experiences in the family, career, and elsewhere, in their full socio-historical-political context.

In summary, in Part II we begin with papers highlighting the interdependency of values, scientific constructs, research questions and interpretation. We see, in Gilligan and Richardson and Kaufman's chapters, illustrations of how gender may stimulate revisions of our measures and inferences in two diverse but prototypical domains—moral development and achievement behavior. We are reminded in their reviews that not only do our values and our gender affect our understandings but they do so in a complex web of dynamic social relationships. The conclusions our authors draw after reviewing the most current and popular research approaches in the field is that our methods are only beginning to tap the wealth of possible information available.

Following this discussion of constructs, concepts, and inference in the area of sex roles and social change, Part III moves directly into the research methods themselves. Barbara Wallston presents an overview of the full range of methodologies in use today. She illustrates her analysis of the appropriateness of various popular methods with reference to current research studies. By pointing out the strengths and weaknesses of an array of approaches,

Wallston hopes to help researchers to "break set," to move away from repeated reliance on a few familiar methods, and to expand their repertoires.

The designs which are discussed include "true" experiments (i.e., random assignment to treatment groups), quasi-experiments, correlational studies with prospective/longitudinal designs and ethnographic/qualitative research strategies. A variety of measurement techniques are described that can be used in conjunction with a range of designs: observation, survey/interview/ questionnaire, historical/archival and ecological methods.

Wallston argues that no one method is intrinsically superior in and of itself. Methods must always be judged in relation to the questions being asked, the state of knowledge in the field, and the practical aspects of undertaking the research. "The best design represents a compromise between the research goal and the possibilities afforded by the situation." Furthermore, despite the frequent association of feminist scholarship with calls for more qualitative research, Wallston rightly points out in Chapter 4 that "no method is inherently feminist and methods should be viewed as tools to answer or generate questions." As Wallston demonstrates, sex role researchers should examine the advantages and disadvantages of methods and designs in relation to their particular research inquiry.

Another new and significant method for studying sex roles and social change is the burgeoning field of evaluation research. Naida Tushnet Bagenstos and Mary Ann Millsap synthesize the current issues and illustrate the potential applications by reviewing the use of evaluation in women's studies programs over the past decade. Unlike research that is designed primarily for the advancement of knowledge, evaluation is designed for decision making. Because of this, people involved with evaluation techniques need to be especially aware of both methodological and political issues as well as the biases and values they bring to their study. Evaluation provides information on the extent to which programs are attaining their objective, on where strengths and weaknesses are, and on what areas require improvement. Bagenstos and Millsap describe a variety of approaches to program evaluation, each with a different purpose and methodology. They compare the advantages and disadvantages of each from the perspective of the user and the researcher.

In Part III we move from Wallston's broad coverage of various designs and methods, to Bagenstos and Millsap's narrower coverage of evaluation methods, to the final chapter in this section on methodological issues that are specific to the study of sex-related differences. Drawing on her extensive familiarity with sex-difference research, Carol Nagy Jacklin identifies ten critical analytic issues in the study of gender development that commonly jeopardize the validity of inferences made in the published literature. One is the conceptualization of the very term "difference," which implies a contrast that may or may not be meaningful to the population as a whole. She argues that we are also often misled by the generalizations from published research literature because there is a tendency to publish and cite only positive findings, i.e., sex differences rather than sex similarities which would be indicated by negative findings. Jacklin concludes that as fewer variables are confounded with sex, sex will account for a smaller percentage of the variance and researchers will begin trying to explain the far greater variance found between individuals within other types of groups.

In Part IV we move away from the general overview of methods and their attendant problems to the specific arena of research methodology concerned with sampling and measurement. In three chapters we cover issues and problems in sampling, instruments and measures, the utility of using psychometric scales in sex roles research, and the relationship between sex-role related attitudes and behaviors.

In their chapter on sampling, Charol Shakeshaft and David Gardner identify four particular weaknesses that have been found in the sampling designs of social research and offer suggestions for dealing with these problems. The four sampling issues discussed all relate to the problem of generalizing from a sample to a larger population. Sampling is a particularly salient issue to researchers studying social processes, since very little can be accomplished until the sample is defined and even less can be said vis-à-vis the larger world if the sample is inadequate. The difficulty lies in selecting a sample that is both economical and representative of the population to which the results of the inquiry are to be generalized.

From sampling issues we move into the problems associated with maintaining the validity of our instruments and measures in a changing, diverse society. Carole Beere presents a number of problems associated with measures utilized in gender-related research. She argues that measures which may have been shown to have adequate reliability and validity at one point in time may not remain valid. In sex role research, many measures that originally were thought reliable and valid for one population are not being questioned or revised as they are used in new groups and situations. Beere also emphasizes the need for sex role scales appropriate to different age groups. The newer and older sex role scales were developed across several decades. They differ in the ways in which they were developed, the assumptions made about age-related variables, the relationship between masculinity and femininity, and the types of items included on the scales. Thus, Beere advises researchers who locate existing measures for their investigations to be careful to ensure that the measures are reliable and valid at the time they are to be used and to examine the relevance of the criteria used for the group of respondents whom they will be studying.

Beere points to the strengths and weaknesses of widely used scales purporting to measure attitudes toward gender-related issues. She is particularly critical of scales with totally unknown psychometric properties, which unfortunately represents a too-frequent occurrence in the field. Another pervasive problem in measuring sex role attitudes is the impact of social desirability bias, or the potential for faking. The question here is not only whether the expressed attitudes are valid, but also whether they have any relationship to the respondents' behaviors.

Reesa M. Vaughter's chapter provides an in-depth examination of the relationship between sex role attitudes and behaviors. Within the broad domain of sex roles, Vaughter focuses on three types of attitudinal measures: measures of gender identity, sex stereotypes, and beliefs about the appropriate social roles for women and men. She asks the question: To what extent do attitude questionnaire data predict sex-typed and sex-biased behaviors?

According to Vaughter, a functional, predictive relationship has been demonstrated between gender identity and *sex-typed behavior*. That is, it has been shown that people who describe themselves as masculine tend to behave in a masculine-typed manner, and similarly for feminine and androgynous individuals.

There is considerably less clarity about the relationship between gender identity and *sex-biased behaviors*. The popular hypothesis that people who are more sex-typed (i.e., the feminine female and the masculine male) will be more sex-biased, has not been empirically supported, according to Vaughter's synthesis of the literature.

A more widely studied relationship is that between peoples' attitudes toward social roles of women and men and their sex-typed behaviors. Clearly, it is of interest to know if those espousing egalitarian attitudes behave in a manner consistent with their ideology. Vaughter reports findings that self-esteem may be a better predictor of women's propensity to engage in traditionally sex-inappropriate but situationally appropriate and self-enhancing behaviors.

In considering the conceptual and methodological issues that could clarify the relationship between attitudes and behavior, Russell Weigel (1983), a participant in the NIE conference on the subject, identified three types of issues worthy of further attention: (1) methodological problems with past attitude-behavior research which could have exaggerated the inconsistencies involved, (2) the role of other variables which, when operative, could counteract and obscure the impact of attitudes on behavior and (3) the need to establish conceptually appropriate behavioral measures.

The problem of establishing a conceptually appropriate behavioral criterion, however critical, has not received much attention until recently. Weigel points out that there has been little conceptual clarity in research studies which attempt to predict a highly specific behavior, versus studies which attempt to predict broad patterns of action. That is, many instances of attitude-behavior inconsistency may be due to the fact that the attitudinal measure is very general, while the behavioral measure is highly specific. For example, subjects' general attitudes toward an entire social group may be utilized to predict behavior toward a particular representative of that group and within a single situational context. Weigel's review of studies in this area leads to the conclusion that more highly focused attitude measures will yield more accurate predictions of the occurrence of specific actions.

Several chapters in Part V, on analysis and inference, focus on the question of causality. Evelyn Rosenthal presents the major statistical techniques for analyzing large numbers of variables and suggests ways that these techniques can be most appropriately applied to the study of sex roles and social change. Gregg Jackson's chapter on "Methods for Integrative Reviews" discusses how to make appropriate inferences of generalizations about substantive issues from a set of studies directly bearing on those issues. Patricia Campbell's chapter analyzes "The Impact of Societal Biases on Research Methods," focusing in particular on the ways that biases affect the objectivity of our analyses and the inferences we draw from those analyses. The final chapter in Part V, "Causal Models: Their Import and Their Triviality" by Robert Boruch, focuses on particular methods that "are designed to make scientific speculation about cause and effect more orderly, coherent, verifiable." Here we briefly outline the major issues raised in each of these chapters.

Evelyn Rosenthal argues that with the wide availability of computers, problems in the analysis of large numbers of variables have shifted from computation to conceptualization. She criticizes researchers for failing to match their statistical analysis techniques to their research questions. Although this failure is not unique to researchers studying sex roles and social change issues, it seems particularly unfortunate, she notes, when "creative and flexible thought yielding exciting new research questions or reconceptualization of old questions is not matched with equally creative and flexible data analysis." Rosenthal focuses on the potential for data analysis strategies to bridge this gap. In so doing she argues explicitly for more *complex* data analysis strategies to address our complex research questions. Ironically, Rosenthal argues that more *complex* data analysis strategies allow for the use of *simpler* statistical models, which in turn are easier to interpret, and provide greater clarity in their explanations of complex phenomena. In her discussion of developing a data analysis plan, Rosenthal notes that regardless of how well we preplan, the data we collect are invariably "a mess"; we should expect them to be "incomplete, error-laden, loose approximations to social reality." The first steps of analysis therefore entail an exploration of the data to reveal the nature of the "mess" and adjustments to clean it up.

To encourage more creative theorizing as well as a better fit between data analysis techniques and research questions, Rosenthal describes several multivariate statistical methods, indicates research situations where each method is most usefully employed, notes the necessary assumptions made for each, and cites an example of each method in use. Even with careful conceptualization of the research questions, however, it is difficult to reveal the full complexity and dynamic quality of the data without equally complex and dynamic data analysis techniques. Rosenthal's chapter makes a significant contribution toward the successful integration of sophisticated theory with equally creative statistical techniques of analysis.

In the next chapter, Gregg Jackson addresses another important problem, that of drawing conclusions and generalizations across a class of studies bearing on the same or similar substantive issues. Jackson describes the lack of explicit methods for doing such integrative reviews, and comments on the need for better guidelines. He argues that in the virtual absence of standards for judging the quality of integrative reviews the accumulation of knowledge in any particular field, as represented in such reviews, is suspect at best, invalid at worst. Jackson's chapter not only describes the state of the art of integrative reviews, but provides concrete steps for improving the validity and usefulness of such syntheses.

In her review of the impact of societal biases on research methods, Patricia Campbell focuses on how bias has and is influencing the questions selected for research, the methods to conduct the research, and the research interpretations and conclusions that are drawn. Campbell uses Harmon's definition of bias: "a particular tendency or inclination which prevents reasonable, knowledgeable, or thoughtful consideration of a question" (see Chapter 12). She argues that people tend to be selective in their perceptions and interpretations of their research, and remain wedded to views with which they are comfortably familiar. As others have pointed out throughout this volume, neither research nor researchers are ever value-free or even value-neutral. Ultimately, the scientist is always conceptually inside the system or phenomena being studied. One's perception of reality must necessarily influence one's research methods, including topic selection, design and data analysis, sampling, measurement, and the generation of conclusions. The continuous challenge, from the scientific perspective, is to move beyond this fact of the human condition to continue the search for "truth."

In the final chapter of Part V, Robert Boruch brings us squarely back to the question of how to determine what causes what. The focus here is on structural equations, a class of causal models used to analyze numerical information usually generated from quasi-experiments and surveys. A structural model is a statistical equation representing a causal linkage among variables. Boruch points out that while this approach does not demonstrate that one variable causes another, it does help determine whether some causal linkages are consonant with the data. The process requires one to be explicit in laying out each causal equation, thus "fostering orderly thinking and opening the process to independent criticism." The process involves sequential testing and fitting in order to gradually develop a verifiable characterization of reality. The method has the disadvantage that it may give more mathematical legitimacy to data than is warranted.

The process involves specifying all causal linkages in a process, and translating those statements into statistical models. The variables, their sequence and placement in causal chains, their cause-effect and noncausal relations should all be based on adequate theory and evidence. The resulting system of equations then forms the basis for testing hypotheses about the causal linkages. Thus, in order to translate theory into workable statistical models the researcher must carefully think through the expected relationships among variables and the possible intervening factors impacting on their reliable estimation.

The issues we address throughout this volume are complex, both conceptually as well as technically. We encourage our readers to use the materials presented here to advance their own ability to think critically and creatively, while conducting the kinds of research that will add new dimensions to our understandings of the dynamics of sex roles and social change.

REFERENCES

Bronfenbrenner, V. Toward an experimental ecology of human development. *American Psychologist* 32 (1977): 513–31.

Gergen, K.J. Social psychology as history. *Journal of Personality and Social Psychology* 26 (1973): 309–20.

Kaufman, D., and B. Richardson. *Achievement and Women: Challenging the Assumptions.* New York: Free Press, 1982.

Leshan, L., and H. Margenau. *Einstein's space and Van Gogh's Sky: Physical reality and beyond.* New York: Macmillan, 1982.

Mishler, E.G. Meaning in context: Is there any other kind? *Harvard Educational Review* 49(1), (1979): 1–19.

Stewart, A., and M. Platt. Studying women in a changing world. *Journal of Social Issues* 38(1), (1982).

Tangri, S.S., and J. Wirtenberg. Women and the future. *Psychology of Women Quarterly* 6(1), (1981) (Special Issue).

Weigel, R. Behavioral implications of knowledge: Lessons from the attitude-behavior controversy. In S. Ward and L. Reed (eds.), *Knowledge structure and use: Implications for synthesis and interpretation.* Philadelphia: Temple University Press, 1983.

PART II

CONTEXTUAL AND CONCEPTUAL ISSUES IN THE STUDY OF SEX ROLES AND SOCIAL CHANGE

2

New Maps of Development: New Visions of Maturity

Carol Gilligan

That development is the aim of a liberal education seems clear until we begin to ask what is a liberal education and what constitutes development. The current spirit of reappraisal in the field of education stems in part from the fact that some old promises have failed and new practices must be found if the vision of education for freedom and for democracy is to be realized or sustained. But this current reappraisal in the field of education finds its parallel in the field of developmental psychology where a similar reassessment is taking place, a reassessment that began in the early 1970s when developmental psychologists began to question the adulthood that formerly they had taken for granted and when the exclusion of women from the research samples from which developmental theories were generated began to be noticed as a serious omission and one that pointed to the exclusion of other groups as well. Thus, if the changing population of students, particularly the larger number of adults and especially of adult women entering postsecondary education, has raised a series of questions about the aims of education and the nature of educational practice, the study of adulthood and of women has generated a new set of questions for theorists of human development.

To ask whether current developmental theories can be applied to understanding or assessing the lives of people who differ from those upon whose experience these theories were based, is only to introduce a problem of far greater magnitude, the adequacy of current theories themselves. The

---

This chapter is reprinted with permission from the *American Journal of Orthopsychiatry* (April 1982) pp. 199–211. Copyright 1982 by the American Orthopsychiatric Association, Inc.

answer to the initial question in one sense is clear, given that these theories are used repeatedly in assessing the development of different groups. But the question asked in such assessment is how much like the original group is the different group being assessed. For example, if the criteria for development are derived from studies of males and these criteria are then used to measure the development of females, the question being asked is how much like men do women develop. The assumption underlying this approach is that there is a universal standard of development and a single scale of measurement along which differences found can be aligned as higher and lower, better and worse. Yet, the initial exclusion of women displays the fallacy of this assumption and indicates a recognition of difference, pointing to the problem I wish to address. While I will use the experience of women to demonstrate how the group left out in the construction of theory calls attention to what is missing in its account, my interest lies not only in women and the perspective they add to the narrative of growth but also in the problem that differences pose for a liberal educational philosophy that strives toward an ideal of equality and for a developmental psychology that posits a universal and invariant sequence of growth. In joining the subjects of morality and women, I focus specifically on the questions of value inherent in education and in developmental psychology, and indicate how the lives of women call into question current maps of development and inform a new vision of human growth.

The repeated marking of women's experience as, in Freud's terms, "a dark continent for psychology"[5] raises a question as to what has shadowed the understanding of women's lives. Since women in fact do not live on a continent apart from men but instead repeatedly engage with them in the activities of everyday life, the mystery deepens and the suggestion emerges that theory may be blinding observation. While the disparity between women's experience and the representation of human development, noted throughout the psychological literature, has generally been seen to signify a problem in women's development, the failure of women to fit existing models of human growth may point to a problem in the representation, a limitation in the conception of the human condition, an omission of certain truths about life. The nature of these truths and their implications for understanding development and thinking about education are the subjects of this paper.

CONSTRUCTION OF RELATIONSHIPS AND THE CONCEPT OF MORALITY

Evidence of sex differences in the findings of psychological research comes mainly from studies that reveal the way in which men and women construct the relation between self and others. While the differences observed in women's experience and understanding of relationships have posed a problem of interpretation that recurs throughout the literature on psychoanalysis and personality psychology, this problem emerges with particular clarity in the field of moral judgment research. Since moral judgments pertain to conflicts in the relation of self to others, a difference in the construction of that relationship would lead to a difference in the conception of the moral domain. This difference would be manifest in the way in which moral problems are seen, in the questions asked which then serve to guide the judgment and resolution of moral dilemmas. While the failure to perceive this difference has led psychologists to apply constructs derived from research on men to the interpretation of women's experience and thought, the recognition of this difference points to the limitation of this approach. If women's moral judgments reflect a different understanding of social relationships, then they may point to a line of social development whose presence in both sexes is currently obscured.

THEORIES OF MORAL DEVELOPMENT

This discussion of moral development takes place against the background of a field where, beginning with Freud's theory that tied superego formation to castration anxiety, extending through Piaget's study of boys' conceptions of the rules of their games, and culminating in Kohlberg's derivation of six stages of moral development from research on adolescent males, the line of development has been shaped by the pattern of male experience and thought. The continual reliance on male experience to build the model of moral growth has been coupled with a continuity in the conception of morality itself. Freud's observation that "the first requisite of civilization is justice, the assurance that a rule once made will not be broken in favour of an individual,"[4] extends through Piaget's conception of morality as consisting in respect for rules[16] and into Kohlberg's claim that justice is the most adequate of moral ideals.[12] The imagery that runs through this equation of morality with justice depicts a world comprised of separate individuals whose claims fundamentally conflict but who find in morality a mode of regulating conflict by agreement that allows the development of life lived in common.

The notion that moral development witnesses the replacement of the rule of brute force with the rule of law, bringing isolated and endangered individuals into a tempered connection with one another, then leads to the observation that women, less aggressive and thus less preoccupied with rules, are as a result less morally developed. The recurrent observations of sex differences that mark the literature on moral development are striking not only in their concurrence but in their reiterative elaboration of a single theme. Whether expressed in the general statement that women show less sense of justice than men[5] or in the particular notion that girls, in contrast to boys, think it better to give back fewer blows than one has received,[16] the direction of these differences is always the same, pointing in women to a greater sense of connection, a concern with relationships more than with rules. But this observation then yields to the paradoxical conclusion that women's preoccupation with relationships constitutes an impediment to the progress of their moral development.

THE MORAL JUDGMENTS OF TWO ELEVEN-YEAR-OLDS

To illustrate how a difference in the understanding of relationships leads to a difference in the conceptions of morality and of self, I begin with the moral judgments of two 11-year-old children, a boy and a girl who see in the same dilemma two very different moral problems. Demonstrating how brightly current theory illuminates the line and the logic of the boy's thought while casting scant light on that of the girl, I will show how the girl's judgments reflect a fundamentally different approach. I have chosen for the purpose of this discussion a girl whose moral judgments elude current categories of developmental assessment, in order to highlight the problem of interpretation rather than to exemplify sex differences per se. My aim is to show how, by adding a new line of interpretation, it becomes possible to see development where previously development was not discerned and to consider differences in the understanding of relationships without lining up these differences on a scale from better to worse.

The two children—Amy and Jake—were in the same sixth grade class at school and participated in a study[8] designed to explore different conceptions of morality and self. The sample selected for study was chosen to focus the variables of gender and age while maximizing developmental potential by holding constant, at a high level, the factors of intelligence, education, and social class that have been associated with moral development, at least as measured by existing scale. The children in question were both bright and articulate and, at least in their 11-year-old aspirations, resisted easy categories of sex-role stereotyping since Amy aspired to become a scientist while Jake preferred English to math. Yet their oral judgments seemed initially to confirm previous findings of differences between the sexes, suggesting that the edge girls have on moral development during the early school years gives way at puberty with the ascendance of formal logical thought in boys.

The dilemma these children were asked to resolve was one in the series devised by Kohlberg to measure moral development in adolescence by presenting a conflict between moral norms and exploring the logic of its resolution. In this particular dilemma, a man named Heinz considers whether or not to steal a drug, which he cannot afford to buy, in order to save the life of his wife. In the standard format of Kohlberg's interviewing procedure, the description of the dilemma, itself—Heinz's predicament, the wife's disease, the druggist's refusal to lower his price—is followed by the question: Should Heinz steal the drug? Then the reasons for and against stealing are explored through a series of further questions, conceived as probes and designed to reveal the underlying structure of moral thought.

Jake

Jake, at 11, is clear from the outset that Heinz should steal the drug. Constructing the dilemma as Kohlberg did as a conflict between the values of property and life, he discerns the logical priority of life and uses that logic to justify his choice:

> For one thing, a human life is worth more than money, and if the druggist only makes $1000, he is still going to live, but if Heinz doesn't steal the drug, his wife is going to die. [*Why is life worth more than money?*] Because the druggist can get a thousand dollars later from rich people with cancer, but Heinz can't get his wife again. [*Why not?*] Because people are all different, and so you couldn't get Heinz's wife again.

Asked if Heinz should steal the drug if he does not love his wife, Jake replies that he should, saying that not only is there "a difference between hating and killing," but also, if Heinz were caught, "the judge would probably think it was the right thing to do." Asked about the fact that, in stealing, Heinz would be breaking the law, he says that "the laws have mistakes and you can't go writing up a law for everything that you can imagine."

Thus, while taking the law into account and recognizing its function in maintaining social order (the judge, he says, "should give Heinz the lightest possible sentence"), he also sees the law as man-made and therefore subject to error and change. Yet his judgment that Heinz should steal the drug, like his view of the law as having mistakes, rests on the assumption of agreement, a societal consensus around moral values that allows one to know and expect others will recognize "the right thing to do."

Fascinated by the power of logic, this 11-year-old boy locates truth in math which, he says, is "the only thing that is totally logical." Considering the moral dilemma to be "sort of like a math problem with humans," he sets it up as an equation and proceeds to work out the solution. Since his solution is rationally derived, he assumed that anyone following reason would arrive at the same conclusion and thus that a judge would also consider stealing to be the right thing for Heinz to do. Yet he is also aware of the limits of logic; asked whether there is a right answer to moral problems, he says that "there can only be right and wrong in judgment," since the parameters of action are variable and complex. Illustrating how actions undertaken with the best of intentions can eventuate in the most disastrous of consequences, he says:

> ...like if you give an old lady your seat on the trolley, if you are in a trolley crash and that seat goes through the window, it might be that reason that the old lady dies.

Theories of developmental psychology illuminate well the position of this child, standing at the juncture of childhood and adolescence, at what Piaget described as the pinnacle of childhood intelligence, and beginning through thought to discover a wider universe of possibility. The moment of pre-adolescence is caught by the conjunction of formal operational thought with a description of self still anchored in the factual parameters of his childhood world, his age, his town, his father's occupation, the substance of his likes, dislikes, and beliefs. Yet as his self-description radiates the self-confidence of a child who has arrived, in Erikson's terms, at a favorable balance of industry over inferiority—competent, sure of himself, and knowing well the rules of the game—so his emergent capacity for formal thought, his ability to think about thinking and to reason things out in a logical way, frees him from dependence on authority and allows him to find solutions to problems by himself.

This emergent autonomy then charts the trajectory that Kohlberg's six stages of moral development trace, a three-level progression from an egocentric understanding of fairness based on individual need (stages one and two), to a conception of fairness anchored in the shared conventions of societal agreement (stages three and four), and finally to a principled understanding of fairness that rests on the free-standing logic of equality and reciprocity (stages five and six). While Jake's judgments at 11 are scored as conventional on Kohlberg's scale, a mixture of stages three and four, his ability to bring deductive logic to bear on the solution of moral dilemmas, to differentiate morality from law, and to see how laws can be considered to have mistakes, points toward the principled conception of justice that Kohlberg equates with moral maturity.

Amy

In contrast, Amy's response to the dilemma conveys a very different impression, an image of development stunted by a failure of logic, an inability to think for herself. Asked if Heinz should steal the drug, she replies in a way that seems evasive and unsure:

> Well, I don't think so. I think there might be other ways besides stealing it, like if he could borrow the money or make a loan or something, but he really shouldn't steal the drug, but his wife shouldn't die either.

Asked why he should not steal the drug, she considers neither property nor law but rather the effect that theft could have on the relationship between Heinz and his wife. If he stole the drug, she explains:

> ...he might save his wife then, but if he did, he might have to go to jail, and then his wife might get sicker again, and he couldn't get more of the drug, and it might not be good. So, they should really just talk it out and find some other way to make the money.

Seeing in the dilemma not a math problem with humans but a narrative of relationships that extends over time, she envisions the wife's continuing need for her husband and the husband's continuing concern for his wife and seeks to respond to the druggist's need in a way that would sustain rather than sever connection. As she ties the wife's survival to the preservation of relationships, so she considers the value of her life in a context of relationships, saying that it would be wrong to let her die because, "if she died, it hurts a lot of people and it hurts her." Since her moral judgment is grounded in the belief that "if somebody has something that would keep somebody alive, then it's not right not to give it to them," she considers the problem in the dilemma to arise not from the druggist's assertion of rights but from his failure of response.

While the interviewer proceeds with the series of questions that follow Kohlberg's construction of the dilemma, Amy's answers remain essentially unchanged, the various probes serving neither to elucidate nor to modify her initial response. Whether or not Heinz loves his wife, he still shouldn't steal or let her die; if it were a stranger dying instead, she says that "if the stranger didn't have anybody near or anyone she knew," then Heinz should try to save her life but he shouldn't steal the drug. But as the interviewer conveys through the repetition of questions that the answers she has given are not heard or not right, Amy's confidence begins to diminish and her replies become more constrained and unsure. Asked again why Heinz should not steal the drug, she simply repeats, "Because it's not right." Asked again to explain why, she states again that theft would not be a good solution, adding lamely, that, "if he took it, he might not know how to give it to his wife, and so his wife might still die." Failing to see the dilemma as a self-contained problem in moral logic, she does not discern the internal structure of its resolution; as she constructs the problem differently herself, Kohlberg's conception completely evades her.

Instead, seeing a world comprised of relationships rather than of people standing alone, a world that coheres through human connection rather than through systems of rules, she finds the puzzle in the dilemma to lie in the failure of the druggist to respond to the wife. Saying that "it is not right for someone to die when their life could be saved," she assumes that if the druggist were to see the consequences of his refusal to lower his price, he would realize that "he should just give it to the wife and then have the husband pay back the money later." Thus she considers the solution to the dilemma to lie in making the wife's condition more salient to the druggist or, that failing, in appealing to others who are in a position to help.

Just as Jake is confident the judge would agree that stealing is the right thing for Heinz to do, so Amy is confident that, "if Heinz and the druggist had talked it out long enough, they could reach something besides stealing." As he considers the law to "have mistakes," so she sees this drama as a mistake, believing that "the world should just share things more and then people wouldn't have to steal." Both children thus recognize the need for agreement but see it as mediated in different ways: he impersonally through systems of logic and law, she personally through communication in relationship. As he relies on the conventions of logic to deduce the solution to this dilemma, assuming these conventions to be shared, so she relies on a process of communication, assuming connection and believing that her voice will be heard. Yet while his assumptions about agreement are confirmed by the convergence in logic between his answers and the questions posed, her assumptions are belied by the failure in communication, the interviewer's inability to understand her response.

MEASURING MORAL DEVELOPMENT: ASSESSING DIVERSE PERCEPTIONS

While the frustration of the interview with Amy is apparent in the repetition of questions and its ultimate circularity, the problem of interpretation arises when it comes to assessing her development. Considered in the light of Kohlberg's conception of the stages and sequence of moral development, her moral judgments are a full stage lower in moral maturity than those of the boy. Scored as a mixture of stages two and three, they seem to reveal a feeling of powerlessness in the world, an inability to think systematically about the concepts of morality or law, a reluctance to challenge authority or to examine the logic of received moral truths, a failure even to conceive of acting directly to save a life or to consider that such action, if taken, could possibly have an effect. As her reliance on relationships seems to reveal a continuing dependence and vulnerability, so her belief in communication as the mode through which to resolve moral dilemmas appears naive and cognitively immature.

Yet her description of herself conveys a markedly different impression. Once again, the hallmarks of the preadolescent child depict a child secure in her sense of herself, confident in the substance of her beliefs, and sure of her ability to do something of value in the world. Describing herself at 11 as "growing and changing," Amy says that she "sees some things differently now, just because I know myself really well now, and I know a lot more about the world." Yet the world she knows is a different world from that refracted by Kohlberg's construction of Heinz's dilemma. Her world is a world of relationships and psychological truths, where an awareness of the connection between people gives rise to a recognition of responsibility for one another, a perception of the need for response. Seen in this light, her view of morality as arising from the recognition of relationship, her belief in communication as the mode of conflict resolution, and her conviction that the solution to the dilemma will follow from its compelling representation seem far from naive or cognitively immature; rather, her judgments contain the insights central to an ethic of care, just as Jake's judgments reflect the logic of the justice approach. Her incipient awareness of the "method of truth," central to nonviolent conflict resolution, and her belief in the restorative activity of care, lead her to see the actors in the dilemma arrayed not as opponents in a contest of rights but as members of a network of relationships on whose continuation they all depend. Consequently, her solution to the dilemma lies in activating the network by communication, securing the inclusion of the wife by strengthening rather than severing the connection.

But the different logic of Amy's response calls attention to a problem in the interpretation of the interview itself. Conceived as an interrogation, it appears as a dialogue that takes on moral dimensions of its own, pertaining to the interviewer's uses of power and to the manifestations of respect. With this shift in the conception of the interview, it immediately becomes clear that the interviewer's problem in hearing Amy's response stems from the fact that Amy is answering a different question from the one the interviewer thought had been posed. Amy is considering not *whether* Heinz should act in this situation (*Should* Heinz steal the drug?) but rather *how* Heinz should act in response to his awareness of his wife's need (Should Heinz *steal* the drug?). The interviewer takes the mode of action for granted, presuming it to be a matter of fact. Amy assumes the necessity for action and considers what form it should take. In the interviewer's failure to imagine a response not dreamt of in Kohlberg's moral philosophy lies the failure to hear Amy's question and to see the logic in her response, to discern that what from one perspective appears to be an evasion of the dilemma, signifies in other terms a recognition of the problem and a search for a more adequate solution.

Thus in Kohlberg's dilemma these two children see two very different moral problems—in Jake a conflict between life and property that can be resolved by logical deduction, in Amy a fracture of human relationship that must be mended with its own thread. Asking different questions that arise from different conceptions of the moral domain, they arrive at answers that fundamentally diverge, and the arrangement of these answers as successive stages on a scale of increasing moral maturity calibrated by the logic of the boy's response misses the different truth revealed in the judgment of the girl. To the question, "What does he see that she does not?", Kohlberg's theory provides a ready response, manifest in the scoring of his judgments a full stage higher than hers in moral maturity; to the question, "What does she see that he does not?", Kohlberg's theory has nothing to say. Since most of her resonses fall through the sieve of Kohlberg's scoring system, here responses appear from his perspective to lie outside the moral domain.

Yet just as Jake reveals a sophisticated understanding of the logic of justification, so Amy is equally sophisticated in her understanding of the nature of choice. Saying that "if both the roads went in totally separate ways, if you pick one, you'll never know what would happen if you went the other way," she explains that "that's the chance you have to take, and like I said, it's just really a guess." To illustrate her point "in a simple way," she describes how, in choosing to spend the summer at camp, she:

> ...will never know what would have happened if I had stayed here, and if something goes wrong at camp, I'll never know if I stayed here if it would have been better. There's really no way around it because there's no way you can do both at once, so you've got to decide, but you'll never know.

In this way, these two 11-year-old children, both highly intelligent, though perceptive about life in different ways, display different modes of moral understanding, different ways of thinking about conflict and choice. Jake, in resolving the dilemma, follows the construction that Kohlberg has posed. Relying on theft to avoid confrontation and turning to the law to mediate the dispute, he transposes a hierarchy of power into a hierarchy of values by recasting a conflict between people into a conflict of claims. Thus abstracting the moral problem from the interpersonal situation, he finds in the logic of fairness an objective means of deciding who will win the dispute. But this hierarchical ordering, with its imagery of winning and losing and the potential for violence which it contains, gives way in Amy's construction of the dilemma to a network of connection, a network sustained by a process of communication. With this shift, the moral problem changes from one of unfair domination, the imposition of property over life, to one of unnecessary exclusion, the failure of the druggist to respond to the wife.

This shift in the formulation of the moral problem and the concomitant change in the imagery of relationships are illustrated as well by the responses of two eight-year-olds who participated in the same study[8] and were asked to describe a situation in which they weren't sure of the right thing to do:

> *Jeffrey* (age 8): When I really want to go to my friends and my mother is cleaning the cellar, I think about my friends, and then I think about my mother, and then I think about the right thing to do. [*But how do you know it's the right thing to do?*] Because some things go before other things.

Karen (age 8): I have a lot of friends, and I can't always play with all of them, so everybody's going to have to take a turn, because they're all my friends. But like if someone's all alone, I'll play with them. [*What kind of things do you think about when you are trying to make that decision?*] Um, someone all alone, loneliness.

While Jeffrey sets up a hierarchical ordering in thinking about the conflict between desire and duty, Karen describes a network of relationships that includes all of her friends. Both children deal with the issues of exclusion and priority created by choice, but while Jeffrey thinks about what goes first, Karen focuses on who is left out.

MORAL JUDGMENT AND SELF-DESCRIPTIONS

In illustrating a difference in children's thinking about moral conflict and choice, I have described two views that are complementary rather than sequential or opposed. In doing so, I go against the bias of developmental theory toward ordering differences in a hierarchical mode. This correspondence between the order of developmental theory and that manifest in the boys' responses contrasts with the disparity between the structure of theory and that manifest in the thought of the girls. Yet, in neither comparison does one child's thought appear as precursor of the other's position. Thus, questions arise about the relation between these perspectives; what is the significance of these differences, and how do these two modes of thinking connect? To pursue these questions, I return to the eleven-year-olds and consider the way they describe themselves.

[*How would you describe yourself to yourself?*]

Jake: Perfect. That's my conceited side. What do you want—any way that I choose to describe myself?

Amy: You mean my character? [*What do you think?*] Well, I don't know. I'd describe myself as, well, what do you mean?

[*If you had to describe the person you are in a way that you yourself would know it was you, what would you say?*]

Jake: I'd start off with eleven years old. Jake [last name]. I'd have to add that I live in [town] because that is a big part of me, and also that my father is a doctor because I think that does change me a little bit, and that I don't believe in crime, except for when your name is Heinz... that I think school is boring because I think that kind of changes your character a little bit. I don't sort of know how to describe myself, because I don't know how to read my personality. [*If you had to describe the way you actually would describe yourself, what would you say?*] I like corny jokes. I don't really like to get down to work, but I can do all the stuff in school. Every single problem that I have seen in school I have been able to do, except for ones that take knowledge, and after I do the reading, I have been able to do them, but sometimes I don't want to waste my time on easy homework. And also I'm crazy about sports. I think, unlike a lot of people, that the world still has hope....Most people that I know I like, and I have the good life, pretty much as good as any I have seen, and I am tall for my age.

Amy: Well, I'd say that I was someone who likes school and studying, and that's what I want to do with my life. I want to be some kind of a scientist or something, and I want to do things, and I want to help people. And I think that's what kind of person I am, or what kind of person I try to be. And that's probably how I'd describe myself. And I want to do something to help other people. [*Why is that?*] Well, because I think that this world has a lot of problems, and I think that everybody should try to help somebody else in some way, and the way I'm choosing is through science.

In the voice of the 11-year-old boy, a familiar form of self-definition appears, resonating to the schoolbook inscription of the young Stephen Daedalus ("himself, his name and where he was")[10] and echoing the descriptions that appear in *Our Town*,[18] laying out across the coordinates of time and space a hierarchical order in which to define one's place. Describing himself as distinct by locating his particular position in the world, Jake sets himself apart from that world by his abilities, his beliefs, and his height. Although Amy also enumerates her likes, her wants, and her beliefs, she locates herself in relation to the world, describing herself in relation to the world, describing herself through actions that bring her into connection with others, elaborating ties through her ability to provide help. To Jake's ideal of perfection against which he measures the worth of himself, Amy counterposes an ideal of care against which she measures the worth of her activity. While she places herself in relation to the world and chooses to help others through science, he places the world in relation to himself as it defines his character, his position, and the quality of life.

CONCLUSIONS

As the voices of these children illuminate two modes of self-description and two modes of moral judgment, so they illustrate how readily we hear the voice that speaks of justice and of separation and the difficulty we encounter in listening to the voice that speaks of care and connection. Listening through developmental theories and through the structures of our educational and social system, we are attuned to a hierarchical ordering that represents development as a progress of separation, a chronicle of individual success. In contrast, the understanding of development as a progress of human relationships, a narrative of expanding connection, is an unimagined representation. The image of network or web thus seems more readily to connote entrapment rather than an alternative and nonhierarchical vision of human connection.

This central limitation in the representation of development is most clearly apparent in recent portrayals of adult life, where the insistent focus on self and on work provides scanty representation of an adulthood spent in the activities of relationship and care. The tendency to chart the unfamiliar waters of adult development with the familiar markers of adolescent separation and growth leads to an equation of development with separation; it results in a failure to represent the reality of connection both in love and in work. Levinson,[15] patterning the stages of adult development on the seasons of a man's life, defined the developmental process explicitly as one of individuation, yet reported his distress at the absence of friendships in men's lives. Vaillant,[17] deriving his account of adaptation to life from the lives of the men who took part in the Grant study, noted that the question these men found most difficult to answer was, "Can you describe your wife?" In this light, the observation that women's embeddedness in lives of relationship, their orientation to interdependence, their subordination of achievement to care, and their conflicts over competitive success leave them personally at risk in mid-life, though generally construed as a problem in women's development, seems more a commentary on our society and on the representation of development itself.

In suggesting that the consideration of women's lives and of adulthood calls attention to the need for an expansion in the mapping of human development, I have pointed to a distinction between two modes of self-definition and two modes of moral judgment and indicated how these modes reflect different ways of imagining relationships. That these modes are tied to different experiences may explain their empirical asociation with gender, though that association is by no means absolute. That they reflect different forms of thought—one relying on a formal logic whose development Piaget has described, the other on a narrative and contextual mode of thought whose development remains to be traced—indicates the implication of this distinction for psychological assessment and education.

The experiences of inequality and of interdependence are embedded in the cycle of life, universal because inherent in the relationship of parent and child. These experiences of inequality and interdependence give rise to the ethics of justice and care, the ideals of human relationship—the vision that self and other will be treated as of equal worth, that despite differences in power, things will be fair; the vision that everyone will be responded to and included, that no one will be left alone or hurt. The adolescent, capable of envisioning the ideal, reflects on the childhood experiences of powerlessness and vulnerability and conceives a utopian world laid out along the coordinates of justice and care. This ability to conceive the hypothetical and to construct contrary-to-fact hypotheses has led the adolescent to be proclaimed a "philosopher,"[11] a "metaphysician par excellence."[9] But the representation of the adolescent's moral philosophy in the literature of developmental psychology has been limited to the portrayal of changes in the conception of justice that supports the adolescent's claim to equality and the separation of other and self. My own work[7] has expanded this description by identifying two different moral languages, the language of rights that protects separation and the language of responsibilities that sustains connection. In dialogue, these languages not only create the ongoing tension of moral discourse, but also reveal how the dynamics of separation and attachment in the process of identity formation relate to the themes of justice and care in moral growth. This expanded representation of identity and moral development allows a more complex rendering of differences, and points to the need to understand and foster the development of both modes.

The old promise of a liberal education, of an education that frees individuals from binding constraints and engenders a questioning of assumptions formerly taken for granted remains a compelling vision. But among the prevailing assumptions that need to be questioned are the assumptions about human development. The lives of women, in pointing to an uncharted path of human growth and one that leads to a less violent mode of life, are particularly compelling at this time in history and thus deserve particular attention. The failure to attend to the voices of women and the difficulty in hearing what they say when they speak has compromised women's development and education, leading them to doubt the veracity of their perceptions and to question the truth of their experience. This problem becomes acute for women in adolescence, when thought becomes reflective and the problem of interpretation thus enters the stream of development itself. But the failure to represent women's experience also contributes to the presentation of competitive relationships and hierarchical modes of social organization as the natural ordering of life. For this reason, the consideration of women's lives brings to the conception of development a much needed corrective, stressing the importance of narrative modes of thought and pointing to the contextual nature of psychological truths and the reality of interdependence in human life.

The process of selection that has shadowed this vision can be seen in Kohlberg's reading of Martin Luther King's letter from the Birmingham jail,[11] since Kohlberg extracted King's justification for breaking the law in the name of justice but omitted the way in which King's vision of justice was embedded in a vision of human connection. Replying to the clergy who criticized his action, King not only offered a justification of his action but also defended the necessity for action, anchoring that necessity in the realization of interdependence:

> I am in Birmingham because injustice is here. I cannot sit idly by in Atlanta and not be concerned about what happens in Birmingham. Injustice anywhere is a threat to justice everywhere. We are caught in an inescapable network of mutuality, tied in a single garment of destiny. Whatever affects one directly, affects all indirectly.

Thus, like Bonhoeffer,[1] who stated that action comes "not from thought but from a readiness for responsibility," King tied his responsiveness to a caring that arises from an understanding of the connection between people's lives, a connection not forged by systems of rules but by a perception of the fact of relationship, a connection not freely contracted but built into the very fabric of life.

The ideals of a liberal democratic society—of freedom and equality—have been mirrored in the developmental vision of autonomy, the image of the educated man thinking for himself, the image of the ideal moral agent acting alone on the basis of his principles, blinding himself with a Rawlsian "veil of ignorance," playing a solitary Kohlbergian game of "moral musical chairs." Yet the developmental psychologists who dared, with Erikson,[3] to "ask what is an adult," immediately began to see the limitations of this vision. Erikson himself has come increasingly to talk about the activity of caretaking and to identify caring as the virtue and strength of maturity.[2] When integrated into a developmental understanding, this insight should spur the search for the antecedents of this strength in childhood and in adolescence. Kohlberg,[13] turning to consider adulthood, tied adult development to the experiences of "sustained responsibility for the welfare of others" and of the irreversible consequences of choice. The resonance of these themes of maturity to the voice of the 11-year-old girl calls into question current assumptions about the sequence of development and suggests a different path of growth.

The story of moral development, as it is presently told, traces the history of human development through shifts in the hierarchy of power relationships, implying that the dissolution of this hierarchy into an order of equality represents the ideal vision of things. But the conception of relationships in terms of hierarchies implies separation as the moral ideal—for everyone to stand alone, independent, self-sufficient, connected to others by the abstractions of logical thought. There is, then, a need to represent in the mapping of development a nonhierarchical image of human connection, and to embody in the vision of maturity the reality of interdependence. This alternate vision of the web of connection is the recognition of relationship that prevents aggression and gives rise to the understanding that generates response.

REFERENCES

1. Bonhoeffer, D. *Letters and Papers from Prison.* New York: Macmillan, 1953.
2. Erikson, E. Reflections on Dr. Borg's life cycle. *Daedalus 105* (1976): 1–29.
3. Erikson, E. Reflections on the dissent of contemporary youth. *Daedalus 99* (1970): 154–76.
4. Freud, S. 1929. Civilization and its discontents. In *Standard Edition of the Complete Psychological Works of Sigmund Freud,* vol. 21, J. Strachey (ed.). London: Hogarth Press, 1961.
5. Freud, S. 1926. The question of lay analysis. In *Standard Edition of the Complete Psychological Works of Sigmund Freud,* vol. 20, J. Strachey (ed.). London: Hogarth Press, 1961.
6. Freud, S. 1925. Some physical consequences of the anatomical distinction between the sexes. In *Standard Edition of the Complete Psychological Works of Sigmund Freud,* vol. 19, J. Strachey (ed.). London: Hogarth Press, 1961.
7. Gilligan, C. *In a Different Voice: Psychological Theory and Women's Development.* Cambridge: Harvard University Press, 1982.
8. Gilligan, C., S. Langdale, and N. Lyons. The contribution of women's thought to developmental theory: The elimination of sex-bias in moral development theory and research. Final report to the National Institute of Education, Washington, D.C., 1982.
9. Inhelder, B., and J. Piaget. *The Growth of Logical Thinking from Childhood to Adolescence.* New York: Basic Books, 1958.
10. Joyce, J. *A Portrait of the Artist as a Young Man.* New York: Viking Press, 1956 (p. 15).
11. King, M., Jr. *Why We Can't Wait.* New York: Harper & Row, 1964.
12. Kohlberg, L. *The Philosophy of Moral Development.* San Francisco: Harper & Row, 1981.
13. Kohlberg, L. Continuities and discontinuities in childhood and adult moral development revisited. In *Life-Span Developmental Psychology: Personality and Socialization,* P. Baltes and K. Schaie (eds.). New York: Academic Press, 1973.
14. Kohlberg, L., and C. Gilligan. The adolescent as a philosopher: The discovery of the self in a post-conventional world. *Daedalus 100* (1971): 1051–86.
15. Levinson, D. *The Seasons of a Man's Life.* New York: Knopf, 1978.
16. Piaget, J. 1932. *The Moral Judgment of the Child.* New York: Free Press, 1965.
17. Vaillant, G. *Adaptation to Life.* Boston: Little, Brown, 1977.
18. Wilder, T. *Our Town.* New York: Coward-McCann, 1938.

3

Social Science Inquiries into Female Achievement: Recurrent Methodological Problems

*Barbara L. Richardson
and
Debra R. Kaufman*

SOCIAL SCIENCE RESEARCH ON WOMEN

Only recently has the female experience become part of the academic consciousness. The impact of this awakening, or consciousness-raising on methodological issues can be well illustrated by a review of developments in one controversial area of research on women—achievement. In this paper we will briefly trace the impact of a growing feminist consciousness as it was gradually revealed in the changing methodological approaches of several disciplines—psychology and sociology—toward the study of achievement and women. Generally, these disciplines have failed to address the types of questions, or to design the kinds of experiments, needed to validly measure the achievement and social progress of women. At stake, theoretically, operationally and politically, is the issue of authenticity, or the question of whose perceptions of reality the current measures of achievement actually best represent.

We emphasize in this paper the methodological importance of considering the entire research process from more than the investigator's point of view. Like other contributors to this volume, our perspective grows out of a tradition of feminist scholarship that favors an interdisciplinary analysis and

---

No official support or endorsement by the National Institute of Education or by the Department of Education of the views expressed herein is intended or should be inferred.

political awareness of our own responsibilities in the research endeavor. Our analysis will illustrate the importance of maintaining the integrity of multiple views of reality when designing research or interpreting data on female aspirations and accomplishments. Embedded as it is in the mainstream of social science, the twentieth-century study of women's achievements illustrates most of the common methodological biases found in research on women and gender roles throughout the 1960s and 1970s. (For excellent discussions of systematic measurement bias in general, see Campbell, Shakeshaft, and Wallston in this volume.)

The traditional approach to studying women's achievement has been heavily influenced by models emphasizing differences between the sexes with norms and reference points based on men's lives and experiences. In the social sciences, the effort to explain differences and make comparisons among various social groups has commonly been hampered by reliance on methods derived from "trait theories." Much of the achievement research we critique in this paper is based on this approach. Trait models look for correlations between and among individual bits of behavior—between personality constructs like dependency to specific achievement behaviors like competitiveness on anagram tasks or persistence after failure. We believe trait theory, as used in the study of achievement, neglects issues of special concern to gender-role researchers and students of social change. Its emphasis on early learning, linear models, internalization, and stabilized traits, provides a restricted view of the achievement process. Our methodological critiques of research on female achievement in psychology and social psychology—of the measurement of need-achievement, self-esteem, attribution, fear-of-success and failure—should be viewed with an appreciation for the pervasive importance of the economic and historical forces shaping women's place in the larger social structure (Kaufman and Richardson 1982).

NEED-ACHIEVEMENT AND MOTIVATION

In psychology, achievement-motivation research was slow to include females in its samples. On the few occasions when women were studied, their patterns of behavior conformed less reliably to the expected models (Lesser 1973; McClelland et al. 1958; McClelland 1961; Veroff 1958; Veroff et al. 1953). Until the 1970s, females were generally the exception, rather than the rule, in most studies of achievement motivation. Thus, much information has been lost on the achievement patterns of females in these age cohorts. The applicability of the classical achievement constructs and measures—the Thematic Apperception Test (TAT), laboratory studies of risk-taking—were not examined with female counterparts at that time. Such methodological issues remained to be explored by a generation of researchers expressly interested in women's own achievement patterns.

Such feminist scholars moved beyond the piecemeal observations of trait theory by drawing on the more integrative concept of gender role. However, even with the new burst in scholarship on female achievement over the past decade, the androcentric biases of the traditional measures of the early expectancy-value school of achievement research were slow to receive acknowledgment—particularly from within the field. Even when confronted with growing empirical evidence concerning the inadequacies of the theories when applied to women, the original formulations of need-achievement have shown little change (Atkinson 1978). This unresponsiveness is due, in part, to the fact that the arguments the critics are raising have implications far beyond those of concern to women and achievement theory alone. This pattern of creative scholarship through reintegration of the female experience with traditional masculine models is a theme that can be illustrated throughout the achievement literature. (Frieze 1975; Hoffman 1974a, 1974b; Kaufman and Richardson 1982; Mednick, Tangri, and Hoffman 1975; Maehr 1974; Weiner 1972, 1974).

Now, nearly three decades after the original research began, we can reexamine those studies contrasting males and females on the need to achieve, with new knowledge based on gender-role research. To take one example, the interpretation of a female's projective responses to achievement cues, stories told for a Thematic Apperception Test, has been admirably reanalyzed by Maccoby and Jacklin (1974). They argue that when girls respond with fewer achievement-related themes to female pictures it may be due to their subjective assessments that girls and women as a social group are not generally achievers in our society and *not* to their *own* low achievement motivation. While a variety of methodological factors have been suggested to account for these findings, the overwhelming evidence suggests that children are displaying a knowledge of which set of gender roles—and consequently which sex—is more valued and therefore destined to achieve in this society (Kaufman and Richardson 1982). A major contribution of Maccoby and Jacklin's analysis is their admonition that projective measures should not necessarily be equated with subjects' own real-life achievement motivation.

In the section to follow, we address another area of social psychological literature commonly used to explain women's achievement motivation and behavior: self-identity. We will see several of the methodological problems already noted in need-achievement research and consider the issue of validity from both a political and methodological perspective.

STEREOTYPES OF SUBJECTS—SELF-ESTEEM AND IDENTITY

In achievement research, especially in experimental situations, there is a tendency to ignore social context and focus on motivation, personality traits, and internal forces. In clinical and qualitative studies, there is often an overdeterministic view about behavior, an assumed correspondence between learned choice and performance. More often than not, learned choice is equated with free will—especially in accounting for women's achievement styles. Too often, a subject's awareness of cultural stereotypes or gender attributes is measured as an irrevocably *internalized* part of the personality (Kaufman and Richardson 1982). When personality measures are assumed to predict long-term achievement behaviors, there are often many hidden stereotypical views about the capacities of the subject and her interest or will to control her own fate. The continuing debates concerning the achievement drives and motives of poor young black women are a case in point.

In the late 1960s, Grier and Cobbs (1968), drawing on much clinical experience, described the self-image of the black adolescent female as one in which "the cards are stacked against her and the achievement of a healthy mature womanhood seems a very long shot indeed" (Grier and Cobbs, cited in Ladner 1972, p. 85). Joyce Ladner critiqued this analysis of the potential of the young black female. Ladner pointed out the stereotypic assumptions about black women guiding such interpretations. She suggested that the degree of impairment to self esteem and motivation has been widely exaggerated and is rarely approximated in real life (Ladner 1972, p. 8).

Countering with evidence from different population samples and other empirical studies, she suggested that when compared to their white counterparts, black children may fare very well. She cites a more representative sample from a study of junior high school students in a rural southern town (Gaughman and Dahlstrom 1968) in which black children described their home lives as happier than average, and themselves as being very satisfied with the kinds of persons they were. Ladner observes, "clearly, if the self-concepts of these children have been unduly damaged, this fact is not reflected in their interview statements about themselves, nor in the educational and vocational aspirations which they report for themselves, and which they seem optimistic about realizing" (Ladner 1972, p. 83).

Ladner's critique also reflects the growing concern in the social sciences with the overdeterministic tone used in explaining the attitudes of individuals toward failure and nonachievement when they are members of an oppressed group. She does not deny that racism has taken a heavy psychological and physical toll on black men and women. Rather, she argues that the measures of attitudes and behaviors used to assess self-esteem underestimate the complexity of feelings and beliefs. She emphasizes the importance of devising indicators that will be sensitive to distinctions between awareness of cultural expectations and personal aspirations; between self-worth and the opportunity to achieve; between theoretical variables and issues of importance to the subjects themselves. The validity of inferences drawn from clinical populations, self-reports of behavior, or attitudes measures in times of stress and social change, go beyond methodological concerns in their potential implications (Guttentag and Salasin 1977).

As explanatory variables, aspirations and expectations may have quite different meanings for youth so far removed from the basic economic resources necessary for contemporary success and achievement.

The research on the correlates of self-esteem and achievement among black females represents one approach found in the achievement literature. Here especially, stereotypical views of subjects and their personalities can lead experimenters to be insensitive to important distinctions among respondents and thereby to the construction of invalid measures. On the other hand, stereotypical views held by subjects for researchers in an experimental situation can also add to systematic misperceptions. The attitudes expressed by young black females to middle-class researchers may not accurately capture their real attitudes. Ladner's critique challenged Grier's and Cobbs's assumption that a black women "does not have standards of her own and experiences self-rejection when she finds herself unable to do more than imitate the standards of white society" (Kaufman and Richardson 1982, p. 56). There is evidence that even when black respondents acknowledge that theirs is not the "more valued race" in society, they have a capacity to maintain a positive self-identity. Similar observations and comparisons have also been made for females of all ages in our culture.

In the area of achievement, where social goals can change so rapidly in their accessibility, it is especially important to allow for differences to emerge between cultural awareness and personal beliefs. Cultural stereotyping is especially evident in the early research on minority female achievement. The research questions asked and the constructs chosen are receiving renewed scrutiny by investigators especially sensitive to these sorts of systematic biases. (McAdoo 1974; Myers 1975; Wright 1975). These controversies over meaning and measurement further illustrate the broader political and philosophical assumptions underpinning our research inquiries. We believe that the entry of women and minorities into developmental research continues to heighten the consciousness of the field and generate far richer understanding of the achieving self.

LUCK, FEAR, AND ACHIEVEMENT ATTRIBUTION

Another active area of research on female achievement grows out of cognitive and social psychology and is known as attribution theory. In the achievement literature generated by attribution theory (Deaux 1976; Deaux and Emswiller 1974; Frieze 1975; O'Leary 1977; Weiner 1972, 1974), women seem to take less personal credit or responsibility for their achievements than do men. The inference problems noted in other areas of achievement research emerge in this aspect of the study of female achievement as well. As greater empirical attention has been given to female attributional patterns, the observed results suggest the need for modifications in the original hypotheses.

An early investigation, influential in the development of an attribution theory of sex differences in achievement was Crandall, Katovsky and Crandall's 1965 study of adolescents between the ages of 11 and 17. This study was one of the first to suggest that females become more anxious and concerned about failure as they progress through school and are more likely to blame themselves rather than others for failure. More recent research has sought to document the same pattern, suggesting that males commonly attribute success to a stable internal factor (ability) and failure to an external unstable factor (e.g., bad luck), whereas females appear to be less likely to credit themselves if they succeed (Bar-tal and Frieze 1977; Deaux 1976; McHugh, Frieze, and Hanusa 1982).

Women's achievement patterns in the attribution research paradigm are ambiguous with regard to the aspects of the experimental situation to which females may be responding (for a more extensive review and critique see McHugh, Frieze, and Hanusa 1982). Considering the range of possible interpretations from the empirical work emerging from this model, Kaufman and Richardson (1982, p. 53) ask:

> Are female subjects responding to attributions about gender role acquired in their earliest socialization or to present assessments of their abilities? Are they feeling the same way that they are responding behaviorally? To what are they responding—a cue, a stereotype, an experimenter in an achievement-specific context? Are their responses merely socially approved tactics or a genuine devaluation of the self? Do women actually feel less pride in their accomplishments or are they simply more modest than men?

O'Leary raises similar questions concerning the failure-related anxieties and attributions of failure among females in this research. She suggests that these behaviors may also represent a "defensive strategy used to avoid being held personally responsible for success and/or failure" (1977, p. 97).

In general, sex difference research has been struggling with the construct validity problems arising from the use of self-report measures. The designs used in attribution research studies often rely upon some form of self-report on the part of subjects. Research on contemporary gender role stereotypes has reliably demonstrated that males are expected to show self-assurance while females are taught to present themselves in a self-effacing fashion (Bem and Bem 1970). Generally, females are also thought to be less defensive in self-report measures than men. Therefore, we may be measuring the subject's sophisticated reading of sex role expectations, rather than her own estimates of personal worth or capability. As a result, research designs that include multiple indicators can provide more sophisticated evaluations of validity (see Beere, Campbell, Jacklin, and Walston in this volume). Through the 1970s, laboratory data on college students were often generalized beyond the experimental setting as evidence that women were less likely than men to view themselves as skilled or competent, showing reluctance to accept personal responsibility for their achievements (Bardwick 1971, 1974, 1979). This conclusion appears unwarranted in view of the heavy reliance much of the work in this area placed upon subjective assessments.

Since achievement research first began including females in its investigations, many more guidelines have emerged to help refine the traditional methods and anticipate systematic biases. More recent research using attribution theory and design is attending to gender role factors as intervening variables. Publications are now availiable to describe the ways in which research situations may differ in their salience, familiarity, relevance, and meaning for males and females (Deaux 1976; Frieze et al. 1978; Frieze, Whitley, and McHugh 1982; O'Leary 1977; Sherif 1979; Sherman and Denmark 1978; Unger and Denmark 1975). These research compendia review a range of social factors now recognized as potential sources of sex-typed variation. They include discussions of the effects various experimental designs may have on subjects. Males and females will react differentially, for instance, in response to the sex of the experimenter and the sex ratio of participants (as noted in Chapter 6).

In its own survey of the available research evidence, the APA Division 35 Task Force on nonsexist guidelines concludes that the data demonstrate that "gender-by-situation" interactions are more the rule than the exception. They write (McHugh, Koeske and Frieze 1981, p. 20) that the problem is widespread:

> The failure to specify or to study the social meanings attached to these varied constituents of a research situation, including its temporal duration, amounts to the "fundamental attributional error" of assigning cause unduly to dispositional determinants of behavior and to neglecting person-environment interactions.

Attribution research has continued to rely heavily on classical research designs and measures of achievement. Consequently, reviewers of this literature tend to urge caution when considering generalizations about women's achievements beyond the laboratory setting.

CONSTRUCT VALIDITY AND THE POLITICS OF POPULAR APPEAL—FEAR OF SUCCESS

Related to the fear of failure and directly derived from the expectancy-value model of achievement is the fear of success or, more accurately, the motive to avoid success (Horner 1968, 1972, 1978). This popular construct has received wide public and professional attention over the past decade, raising new controversies over the classical measures of need-achievement research, and their applicability to women. We choose here to emphasize the positive contribution the dialogues surrounding this theory have had for the development of research on female achievement and feminist scholarship. For more detailed methodological critiques of the fear-of-success construct and its validity, we refer the reader to analyses in this volume and elsewhere (Beere 1983; Campbell 1983; Paludi 1982; Tresemer 1977). The interest in the fear-of-success concept has continued, despite the fact that subsequent research has not confirmed some of the earliest formulations about the motive (Hoffman 1974a, 1974b, 1975; Condry and Dyer 1976). Two propositions critical to the construct validity of Horner's original formulation have not been clearly and repeatedly supported: that the motive to avoid success was inextricably tied to a woman's feelings of femininity, and that it was a stable characteristic of the personality that was being tapped through projective and competitive measures (Kaufman and Richardson 1982).

While major sex differences have not been consistently supported over time, the continuing methodological controversies surrounding the motive to avoid success have spurred some important questions which helped refine achievement theory for both sexes. For instance, Depner and O'Leary called for a more interdisciplinary direction when their data did not support Horner's original formulations (1976). These authors suggest that women's psychological barriers to entry into male-dominated occupational roles need not be limited "to the realms of achievement motivation or motivation alone" (1976, p. 267). They argue that the issue of achievement among women is broader than the question of why women fail to strive for success: "Individuals often fail to aspire to roles which they view as attractive. There are probably many reasons for this, some of them motivational or otherwise intrapsychic, others are better understood at a macro level" (1976, p. 267). These concerns with the fear-of-success construct echo Ladner's reservations with the measures of identity. Both focus on very narrow dimensions of achievement.

Currently, many young scholars based in experimentally oriented fields but familiar with the broader perspectives of women's studies are expanding their field's research parameters. Feminist researchers are reanalyzing and reinterpreting the existing literature. We also see a shift outward from individual to social variables and formulations. This tendency to move toward multilevel interdisciplinary research designs is characteristic both of feminist scholarship and of much social change research. Increasingly research guided by this more interdisciplinary or feminist perspective is generating questions about the value of success itself. There is a wide range of variables that help determine achievement expectancies, many of which are likely to shift in importance over the course of a lifetime and across generations. Hoffman's work on changes in individuals and across age groups grew directly out of her interest in replicating the earlier fear-of-success findings. There is a definite momentum to move beyond experimental definitions of achievement to women's life experiences, family situations, and actual career opportunities. New guidelines are developing for framing research questions and shaping inquiry. From the methodological controversies of the 1970s there appears to be a newly emerging approach to female achievement research. It is grounded in gender-role theory and sensitive to the sociohistorical context (Duberman 1975; Gordon 1977; Hochschild 1975; Howe 1975; Kanter 1978; Kaplan and Bean 1976; Lipman-Blumen 1976; O'Leary 1977; Parlee 1975; Thorne and Henley 1975).

FEMALE ACHIEVEMENT AND STATUS ATTAINMENT IN THE SOCIOLOGICAL PERSPECTIVE

Women's achievements are difficult to analyze within the theoretical models and methods available in the literature on the sociology of work, mobility, and stratification (Blau 1978; Duncan, Featherman, and Duncan 1972; Featherman 1978; Haller and Portes 1973; Sewell and Hauser 1972, 1975; Treiman and Terrell 1975). Operational definitions, scales, and measures are based on the patterns of male career paths. For example, the accepted sociological definition of the labor force is restricted to those working for pay or actively seeking work (Hauser and Featherman 1977; U.S. Congress: Senate Committee on Labor and Human Resources 1979; U.S. Department of Labor 1978). Acker warns of the biases likely to surround research inferences drawn from inquiries that systematically exclude unpaid work as an analytic category in labor force analysis. (Acker 1978).

It has taken some time for the field to appreciate the methodological hazards of attempting to generalize directly from men's to women's experiences. A striking example of a research area ripe for constructive change is the field of social stratification, an area of great prestige in sociology and heavily influenced by male investigators. Over the past decade, literature dealing with occupational and eductational choice, and/or social mobility, has come to be referred to as status attainment, or more generally, stratification research. Mobility, in the sociological sense, simply refers to the process by which one comes to attain or achieve a particular occupational or educational level in society. Research inquiries are predicated on the untested assumption that male experiences are representative for the population at large. The committee reviewing sexist biases in sociological research describes this issue as "inadequate specification of the research problem," and recommends greater attention to variables that transcend sex-stereotyped divisions.

In the stratification literature, both educational and occupational achievements are conceptualized as a part of a long-range process. We will concentrate on two measurement issues—timing and choice—and refer the reader to several excellent reviews that detail an even broader range of methodological concerns (Alexander and Eckland 1974; Bibb and Form 1977; Kaufman and Richardson 1982; Keller and Zavarolli 1964; Laws 1975, 1976, 1978; Marini and Greenberger 1976; Wolf and Rosenfeld 1978). Several philosophical assumptions about achievement in the American system are worth noting. In both the achievement motivation literature and the stratification literature, there is an assumption that the processes involved in social mobility and success are based primarily on universalistic criteria. Competence, ability, performance, and the timing of a career choice rests primarily within the control of the individual. Work in these areas gives little attention to the different effects that gender has on the decisions and career paths of each sex. This is a serious oversight, given the clear evidence that gender roles act as intervening variables, in accounting for women's individual routes to achievement and their quite different paths from men's (Baruch 1974; Birnbaum 1975; Ellis 1952; Epstein 1970; Frieze et al 1978; Mednick, Tangri, and Hoffman 1975; Oppenheimer 1968; Stein and Bailey 1976; Unger and Denmark 1975).

A critical methodological issue in social science research is devising measures that are sensitive to individual values which shift in relation to changing historical, cultural, and economic factors. Most researchers attempting to study achievement or mobility are faced with the need to separate hopes and aspirations of individuals from the realistic expectations they may have, given the actual opportunities available in the opportunity structure. The illustration that follows from the status-attainment literature points to the importance of this issue in the research on career goals and occupational accomplishments.

The dynamic relationship among and between gender role and career choice variables is poorly accounted for in the current status attainment literature. That is, an individual's goals, values, and perceptions of both the opportunity structure and her/his ability (at any particular point) are ordinarily combined and evaluated in one single measure, with insufficient regard to the impact gender roles may have at different points in the life cycle. This combining of qualitatively different and changing variables into a single dimension of aspiration has been critiqued in social-stratification research before. The practice tends to underestimate the ambitions (as tempered by reality) characteristic of social groups experiencing racial, ethnic, or age discrimination in a culture (Elder 1968, 1974; Empey 1956; Han 1969; Rosen 1969). What one hopes for may be quite different from what one expects, and this is particularly true during periods of rapid social change. For example, high scores on the Strong Vocational Interest form did not predict the occupations pursued by those who worked most of the time since graduating from college. Variables measuring "choice" or "timing" seem especially problematic. Birnbaum's (1975) data (cited in Laws 1975, p. 31) on homemakers, married professionals, and single professionals, illustrate the difficulty:

> ...the three groups showed little difference in the occupations they reported having considered as children. All had considered wife and mother (homemaker most frequently); and all had considered professional careers (the married professionals most). The most career-oriented (single professionals) had the highest proportion undecided at the early stage, suggesting that their career choices entered their life later than the standard female occupational map....

Women's occupational outcomes can rarely be attributed to early expressions of aspirations measured at a single point in time. Given the different pressures and decision points affecting the two sexes in our culture, the timing and importance of key life events needs to be considered for each.

Until researchers take into account a more realistic and common understanding of the female experience, our efforts at explaining women's achievement patterns will have little practical utility. In 1976 some researchers were suggesting that "even with the tremendous growth in the number and visibility of status attainment researchers, the present hypothesized paradigm is inadequate" (Falk and Cosby 1975, p. 314). There is evidence, as in the achievement literature, of methodologies better designed for the study of women. One that is illustrative of promising work in this area is being developed by Falk and Cosby (1975). Their reworking of earlier status-attainment models includes new and relevant items such as an individual's marital status, sex of sibling(s), and stage in family life cycle. The improvement of this model over the ones described earlier are readily apparent. They give new consideration to the roles women play—sister, girlfriend, wife, and mother.

SUMMARY AND CONCLUSION

Despite the recent outpouring of popular and academic works explaining women and their achievements, the social sciences have yet to develop measures and methods that authentically describe as well as predict female achievement. Even with rapidly accumulating empirical information there is continuing theoretical, philosophical and political disagreement about women and their achievements. The findings on female achievement which we have reported here have generally been gathered while using narrow experimental definitions, and college-aged samples. Less studied, but more representative adult populations, for whom sex differences are generally less consistent, should provide some useful information on the validity of both theory and method. The premium contemporary researchers place upon predictable results contributes to the tendency on the part of researchers to return repeatedly to similar sampling populations. In the expectancy-value tradition, when data on females did not conform to those on white college males, the women, rather than the theory were regarded as the source of error. Females were singled out as being different from males because they did not fit a model that was already proving inadequate for expanded samples of male subjects.

Without representative sampling and broader validation of instruments, theorists remain at odds in their interpretations. The predictive validity of our measures becomes particularly critical if we are concerned with anticipating how much carryover exists between the experimental context and the objective realities women face in their daily lives. Even when we are convinced that we have adequately constructed our measures it is critical to remember that our sampling procedures may have unintentionally minimized variation, conflict, and ambiguity. What consensus we have achieved may be an outcome of having focused on a limited range of age, class and ethnic groups. Although feminist scholars are generally advocates for more inclusive models, they too, are often tempted by the convenience of captive college populations.

The most popular theories of female achievement in both psychology and sociology have been slowly moving to develop, modify, and expand existing methods and theories to incorporate both male and female experiences. There are, however, some methodological pitfalls that social change researchers of all persuasions need to resolve. Social desirability and stereotyping are both persistent problems. Projective measures are often ambiguous and difficult to interpret, as are self-reports and attitude scales—particularly when removed from any measures of real-life behavior. Sample populations for studying both male and female achievement remain narrow in age and background. Our statistical techniques are designed for charting "linear career trajectories" rather than the timing and choices characteristic of most women's actual experiences in today's job market. The continued growth of women's caucuses and sections on gender role research in our professional organizations is needed. They should begin to provide a forum for critical evaluation and development of the emerging models and methodologies in achievement research. To date, the findings on female achievement have been confounded by a legacy of measurement problems familiar to social change researchers working in related areas. What is called for now is persistence in refining our methods, measures, and constructs, as well as our theories.

REFERENCES

Acker, J. Issues in the sociological study of women's work. In A. Stromberg and S. Harkess (eds.), *Women Working.* Palo Alto: Mayfield, 1978.
Alexander, J., and B. Eckland. Sex differences in the educational attainment process. *American Sociological Review* 39 (5), 1974:668–82.
Atkinson, J. *Personality, Motivation, and Achievement.* New York: Wiley, 1978.
Bardwick, J. *Psychology of Women: A Study of Bio-cultural Conflicts.* New York: Harper & Row, 1971.
———— The dynamics of successful people. In D.C. McGuigan (ed.), *New Research on Women at the University of Michigan,* Ann Arbor: Center for Continuing Education of Women, University of Michigan, 1974.
———— *In Transition: How the Feminist Movement, Sexual Liberation, and the Search for Fulfillment Have Altered Our Lives.* New York: Holt, Rinehart & Winston, 1979.
Bar-Tal, D., and I. Frieze. Achievement motivation for males and females as a determinant of attributions for success and failure. *Sex Roles* 3(3), (1977):301–13.
Baruch, G.K. Maternal career-orientation as related to parental identification in college women. *Journal of Vocational Behavior* 4(2), (1974):173–80.
Bem, S.L., and D.J. Bem. Training the woman to know her place. In D.J. Bem (ed.), *Beliefs, Attitudes, and Human Affairs.* Belmont: Brooks/Cole, 1970.
Bibb, R., and W. Form. The effects of industrial, occupational, and sexual stratification on wages in blue collar markets, *Social Forces* 55 (1977):974–96.
Birnbaum, J.A. Life patterns and self-esteem in gifted family-oriented and career-commited Women. In M. Mednick, S. Tangri, and L. Hoffman (eds.), *Women and Achievement.* New York: Wiley, 1975.
Blau, F.D. The data on women workers, past, present, and future. In A. Stromberg and S. Harkess (eds.), *Women Working.* Palo Alto: Mayfield, 1978.
Condry, J. and S. Dyer. Fear of success: attribution of cause to the victim. *Journal of Social Issues,* 32(3), 1976:63–83.
Crandall, V.C., W. Katovsky, and V.J. Crandall. Children's belief in their own control of reinforcement in intellectual-academic achievement situations. *Child Development,* 36(1), (1965):91–109.
Deaux, K. *The Behavior of Women and Men.* Monterey: Brooks Cole, 1976.
Deaux, K. and T. Emswiller. Explanations of successful performance on sex-linked tasks: What's skill for the male is luck for the female. *Journal of Personality and Social Psychology* 29(1), (1974):80–85.
Depner, C., and V. O'Leary. Understanding female careerism: Fear of success and new directions. *Sex Roles* 2(3), (1976):259–68.
Duberman, L. *Gender and Sex in Society.* New York: Praeger, 1975.
Duncan, O.D., D.L. Featherman, and B. Duncan. *Socioeconomic Background and Achievement.* New York: Seminar, 1972.
———— *Children of the Great Depression.* Chicago: University of Chicago Press, 1974.
Elder, G.H., Jr. Achievement motivation and intelligence in occupational mobility: A longitudinal analysis. *Sociometry* 31(4), (1968):327–54.

Ellis, E. Social psychological correlates of upward social mobility among married career women. *American Sociological Review* 17(5), (1952):558–63.

Empey, L. Social class and occupational aspiration: A comparison of absolute and relative measurement. *American Sociological Review* 21(6), (1956):703–9.

Epstein, C. *Woman's Place: Options and Limits in Professional Careers.* Berkeley: University of California Press, 1970.

Falk, W. and A. Cosby. Women and the status attainment process. *Social Science Quarterly* 56 (September 1975):307–14.

Featherman, D. Schooling and occupational careers: Constancy and change in worldly success. Center for Demography and Ecology. University of Wisconsin, 1978.

Frieze, I.H. Women's expectations for and causal attributions of success and failure. In M. Mednick, S. Tangri, and L. Hoffman (eds.), *Women and Achievement.* New York: Wiley, 1975.

Frieze, I.H., P.B. Johnson, J.E. Parsons, D.N. Ruble, and G.L. Zellman. *Women and Sex Roles: A Social Psychological Perspective.* New York: Norton, 1978.

Frieze, I.H., B. Whitley and M. McHugh. Assessing the theoretical models for sex differences in causal attributions for success and failure, *Sex Roles* 8(4), (1982):33–43.

Gaughman, E.E., and W.G. Dahlstrom. *Negro and White Children.* New York: Academic, 1968.

Gordon, L. *Woman's Body, Woman's Right: A Social History of Birth Control in America.* Baltimore: Penguin, 1977.

Grier, W.H. and P.M. Cobbs. *Black Rage.* New York: Basic Books, 1968.

Guttentag, M., and S. Salasin. Women, men, and mental health. In L. Cater, A. Scott, and W. Martyna (eds.), *Women and Men: Changing Roles.* New York: Praeger, 1977.

Haller, A.O., and A. Portes. Status attainment processes. *Sociology of Education* 46 (Winter 1973):51–91.

Han, W.S. Two conflicting themes: Common values versus class differential values. *American Sociological Review* 34(5), (1969):679–90.

Hauser, R., and D. Featherman. *The Process of Stratification.* New York: Academic, 1977.

Hochschild, A. The sociology of feeling and emotion: Selected possibilities. In M. Millman and R. Kanter (eds.), *Another Voice.* New York: Doubleday Anchor, 1975.

Hoffman, L.W. Psychology looks at the female. In D.C. McGuigan (ed.), *New Research on Women at the University of Michigan.* Ann Arbor: University of Michigan, 1974a.

——— A re-examination of the fear of success. In D.C. McGuigan (ed.), *New Research on Women at the University of Michigan.* Ann Arbor: Center for Continuing Education of Women, University of Michigan, 1974b.

——— Early childhood experiences and women's achievement motives. In M. Mednick, S. Tangri, and L. Hoffman (eds.), *Women and Achievement.* New York: Wiley, 1975.

Horner, M. Sex differences in achievement motivation and performance in competitive and non-competitive situations. Ph.D. diss., University of Michigan, 1968.

——— Toward an understanding of achievement-related conflicts in women. *Journal of Social Issues* 28(2), (1972):157-75.

──── The measurement and behavioral implications of fear of success in women. In J.W. Atkinson and J.O. Raynor (eds.), *Personality, Motivation, and Achievement.* New York: Wiley, 1978.

Howe, F. (ed.). *Women and the Power to Change.* New York: McGraw Hill, 1975.

Kanter, R. Work in a new America. *Daedalus* 107(1), (1978):47-78.

Kaplan, A., and J. Bean. (eds.). *Beyond Sex-Role Stereotypes: Readings Toward a Psychology of Androgyny.* Boston: Little, Brown, 1976.

Kaufman, D., and B. Richardson. *Achievement and Women.* New York: Free Press, 1982.

Keller, S., and M. Zavarolli. Ambition and social class: A respecification. *Social Forces* 43(1), (1964):58-70.

Ladner, J.A. *Tomorrow's Tomorrow.* New York: Anchor Books, 1972.

Laws, J.L. Work motivation and work behavior of women: New perspectives. In J. Sherman and F. Denmark (eds.), *The Psychology of Women: Future Directions in Research.* New York: Psychological Dimensions, 1978.

──── Work aspiration of women: False leads and new starts. In M. Blaxall and B. Reagan (eds.), *Women and the Workplace.* Chicago: University of Chicago Press, 1976.

──── The psychology of tokenism: an analysis. *Sex Roles* 1(1), (1975):51-67.

Lesser, G.S. Achievement motivation in women. In D.C. McClelland and R. Steele (eds.), *Human Motivation.* Morristown: General Learning Press, 1973.

Lipman-Blumen, J. Toward a homosocial theory of sex roles. In M. Blaxall and B. Reagan (eds.), *Women and the Workplace.* Chicago: University of Chicago Press, 1976.

Maccoby, E., and C. Jacklin. *The Psychology of Sex Differences.* Stanford: Stanford University Press, 1974.

Maehr, M. Culture and achievement motivation. *American Psychologist* 29(12), (1974):887-96.

Marini, M., and E. Greenberger. Differences in occupational aspirations and expectations. Paper presented to the Sixty-fourth American Sociological Association, New York City, August 1976.

McAdoo, H. Race and sex-typing in young black children. Paper presented to the Annual Meeting of the National Conference of Social Welfare, Cincinnati, May 1974.

McClelland, D.C. *The Achieving Society.* Princeton: Van Nostrand, 1961.

McClelland, D.C., A.L. Baldwin, U. Bronfenbrenner, and F.L. Strodtbeck. *Talent and Society.* Princeton: Van Nostrand, 1958.

McHugh, M., I. Frieze, and B. Hanusa. Attributions and sex differences in achievement: Problems and new perspectives. *Sex Roles* 8(4), (1982):467-97.

McHugh, M., R. Koeske and I. Frieze. Nonsexist guidelines for research in psychology: Introduction. Report of Division 35 Task Force of the American Psychological Association, Washington, D.C., December 1981.

Mednick, M., S. Tangri and L. Hoffman (eds.) *Women and Achievement.* New York: Wiley, 1975.

Myers, L. Black women: Selectivity among roles and reference groups in the maintenance of self-esteem. *Journal of Social and Behavioral Sciences* 21(2), (1975):39-47.

O'Leary, V. *Toward Understanding Women.* Monterey, Calif.: Brooks/Cole, 1977.
Oppenheimer, V.K. The Sex-Labelling of Jobs. *Industrial Relations* 7(3), (1968):219–34.
Paludi, M. An idiographic approach to the study of success and fear of success. Paper read at the American Educational Research Association Special Interest Group on Women Conference, Philadelphia, November 1982.
Parlee, M.B. The new scholarship: review essays in the social sciences. *Signs* 1(1), (1975):110–38.
Rosen, B. Introduction in B.C. Rosen, H. Crockett, and C. Nunn (eds.), *Achievement in American Society.* Cambridge: Schenkman, 1969.
Sewell, W.H., and R.M. Hauser. *Education, Occupation, and Earnings.* New York: Academic, 1975.
——— Causes and consequences of high education: Models of the status attainment process. *American Journal of Agricultural Economics* (December 1972):851–61.
Sherif, C. Bias in psychology. In J. Sherman and E. Beck. *The Prism of Sex,* Madison: University of Wisconsin Press, 1979.
Sherman, J., and F. Denmark (eds.). *The Psychology of Women: Future Directions in Research.* New York: Psychological Dimensions, 1978.
Stein, A., and M. Bailey, The socialization and achievement orientation in females. In A. Kaplan and J. Bean (eds.), *Beyond Sex-Role Stereotypes: Readings toward a Psychology of Androgyny.* Boston: Little, Brown, 1976.
Thorne, B., and N. Henley. *Language and Sex: Difference and Dominance.* Rowley: Newbury House, 1975.
Treiman, J., and K. Terrell. Sex and the process of status attainment: A comparison of working women and men. *American Sociological Review* 40(2), (1975):174–200.
Tresemer, D.W. *Fear of Success,* New York: Plenum, 1977.
Unger, R.K., and F.L. Denmark. *Women: Dependent or Independent Variable?* New York: Psychological Dimensions, 1975.
U.S. Congress, Senate Committee on Labor and Human Resources. Hearings on the coming decade: American women and human resources policies and programs. Ninety-sixth Congress, first session. Washington, D.C.: Government Printing Office, 1979.
U.S. Department of Labor, Women's Bureau. Employment and earnings 1970–1977. Bulletin no. 25. Washington, D.C.: Government Printing Office, January 1978.
Veroff, J. Scoring manual for the power motive. In J.W. Atkinson (ed.), *Motives in Fantasy, Action, and Society.* Princeton: Van Nostrand, 1958.
Veroff, J., S. Wilcox, and J.W. Atkinson. The achievement motive in high school and college age women. *Journal of Abnormal and Social Psychology* 48(1), (1953):108–19.
Weiner, B. *Theories of Motivation: From Mechanism to Cognition.* Chicago: Markham, 1972.
——— Achievement motivation as conceptualized by an attribution theorist. In B. Weiner (ed.) *Achievement Motivation and Attribution Theory.* Morristown, N.J.: General Learning Press, 1974.
Wolf, W.C., and R. Rosenfeld. Sex structure of occupational and job mobility. *Social Forces* 56(3), (1978):823–44.
Wright, M. Self-concept and the coping process of black undergraduate women at a predominantly white university. Ph.D. diss., University of Michigan, 1975.

PART III

OVERVIEW OF RESEARCH METHODS IN SEX ROLES AND SOCIAL CHANGE

4

Overview of Research Methods

Barbara Strudler Wallston

OVERVIEW OF RESEARCH METHODS

Given the numerous books, articles, and journals devoted to research methodology, it is an audacious undertaking to provide an overview of methods in this brief chapter. The risk of superficiality is tremendous. Therefore, one cannot hope to learn how to carry out any of the methods discussed from this brief treatment. However, by pointing out some of the strengths and weaknesses of a variety of approaches, it is hoped to expand the range of potential methods considered to address a research question. Researchers tend to rely on a few methods based on training and experience; this chapter is an attempt to help us break this set. By providing appropriate references that discuss the techniques in greater detail, as well as examples of studies that utilize the methods, the chapter will provide the tools to access the literature on methods of interest.

Because of space constraints, the need to limit this undertaking, and knowledge of the material covered in other chapters in this book, little attention will be given to statistical analysis (see the Rosenthal chapter, this volume), sampling (see Shakeshaft chapter, this volume), operationalizing variables (see Vaughter chapter, this volume), instruments and measures (see

---

This chapter is a revised version of a paper written pursuant to Contract No. NIE-P-81-0081 of the National Institute of Education. It does not, however, necessarily reflect the views of that agency. The work was completed while the author was on leave at the Department of Medical Psychology, University of Health Sciences, Bethesda, Maryland, and the Department of Psychology, University of Maryland, College Park.

Beere chapter, this volume), or inferences with respect to causality (see Boruch chapter, this volume). Some selection with respect to methods was also necessary.

A distinction is made between design and research techniques. The designs discussed include true experiments, where random assignment to treatment occurs, quasi-experiments, correlational studies with prospective/ longitudinal designs and ethnographic/qualitative research. A number of research techniques are then discussed that can be used with a variety of designs: observation, survey/interview/questionnaire, historical/archival research, and ecological techniques. For example, Goldstein's (1979) archival data involve a prospective correlational design. Although surveys generally involve a correlational design (e.g., Carvell and Kerr 1980), Biddle et al. (1981) used a quasi-experimental design and Wallston, Foster, and Berger (1978) included a true experiment in their survey of dual career couples. Similarly, observation may be used in correlational studies (e.g., Serbin et al. 1973), quasi-experiments (e.g., Seaver 1973), true experiments (e.g., Sarason and Ganzer 1973; Zahavi and Asher 1978), and is an important part of ethnographic research (e.g., Corsaro 1981).

There is sometimes a tendency to confuse design with statistical analysis strategy. In fact, referring to designs as "correlational" adds to such confusion. The use of analysis of variance does not necessarily imply that an experiment was carried out (e.g., Goldstein 1979). It is important that conclusions reflect the actual design as well as the statistics employed (cf. Boruch and Rosenthal chapters, this volume).

Because this chapter focuses on research relevant to sex-roles and social problems, techniques useful in the field will be emphasized. This does not suggest that laboratory experimentation may not be an important strategy for investigating some questions relevant to social problems (cf. Leinhardt 1978; Unger, 1981). Moreover, the field/laboratory distinction is overly simplistic. Tunnell (1977) discussed three dimensions of naturalness: behavior, setting, and treatment. Experiments may use natural treatments in a natural setting (e.g., school desegregation) but rarely study natural behavior. Observation and ethnography are the most common techniques for the study of natural behavior. Each element of naturalness typically adds to our ability to generalize from our data across populations, settings and times, termed external validity.

In discussing disadvantages of various methods, Cook and Campbell's (1979) terminology regarding validity will be employed. In addition to external validity, designs vary in their statistical conclusion validity (is there a relationship between variables?), internal validity (is the relationship causal?) and construct validity (can a generalization be made about higher-order constructs from the research operations?). Other chapters focus on aspects of statistical-conclusion validity and construct validity. The focus here will be on internal and external validity.

While this chapter emphasizes research methods, one must remember that question generation is an equally important aspect of research (cf. Wallston 1981). In fact, questions and method are inextricably intertwined. Our questions may be limited by the types of methods we tend to employ. Brief discussion of such limitations of designs will follow but extensive discussion of questions is beyond the scope of this chapter (cf. McGuire 1973; Wallston 1981; Wallston and Grady, in press; Wrightsman and Deaux 1981).

None of the discussion to follow should be taken to suggest that some research methods are inherently superior in and of themselves. Validity issues must always be considered in terms of validity for what. Methods must be considered, in terms of the question being asked, the state of knowledge in the field, and the practical aspects of undertaking research. The best design represents a compromise between the research goal and the possibilities afforded by the situation (Glass and Ellett 1980). While calls for more qualitative research approaches have come from feminists (e.g., Carlson 1972; Weiss 1981), thorough reading of these critiques recognizes their argument for the integration of a variety of methods (Wallston 1981). Methods have frequently been aligned with particular disciplines, and until recently, all disciplines had masculine patriarchal biases (e.g., Laws 1976; Sherman and Beck 1979). Thus, no method is inherently feminist and methods should be viewed as tools to answer or generate questions.

Before turning to the discussion of specific methods, a brief additional discussion of my perspective is in order. Since values are an inherent part of science (cf. Sherif 1979; Shields 1975; Wallston 1979, 1981; Wallston and Grady, in press), my discussion of methods should be read in light of my background, values and biases.*

The chapter will begin with a discussion of selected designs, followed by a discussion of selected techniques. A discussion of the value and importance of method triangulation will conclude the chapter. Following the research design section, examples will be presented using the designs. Because of the variety of available literature on school desegregation, this was selected as the example topic to show the reader the variety of possible approaches using different designs. One should be able to extrapolate to sex roles research.

---

*My training was in experimental social psychology. Most of my own research involves true experiments, although I've done quasi-experiments, and correlational studies as well. I've had extensive experience in scale development and I've done research using mail surveys, interviews, content analyses and observational techniques. Thus, I lack experience in ethnographic/qualitative research and ecological techniques. These are important approaches and I have argued for their utilization (Wallston 1981), but my experience with them is secondhand. Other biases and values should be clear from the discussion thus far.

RESEARCH DESIGNS

True Experiments

Random assignment of participants to treatment and control groups characterize the experimental method. Such assignment allows at least probabilistic comparability between groups at pretreatment and thus provides relatively strong internal validity. However, relatively large sample sizes are needed to obtain actual comparability, and testing whether random assignment worked in terms of important dimensions is essential (Cook and Campbell 1979). For further details on how to achieve random assignment and field conditions which are conducive to this research strategy, Cook and Campbell (1979) is an excellent resource. Where true experiments are possible, they provide the strongest evidence for the conclusion that a causes b. Treatments generally involve the manipulation of some variable by the experimenter. Control groups are discussed further in the section on quasi-experiments.

Although random assignment rules out the majority of threats to internal validity listed by Cook and Campbell (1979), some threats remain. There may be differential "mortality" between treatment and control groups. It is essential to collect data on attrition and test for this effect. Four other threats remain: (1) "compensatory equalization of treatments," (2) "compensatory rivalry by respondents receiving less desirable treatments," (3) "resentful demoralization of respondents receiving less desirable treatment," and (4) "diffusion" where control participants interact with those in the treatment and receive some benefits. Cook and Campbell (1979) provide further details on these threats and suggest assessing the nature of participants' experience as one means of examining and ruling out these threats to validity.

Numerous resources exist on the conduct of true experiments (e.g., Campbell and Stanley 1963; Carlsmith, Ellsworth and Aronson 1976; Kerlinger 1979). Experiments, however, are not always possible. Many powerful treatments cannot be randomly assigned because of lack of control of the field setting, resistance of administrators, or ethical considerations (cf. Cook and Campbell 1979). Moreover, experiments may be time-consuming, laborious, costly, and most importantly, what is gained in control may be lost in impact (cf. Carlsmith, Ellsworth and Aronson 1976).

Glass and Ellett (1980) note that experiments are awkward and insensitive, involving such inadequate description of treatments that replication is impossible. They "risk overlooking small signals in noisy messages" (Glass and Ellett, 1980, p. 223). Cronbach (1975) notes the limited ability to detect interactions since the number of independent variables must be kept small.

Complex treatments are likely to have multiple meanings and participants' interpretations of the same situation may vary systematically or in relation to their individual history (cf. Carlsmith, Ellsworth, and Aronson 1976; Grady 1981).

Because they are obtrusive, experiments have the potential for bias in terms of demand characteristics of the experimental situation and the nature of the researcher/participant interaction (cf. Rosenthal and Rosnow 1969; Unger 1981; Wallston and Grady, in press). In laboratory research, experimenters may be "blind" to the experimental treatment but this is much more difficult to accomplish in field settings. On the other hand, because field settings add a dimension of naturalness and frequently occur over time, artificial responses by participants due to being in an experiment may be less likely. The investment in a treatment by those who carry it out may be higher, so "experimenter effects" may be more likely. Carlsmith, Ellsworth, and Aronson (1976) provide further suggestions to control for such bias.

Experiments may be premature (cf. Depner 1981; Petronovich 1979; Wallston 1981), and, therefore, the choice of variables to manipulate may be arbitrary. Unlikely situations may be created, thus teaching us about the possible but not the probable importance of variables. The context is frequently lost in experiments, and complex, dynamic processes may not be adequately understood with the static experimental method (cf. Bronfenbrenner 1977; Petronovich 1979). Further discussion of these issues will be presented under the advantages of qualitative and ecological approaches. Experiments have frequently been used to investigate sex-role issues (e.g., Goldstein 1979; Wallston, Foster, and Berger 1978).

Quasi-experiments

Numerous designs are classified as quasi-experiments. The most complete treatment of design issues is found in Cook and Campbell (1979). Two major types of designs, nonequivalent control groups, and time series will be discussed. Only a few designs under each heading will be covered. Mahoney (1978) provides an excellent brief treatment of these designs.

Nonequivalent control groups. The untreated control group with pretest and posttest is similar to a true experimental design, except that the untreated group is constituted in some way other than random assignment. In addition to all the threats to validity discussed above, "maturation," "instrumentation," "differential statistical regression," and the interaction of "selection" and "history" pose threats to internal validity. Since both groups receive the pretest and posttest, there is control for the effect of testing and it is possible to test for selection effects. History, social change over time that may affect the experimental outcome, is not a problem since both groups experience any historical factors. However, maturation, or developmental change, may be differential for treatment and control groups or history may interact with the treatment. Differential statistical regression would mean that there was change in the dependent measure in the experimental or control groups for artifactual statistical reasons. Such threats may be ruled out through appeals to logic. Are they reasonable alternative explanations of the findings? The addition of multiple pretests to the design, particularly possible when available from archives, allows one to test the effects of maturation (Cook and Campbell 1979).

Because of the problem of selection effects, findings from the nonequivalent control groups with posttest only design are difficult to interpret. However, when higher-order interactions are predicted, relatively stronger causal inference is possible (Cook and Campbell 1979). That is, persons in experimental groups may differ from the control groups at the outset. This is more plausible when a simple outcome such as higher test scores is found. However, when a variety of variables interact, it is less likely that simple selection could lead to such a result. Seaver's (1973) study of teacher-expectancy effects illustrates this principle. She provides an excellent discussion of potential threats to validity in this natural quasi-experiment using archival data.

In situations where random assignment is not possible ethically or practically, quasi-experiments make it possible to draw relatively strong causal conclusions. Appropriate contrast or control groups are of central importance in allowing such influence.

Control groups. A complete discussion of control groups is beyond the scope of this chapter, but clearly the choice of an appropriate control group is essential to a good quasi-experiment. Parlee (1981) raises important issues regarding the underlying theoretical assumptions in selection of a control group.* (See also Cook and Campbell 1979; Ellsworth 1977.)

Sex and quasi-experimental design. In some sense, any study of sex differences can be considered a quasi-experimental design. Persons cannot be randomly assigned to a sex, and cross-sex comparisons are always, therefore, comparisons of nonequivalent control groups. Grady (1981) has discussed the way sexist institutions prescreen individuals creating potentially nonequivalent groups. Causal inferences with respect to sex should be made in light of the threats to internal validity discussed above.†

Thus, before a conclusion is drawn that males and females differ, it is important to consider differential selection to the sample, how recent history may have had different effects on the groups, and how maturation of the

---

*Control groups are an issue in all research designs, but discussion at this point seemed most parsimonious.

†For discussions of other issues related to sex difference in conclusions, see Eagley and Wood, in press; Grady 1979; Jacklin 1979; Unger 1981; Wallston 1981; Wallston and Grady, in press.

groups might be different. All of these and all the other threats to internal validity discussed by Cook and Campbell are potential alternative explanations of the conclusion that males and females differ.

Time-series designs. The simple interrupted time-series design involves a number of pretests, the treatment and a number of posttests. That is, multiple measures are made over time. Cook and Campbell (1979) provide extensive discussion of such techniques and data analysis strategies are detailed by Glass, Willson, and Gottman (1975). The multiple measures allow the assessment of maturational trends prior to the intervention. However, sufficient observations need to be collected to consider the possibility of seasonal, or cyclic, trends. History is the major threat to internal validity since specific other factors during the experimental treatment could affect the dependent measures. However, the use of the addition of a nonequivalent no treatment control can counter this threat to validity as well as the issue of selection.

Instrumentation is, however, an issue since the intervention may affect record keeping. Attention to the issues of the study may cause more careful records and this alone could change numbers. These designs are most easily accomplished with archival data or the repeated measures can become costly and time-consuming.

Data in time series are used to detect changes in the slope and/or the level subsequent to intervention. Details on a variety of findings and their possible interpretation are provided by Cook and Campbell.

Single subject or case-study designs, frequently termed ABA or ABAB in the literature, are a common type of time-series design (cf. Hayes 1981; Levy and Olson 1979; Tripodi and Harrington 1979). Kazdin (1981) discusses means to improve inferences from such designs including the use of systematic quantitative data. Such designs may be appropriate for studying clinical interventions such as assertiveness training, or work with anorexics (cf. Brodsky and Hare-Mustin 1980).

Correlational Studies

Because data collection at a single point in time provides the weakest basis for causal inference, the emphasis will be on prospective or longitudinal studies. These terms may be interchanged, although prospective designs imply that data on the "independent" varibles are collected at some point in time prior to data on the "dependent" variable;* longitudinal designs merely imply more than one measurement time, and in fact, the quasi-experimental designs

---

*This distinction is particularly arbitrary for correlational data. It can also be arbitrary in experimental design (Wallston 1981).

already discussed are longitudinal designs. The distinction here is that in correlational studies, the independent variables are generally measured rather than manipulated experimentally or found to occur naturally.

The parallel designs that raise more serious threats to internal validity are retrospective and cross-sectional designs.* Further discussion of some problems will be covered under survey techniques.

Longitudinal designs present numerous practical problems (cf. Wohlwill 1973). They require extensive commitment of time, money, and resources. Participant attrition is a major problem. Freedman, Thornton, and Camburn (1980) provide an excellent discussion of techniques for maintaining long-term contact. They discussed the importance of maintaining rapport, personalizing each interaction with data from the previous interaction, and obtaining names and addresses of other individuals to assist in future location. Using these techniques they were able to maintain contact with more than 80 percent of their sample for four interviews spanning 15 years.

Longitudinal designs are necessary to provide evidence on changes. They also allow inferences regarding the relation between early behavior and/or conditions and later behavior, with the individual serving as his or her own control. Information on the shape of developmental functions can only be obtained from a longitudinal design (Wohlwill 1973).

The threats to internal validity with longitudinal designs include selection, history, testing, instrumentation, mortality (i.e., loss of subjects), and the interaction of these threats with selection and ambiguity regarding the direction of causal inference. Cross-sectional designs have differential maturation as an additional threat to internal validity. Effects of history may be ruled out by using what is termed a convergence method (Wohlwill 1973). A cross-sectional design is superimposed on a longitudinal design. If changes over time (e.g., as girls grow from 12 to 13) parallel changes originally found between groups, history is a less plausible explanation.

Angle and Wissman (1981) illustrate the use of data from existing national longitudinal data bases. They found a large negative effect on earnings of being female, even with numerous other factors controlled. Such secondary analysis (cf. Boruch, Wortman and Cordray 1981) of existing data has important potential for sex roles research.

Ethnographic/Qualitative Research

The broad rubric of qualitative research is not a design in the same sense as the other designs here, but it does connote some overall approaches to

---

*For discussions of problems with retrospective data, see Wallston et al. (1983) and Wohlwill (1973). Numerous treatments of cross-sectional versus longitudinal designs are found in the developmental literature (e.g., Baltes 1968; Baltes, Reese and Lipsitt 1980; McCall 1977).

research that differ substantially from those discussed and thus is not a technique by my technique/design distinction. Ethnography stems from a different conception of science (Hutson 1981). The goal is to understand an event and create appropriate metaphors to give it logical coherence.

Sanday (1979) provides an excellent overview of ethnographic paradigms, noting areas of agreement and distinctions. Extended participant observation is central to all ethnography which is primarily derived from work in anthropology. The ethnomethodology of sociologists has commonality with these techniques (cf. Garfinkle and Sacks 1969). Recently educational ethnography has become more popular (cf. Green and Wallat 1981a; Lancy 1978; Rist 1977; Tikunoff and Ward 1977). Numerous sources on qualitative methods exist (e.g., Bogdan and Taylor 1975; Glaser 1978; Glaser and Strauss 1967; Harre 1977; Patton 1980; Van Maanen 1979b; Walcott 1975). Several briefer treatments form the basis for much of my discussion (e.g., Lancy 1978; Lutz 1981; Miles 1979; Sanday 1979; Van Maanen 1979a; Weiss 1980, 1981).

Ethnography has been termed thick description (Geertz 1973). Its focus is on meaning, context, subjective experience, and connections. The emphasis is on understanding the phenomenology of respondents (Weiss 1981). Thus, its advantages are in direct contrast to the disadvantages of experiments and vice versa. Discovery and exploration, rather than hypothesis testing, is the goal. Although statistics are not used, it is important to provide detailed information on the means of obtaining and analyzing data (Weiss 1981).

In addition to participant observation, ethnography may include informant interviews, mapping, and charting, and use of archival data (cf. Green and Wallat 1981b; Lutz 1981; Sanday 1979). Although the term ethnography has usually been applied to study of a culture as a whole, microethnography constitutes such work when a smaller unit of analysis is used (Green and Wallat 1981b). I won't adhere to this distinction here. An important aspect of ethnography is validation of the description that has been constructed by the participants (Green and Wallat 1981b). However, Miles (1979) notes the difficulties of this because of the potential for lack of anonymity even with pseudonyms and the participants' desire for positive self-presentation.

While not statistical ethnography is empirical. The principal data document is the diary or field notes. Training in ethnography is essential (Lutz 1981).

The advantages of ethnography are its preservation of the chronological flow. It is full, holistic and real. Minimal instrumentation is necessary at the outset. Examples lend credence to reports (Miles 1979). There is some disagreement regarding the extent to which the ethnographer begins with any conceptual notions or whether these develop from the data (cf. Lutz 1981; McClintock, Brannon, and Maynard-Moody 1979; Sanday 1979).

Ethnography is extremely time-consuming and may cause culture shock and disorientation (Sanday 1979). The data overload can be overwhelming and the methods of analysis are not well-formulated (Miles 1979).

The concepts of internal validity are not particularly appropriate for a discussion of ethnography since causality is not the issue. However, replicability is important and potentially difficult. Some argue that ethnography must be more accountable in terms of verification and falsification (Hutson 1981). McClintock, Brannon, and Maynard-Moody (1979) provide suggestions for this by adding notions of survey sampling to ethnographic procedures. They refer to this as a case cluster method and provide three examples. They argue persuasively that perception is always an organizing process (cf. Neisser 1976), and their procedures formulate this process publicly rather than leaving it as tacit or nonconscious. From research in cognitive social psychology, we know that perceptions of actors and observers differ in systematic ways (cf. Jones and Nisbett 1972; Monson and Snyder 1977) which need to be considered by participant observers. There is also extensive research showing that persons do not take sufficient account of base-rate information (cf. Kahneman and Tversky 1973; Taylor and Fiske 1978). Thus, in ethnographic as well as other research methods, we must be aware of the influence of the researcher and the researcher's cognitive and perceptual process (cf. Ogbu 1981; Van Maanen 1979a).

Goetz and Le Compte (1981) provide an excellent synthesis of data analysis and reduction strategies for ethnographers. They suggest some ways to control or test for the reactive effects of observer bias. Bunster (1977) provides an interesting discussion of her use of still photography to interview proletarian working mothers in Lima, Peru.

Research Comparison

A series of studies has investigated the conditions of effective school desegregation. Hansell and Slavin's (1981) true experiment provides better inference than efforts by Aronson and colleagues (e.g., Aronson and Bridgeman 1979; Aronson and Geffner 1978; Aronson and Osherow 1980; Blaney et al. 1977) that were quasi-experiments. While Hansell and Slavin randomly assigned classes to treatment and control groups, with teachers teaching both an experimental and a control class, in the Aronson research, teachers who attended a workshop formed the experimental treatment group. They were asked to nominate other competent teachers in their school to form the control group. Thus, teacher selection may have contributed to the success of their intervention, termed the jigsaw classroom.

Rosenfield et al. (1981) also studied desegregation, but they investigated variables not amenable to experimental manipulation (e.g., racial structure and relative status in classrooms). They used a correlational design employing the convergence method with a cross-sectional sample and a longitudinal replication. Their discussion of issues of causal inference is particularly valuable.

Schofield and Sager's (1977) time-series design illustrates another approach to school desegregation, taking advantage of a naturally occurring experiment. The study illustrates how multiple measures over time allow the investigation of behavior patterns. Lunchtime seating as an indicator of friendship choice is a natural behavior in a natural setting in contrast to sociograms used in some of the other studies. While the study is flawed, the lack of pretest data and a comparison group are discussed appropriately.

Ethnographies can provide a very different perspective of desegregated schools (Metz 1978), resegregated schools (Collins and Noblit 1977), and de facto segregated schools (Rosenfield 1971). Within ethnographic studies, comparisons across cultures add perspective on minority issues in education (e.g., Lewis 1981; Ogbu 1978).

The full flavor of the different questions and findings from these varied designs cannot be provided in these few paragraphs. They are meant to illustrate that similar problems may be attacked in very different ways with different outcomes. Interested readers will need to consult the original sources for the total perspective.

RESEARCH TECHNIQUES

As already noted, the techniques to be discussed can be used within the research designs already delineated.

Observation

Observational techniques are a broad rubric covering any "planned, methodological watching that involves constraints to improve accuracy" (Weick 1968, p. 388). Observation may involve structured or unstructured interaction in laboratory or field settings (cf. Lytton 1971). Generally, only public events can be observed. Numerous reviews of methods of behavioral observation exist (e.g., Bakeman and Dabbs 1976; Lytton 1971; Sackett 1978; Veit 1979; Weick 1968).

Category selection is an important aspect of observational methodology. Veit (1979) suggests that this process can be considered a form of theory construction; validity as well as reliability of category must be considered. Simon and Boyer (1974) have reviewed instruments used for observation. Careful definition of behavioral elements are central to category selection criteria (cf. Gellert 1955; Rosenblum 1978; Weick 1968).

Sampling strategies (cf. Altman 1974; Bakeman 1978; Veit 1979) are important to consider and have implications for data analysis. Data recording techniques also influence the form of the resulting data (cf. Veit 1979).

Reliability is probably the aspect of observation that has received the most attention (cf. Veit 1979). Observer bias is a major problem that may influence reliability (cf., Berman and Kenny 1976; Reid 1970; Saal, Downey and Lahey 1980; Taplin and Reid 1973; Unger 1981; Veit 1979). Some of the issues were discussed earlier in the section on ethnography. Reactivity is also an important issue (e.g., Smith, McPhail, and Pickens 1975; Spencer et al. 1974; Veit 1979). Calculations of reliability should correct for chance agreement between observers (Cohen 1960; Light 1971) but simple percentage agreement is too frequently used (see Veit 1979).

Observations allow us information about actual ongoing behavior. We can investigate patterns of interaction. Processes which are subtle or not fully conscious for participants can be extracted through observational procedures. They are an important technique for sex role researchers.

While research examples cited in the last section use observational techniques (e.g., Metz 1978; Schofield and Sagar 1977), Serbin et al. (1973) provide a particularly good illustration of a study of sex bias that uses observation. Differences in responses to males and females are frequently nonconscious, so observation in contrast to verbal self-reports may be critical to investigate such issues.

Survey/Interview/Questionnaire

Asking people questions is part of most research endeavors. Dillman (1978) provides an excellent step-by-step approach to survey research. Cannell and Kahn's (1968) discussion of interviewing provides a good overview of issues and techniques. Several recent articles have discussed issues specific to surveys of minority populations (cf. Myers 1977; Weiss 1977; Zusman and Olson 1977).

A major issue with surveys is the extent to which self-reports reflect behavior (cf. Cannell and Kahn 1968; Cherlin and Horiuchi 1980; Hook and Rosenshine 1979; Newfield 1980). Memory lapse and motivational factors contribute to reporting errors (Wyner 1980). Characteristics of interviewers and respondents also affect the validity of interview data (cf. Cannell and Kahn 1968; Schaeffer 1980; Unger 1981). Construction of the questions is also an important element (cf. Cannell and Kahn 1968; Schuman and Presser 1978).

Self-report techniques allow access to a range of experiences that cannot be observed. Access to the phenomenology of the participant is only possible through direct questioning. We must, however, be aware of the interview as a social situation and consider how this influences the data obtained.

Many of the research examples already provided used some form of questionnaire (Hansell and Slavin 1981; Rosenfield et al. 1981) or interview (Angle and Wissman 1981; Bunster 1977).

Frieze's (1979) work on battering shows the advantages of in depth interviews in gathering information on important social problems. It would have been impossible to observe battering instances. Only direct questioning could provide the variety of data gathered by Frieze and her colleages.

Historical/Archival Research

Historical research uses data already collected from other sources. A major advantage is the potential time saved in collecting data. A major disadvantage is that questions are limited by the data that are available.

Use of primary rather than secondary sources is important for accuracy of conclusions (Kerlinger 1979). While much archival research involves content analysis (e.g., Holsti, Loomba, and North 1968; Krippendorff 1980; Sanders 1974), the nature of the available archival data and the research questions influence the technique. Secondary analysis of data is becoming a popular technique (cf. Borgatta and Jackson 1980; Kerlinger 1979). When you have not collected your own data, the validity and reliability of the archives are important to assess. Institutional records vary considerably in their accuracy.

Content analysis is a technique for making inferences by systematically identifying specified characteristics of messages. Issues of coding, categories, reliability and validity are similar to issues with observational categories. The definition of the categories, the units of analysis and sampling are critical issues (cf. Holsti, Loomba and North 1968).

There have been numerous content analyses showing differential media portrayals of males and females (e.g., Busby 1975; Sternglanz and Serbin 1974; Weitzman et al. 1972). Goldstein (1979) provides an excellent example where archival data *(Psychological Abstracts)* were a better source than questionnaires to study the relation of same- and other-sex advisors to postdegree publication. Her method eliminated problems of nonrespondents as well as potential unreliability of self-reports. Goldstein (1979) was appropriately cautious regarding causal inference from this prospective correlational design (although she analyzed using analysis of variance).

Ecological Research

The discussion here will not be of techniques in quite the same sense as the techniques described above. They are also not quite designs. There is some commonality with the previous discussion of qualitative research, but ecological inquiry involves quantitative methods as well.

Ecological psychology is the study of human behavior in natural contexts. Human environments are analyzed at a molar rather than a molecular level (Wicker 1979). Alternative techniques have been criticized for their failure to consider the environmental context of research (e.g., Ogbu 1981; Petronovich 1979; Willems 1974). For example, Bronfenbrenner (1977, p. 513) described developmental psychology as the "science of the strange behavior of children in strange situations with strange adults for the briefest possible periods of time."

Two conceptual schemes or techniques form the basis of much ecological research, Barker's work on behavioral settings (e.g., Barker 1968; Barker and Schoggen 1973) and Brunswik's "representative design" (cf. Hammond and Wascoe 1980; Petronovich 1979; Tyler 1981).

Behavior settings, a concept developed by Barker, refer to the miniature social systems or environments in which we are involved in day-to-day living. Naturalistic observation is generally used to describe behavior settings. Records are made of all occurrences and there are many parallels to ethnography. However, quantitative analyses are carried out. A major focus of work using these techniques has been the relationship of setting density, in terms of roles and persons to fill them, and individuals' involvement in the settings (e.g., Barker and Gump 1964; Wicker 1969).

Major implications of research stemming from Brunswikian notions are: the importance of sampling settings, the inappropriateness of much experimental molecular reductionism, and the importance of external validity (Petronovich 1979). "Representative design" captures the first of these issues, the need to sample from stimuli just as we sometimes recognize the need to sample from subjects (cf. Maher 1978a; Petronovich 1979). A complex lens model technique developed by Brunswik preserves the complexity of behavioral episodes (e.g., Davis and Plas, in press; Petronovich 1979; Tyler 1981) in contrast to static studies of necessarily dynamic processes.

CONCLUSION

I began with the concept that design and technique should fit the research question. The discussion of the various methods should assist in making method decisions. All methods have advantages and disadvantages. Certainly we know the most about a particular problem or issue when we have considered it from a variety of perspectives. The multiple research examples from the school-desegregation literature were meant to illustrate this point. The use of multiple methodologies within the same research project, sometimes termed "triangulation," will be discussed here briefly.

Triangulation

The call for triangulation has now become extremely popular (e.g., Jick 1979; Macke, Richardson and Cook 1980; McCall 1977; McClintock, Brannon, and Maynard-Moody 1979; Miles 1979; Sevigny 1981; Trend 1978; Tsukashima 1977; Weiss 1980). "Converging operations" is a parallel term (McCall 1977). Although the idea of the multitrait-multimethod matrix (Campbell and Fiske 1959) was developed for the assessment of scale validity, it can provide a framework for triangulated inquiry within quantitative methods (Jick 1979). Much of the call for triangulation, however, argues for the value of combining quantitative and qualitative techniques.

Jick's (1979) discussion of triangulation is excellent. He notes that determining convergence of findings is a subjective exercise without good guidelines. However, divergence can provide an opportunity for richer, more complex explanations. Triangulation is, however, costly and time-consuming. Moreover, Jick (1979) notes the importance of equally valuing the methods utilized rather than using one as "window dressing" for the other. The advantages of triangulation are relatively obvious. They allow us to bring the advantages of each of the methods we use to our research endeavor. They provide data that are "'real, deep, *and* hard'" (Zelditch 1962, p. 567) (cited in McClintock, Brannon, and Maynard-Moody 1979, p. 612).

On Dichotomies

My discussion and other discussions of research methods frequently focus on dichotomies that may be better considered as continua or may fail to acknowledge more appropriate distinctions. Elsewhere I have discussed the labeling of hard and soft science that Bart (1973) has termed dry and wet, and called for a science that is hard and wet (Wallston 1981). Bronfenbrenner similarly notes, "We risk being caught between a rock and a *soft* place. The rock is *rigor* and the soft place *relevance*" (1977, p. 513) in his call for an experimental ecology of human development.

The qualitative/quantitative distinction may be overdrawn. "Naive social quantifiers continue to overlook the presumptive, qualitatively judgmental nature of *all* science;...the scientist must continually judge whether a given rival hypothesis will explain the data. Qualitative contextual information (as well as quantitative evidence on tangential variables) has long been recognized as relevant to such judgments" (Cook and Campbell 1979, p. 95). Moreover, quantitative researchers use qualitative judgments throughout the research process, though we rarely acknowledge their importance in print. In fact, our belief or disbelief of our findings is frequently a subjective judgment that dictates continuing statistical analysis, the decision to attempt a replication or to publish. Koch (1981) has noted a problematic move away from such judgments as part of the "pathology of knowledge" resulting in "the *total abrogation* of the criterion that knowledge should make sense and in an ultimate distrust of one's own experience" (p. 258).

Smith and Sluckin (1979) provide an interesting discussion of false dichotomies focusing on four distinctions. Continua provide a better framework for considering these distinctions that provide a basis for categorizing research. Rather than asking are categories subjective (actor determined) or objective (researcher determined), we might better discuss the amount of agreement and the perspective taken to determine categories. Rather than considering description as direct or inferential, we can discuss the level of inference involved. The actor/observer distinction can also be overdrawn since people can participate at a variety of levels. Even verbal and nonverbal behavior cannot always be easily dichotomized.

Thus, although qualitative research may sometimes be distinguished from quantitative by its use of actor categories and behavior that is directly described, the level of inference may not be fully clear and quantitative approaches are sometimes phenomenological. As already discussed, ecological approaches and ethnographic approaches clearly value the subjective and phenomenological, and other methods such as the Q-sort have been touted as means of assessing the subjective (e.g., Stephenson 1980). However, survey techniques are designs to assess experience from the perspective of the actor and may vary on how categories are determined. Moreover, as already noted, these techniques may be part of any of the designs discussed. Thus, a clarification of the goals of our research and a recognition of the potentialities of a variety of methods will allow us to better fit the method to the question.

Some have suggested that qualitative descriptive information should always form the basis of experimental operations (e.g., McCall 1977). While this is a good rule of thumb, we should not restrict ourselves to specifying when and where to use each method. As Trend (1978) noted: "Commonly, however, observational data are used for 'generating hypotheses,' or describing *process*. Quantitative data are used to 'analyze *outcomes*,' or verify hypotheses. I feel that this division of labor is rigid and limiting" (p. 352).

Summary

True experiments provide the best ability to draw conclusions regarding causal relationships. Quasi-experiments are often important substitutes for experiments where random assignment is not possible. Since persons can never be randomly assigned to the classification of male and female, all sex differences studies are quasi-experiments and the threats to validity, particularly in terms of differential selection, must be considered in drawing conclusions regarding sex differences.

Longitudinal and prospective designs are important approaches to studying change over time. Many variables of interest in research on social change are not amenable to experimental manipulation, and thus such correlational designs are an important source of research information.

Qualitative research provides information that cannot be gathered using the other quantitative designs. The richness of the context may best be assessed by using qualitative methods. As already emphasized, triangulation, combining the best aspects of quantitative and qualitative models, will give the most complete research information.

Techniques such as observation, surveys, and archival research can be used with all the designs discussed. Observation provides information on ongoing behavior. Subtle processes and patterns of interaction can be ascertained through observational procedures. Surveys provide information on individuals' perceptions. Participants' phenomenology is only accessible through such direct questioning. Thus, a combination of observation and interviews provides a better picture of what is happening than can be provided by either technique alone.

Archival research allows the understanding of issues over time without the time-consuming longitudinal data collection. Representative design and behavior-setting research are quantitative approaches with some of the advantages of qualitative research. Researchers should consider all of these designs and techniques in relation to the question of interest.

Implications

Triangulation should be used where possible. Where it is not feasible, we should be open to a variety of approaches. Koch's (1981) prescriptions for psychologists are relevant to all sex role researchers: "Psychological events...are multiply determined, ambiguous in their human meaning, polymorphous, contextually environed or embedded in complex and vaguely bounded ways, evanescent and labile in the extreme;...extensive and important sectors of psychological study require modes of inquiry rather more like those of the humanities than the sciences" (pp. 268–69). Cook and Campbell's (1979) prescription—"Field experimentation should always include qualitative research to describe and illuminate the context and conditions under which research is conducted" (p. 93)—recognizes this. But, Miles (1979) equally cautions those involved in qualitative approaches that systematization is necessary so that such work can transcend storytelling.

Using Pepper's (1942) world hypotheses, Tyler's (1981) analysis of research approaches is useful. She notes an overreliance on the metaphor of the machine and the value of the alternative metaphor of the living creature adapting to the environment. But neither metaphor needs to be directly linked to a specific method. "Neither formism nor mechanism is obsolete. Some phenomena called for observation and classification.... Some problems lend themselves to experimental manipulation and mechanistic conclusions. But to be able to shift to a contextual or organic orientation when it is needed is an advantage for the scientist" (Tyler 1981, p. 18). This overview of a variety of research methods has been geared toward the development of such openness to methods and conceptualizations beyond those which we utilize out of habit and training.

REFERENCES

Altman, J. Observational study of behavior: Sampling methods. *Behaviour* 49 (1974):227–67.
Angle, J., and D.A. Wissman. Gender, college major, and earnings. *Sociology of Education* 54 (1981):25–33.
Aronson, E., and D. Bridgeman. Jigsaw groups and the desegregated classroom: In pursuit of common goals. *Personality and Social Psychology Bulletin* 5 (1979):438–46.
Aronson, E., and R. Geffner. Interdependent interactions and prosocial behavior. *Journal of Research and Development in Education* 12 (1978):16–27.
Aronson, E., and N. Osherow. Cooperation, prosocial behavior and academic performance: Experiments in the desegregated classroom. In L. Bickman (ed.), *Applied social psychology annual,* vol. 1. Beverly Hills: Sage, 1980.
Bakeman, R. Untangling streams of behavior: Sequential analysis of observation data. In G.P. Sackett (ed.), *Observing behavior* (vol. 2) Baltimore: University Park Press, 1978.
Bakeman, R., and J.M. Dabbs. Social interaction observed: Some approaches to the analysis of behavior streams. *Personality and Social Psychology Bulletin* 2 (1976):335–45.
Baltes, P.B. Longitudinal and cross-sectional sequences in the study of age and generation effects. *Human Development* 11 (1968):145–71.
Baltes, P.B., H.W. Reese, and L.P. Lipsitt. Life-span developmental psychology. In M.R. Rosenzweig and L.W. Porter (eds.), *Annual review of psychology.* Palo Alto: Annual Reviews 31 (1980):65–110.
Barker, R.G. *Ecological psychology.* Stanford: Stanford University Press, 1968.
Barker, R.G., and P.V. Gump. *Big school, small school.* Stanford: Stanford University Press, 1964.
Barker, R.G., and P. Schoggen. *Qualities of community life.* San Francisco: Jossey-Bass, 1973.
Bart, P. Psychotherapy, sexism, and social control: A review of *Women and Madness. Society,* 1973.
Berman, J.S., and D.A. Kenny. Correlational bias in observer ratings. *Journal of Personality and Social Psychology* 34 (1976):263–73.
Biddle, B.J., B.J. Bank, D.S. Anderson, J.A. Keats and D.M. Keats. The structure of idleness. In school and dropout adolescent activities in the United States and Australia. *Sociology of Education* 54 1981:106–19.

Blaney, N.T., C. Stephan, D. Rosenfield, E. Aronson and J. Sikes. Interdependence in the classroom: A field study. *Journal of Educational Psychology* 69 (1977):139–46.

Bogdan, R., and S.J. Taylor. *Introduction to qualitative methods.* New York: Wiley, 1975.

Borgatta, E.F., and D.J. Jackson (eds.). *Aggregate data: Analysis and intepretation.* Beverly Hills: Sage, 1980.

Brodsky, A.M., and R. Hare-Mustin. *Women and psychotherapy: An assessment of research and practice.* New York: Guilford, 1980.

Bronfenbrenner, U. Toward an experimental ecology of human development. *American Psychologist* 32 (1977):513–31.

Bunster, B.X. Talking pictures: Field method and visual mode. *Signs* 3 (1977):278–93.

Busby, L.J. Sex-role research on the mass media. *Journal of Communication* 25 (1975):107–31.

Campbell, D.T., and D.W. Fiske. Convergent and discriminant validation by the multitrait-multimethod matrix. *Psychological Bulletin* 56 (1959):81–105.

Campbell, D.T., and J.C. Stanley. Experimental and quasi-experimental designs for research on teaching. In N.L. Gage (ed.) *Handbook of research on teaching.* Chicago: Rand McNally, 1963. Also published as *Experimental and quasi-experimental designs for research.* Chicago: Rand McNally, 1966.

Cannell, C.F., and R.L. Kahn. Interviewing. In G. Lindzey and E. Aronson (eds.) *The handbook of social psychology* (2nd ed.) Reading, Mass: Addison-Wesley, 1968.

Carlsmith, J.M., P.C. Ellsworth, and E. Aronson. *Methods of research in social psychology.* Reading, Mass: Addison-Wesley, 1976.

Carlson, R. Understanding women: Implications for personality theory and research. *Journal of Social Issues* 28(2), (1972):17–32.

Carvell, R., and M.A. Kerr. A self-appraisal survey of reading specialists: Education in the least restrictive environment. *Journal of Educational Research* 74 (1980):120–24.

Cherlin, A., and S. Horiuchi. Retrospective reports of family structure: A methodological assessment. *Sociological Methods and Research* 8(4) (1980).

Cohen, J. A coefficient of agreement for nominal scales. *Educational and Psychological Measurement* 20 (1960):37–46.

Coleman, J.S., E.O. Campbell, C.J. Hobson, J. McPartland, A.M. Mood, C.D. Weinfeld, and R.L. York. *Equality of educational opportunity.* Washington, D.C.: Government Printing Office, 1966.

Collins, T.W., and C.W. Noblit. Stratification and resegregation. The case of crossover high school, Memphis, Tenn.: Final Report, NIE Contract 400-76-009. Washington, D.C.: NIE, 1977.

Cook, T.D., and D.J. Campbell. *Quasi-experimentation: Design, and analysis issues for field settings.* Chicago: Rand McNally, 1979.

Corsaro, W.A. Entering the child's world—research strategies for field entry and data collection in a preschool setting. In J.L. Green and C. Wallat (eds.) *Ethnography and language in educational settings.* Norwood, N.J.: Ablex, 1981.

Crain, R.L. Racial tension in high schools: Pushing the survey method closer to reality. *Anthropology and Education Quarterly* 8 (1977):142–51.

Cronbach, L.J. Beyond the two disciplines of scientific psychology. *American*

Psychologist 30 (1975):116–27.
Davis, J.A., and J.M. Plas. A lens model approach to the evaluation of consumer experience with special education service delivery. *Journal of Special Education*. In Press.
Depner, C. Toward the further development of feminist psychologist. Paper presented at the annual meeting of the Association for Women in Psychology, Boston, March 1981.
Dillman, D. *Mail and telephone surveys: The total design method.* New York: Wiley, 1978.
Eagly, A.H., and W. Wood. Gender and influenceability: Stereotype vs. behavior. In V.E. O'Leary, R.K. Unger, and B.S. Wallston (eds.), *Women, gender and social psychology*. Hillsdale, N.J.: Lawrence Erlbaum, in press.
Ellsworth, P.C. From abstract ideas to concrete instances: Some guidelines for choosing natural research setting. *American Psychologist* 32 (1977):604–15.
Freedman, D.S., A. Thornton, and D. Camburn Maintaining response rates in longitudinal studies. *Sociological Methods and Research* 9 (1980):87–90.
Frieze, I.H. Perceptions of battered wives. In I.H. Frieze, D. Bar-Tal, and J.S. Carroll (eds.), *New approaches to social problems: applications of attribution theory*. San Francisco: Jossey-Bass, 1979.
Garfinkle, H., and H. Sacks. *Contributions to ethnomethodology*. Bloomington: Indiana University Press, 1969.
Geertz, C. *The interpretation of cultures.* New York: Random House, 1973.
Gellert, E. Systematic observation: A method in child study. *Harvard Educational Review* 25 (1955):179–95.
Gerard, H.B., and N. Miller. *School desegregation: A long-range study.* New York: Plenum, 1975.
Glaser, B. *Theoretical sensitivity: Advances in the methodology of grounded theory.* Mill Valley, Calif.: Sociology Press, 1978.
Glaser, B.G., and A. Strauss. *The discovery of grounded theory.* Chicago: Aldine, 1967.
Glass, G.V., and F.S. Ellett. Evaluation research. In M.R. Rosenzweig, and L.W. Porter (eds.), *Annual review of psychology* (vol. 31). Palo Alto: Annual Reviews, 1980:211–88.
Glass, G.V., V.L. Willson, and J.M. Gottman. *Design and analysis of time-series experiments.* Boulder: Colorado Associated University Press, 1975.
Goetz, J.P., and M.D. Le Compte. Ethnographic research and the problem of data reduction. *Anthropology and Education Quarterly* 12 (1981):51–70.
Goldstein, E. Effect of same-sex role models on the subsequent academic productivity of scholars. *American Psychologist* 34 (1979):407–10.
Grady, K.E. Sex bias in research design, *Psychology of Women Quarterly* 5(4), 1981:628–36.
Grady, K.E. Androgyny reconsidered. In J.H. Williams (ed.) *Psychology of women: Selected readings.* New York: Norton, 1979.
Green, J.L., and C. Wallat (eds.). *Ethnography and language in educational settings.* Norwood, N.J.: Ablex, 1981a.
Green, J.L., and C. Wallat, Introduction. In J.L. Green and C. Wallat (eds.), *Ethnography and language in educational settings.* Norwood, N.J.: Ablex, 1981b.

Hammond, H.R., and N.E. Wascoe (eds.). *New directions for methodology of social and behavioral science: Realizations of Brunswik's design*. San Francisco: Jossey-Bass, 1980.

Hansell, S., and R.E. Slavin. "Cooperative learning and the structure of interracial friendships." *Sociology of Education* 54 (1981):98–106.

Harre, R. The ethogenic approach: Theory and practice. In L. Berkowitz (ed.), *Advances in experimental social psychology* (vol. 10). New York: Academic Press, 1977.

Hayes, S.C. Single case experimental design and empirical clinical practice. *Journal of Consulting and Clinical Psychology* 49 (1981):193–211.

Hennigan, K.M., B.R. Flay, and T.D. Cook. "Give me the facts": Some suggestions for using social science knowledge in national policymaking. In R.F. Kidd and M.T. Saks (eds.), *Advances in Applied Social Psychology* (vol. 1). Hillsdale, N.J.: Lawrence Erlbaum, 1980, 113–47.

Holsti, O.R., J.K. Loomba, and R.C. North. Content analysis. In G. Lindzey and E. Aronson (eds.) *The handbook of social psychology* (vol. 2) Reading, Mass.: Addison-Wesley, 1968.

Hook, C.M., and B.V. Rosenshine. Accuracy of teacher reports of their classroom behavior. *Review of Educational Research* 49 (1979):1–11.

Hutson, B. (ed.). Discussion—Needed directions in face-to-face interaction in educational settings (This is an edited version of the conference discussion). In J.L. Green and C. Wallat (eds.), *Ethnography and language in educational settings*. Norwood, N.J.: Ablex, 1981.

Jacklin, C.N. Epilogue. In M.A. Wittig and A.C. Peterson (eds.), *Sex-related differences in cognitive functioning: Developmental issues*. New York: Academic Press, 1979.

Jick, J. Mixing qualitative and quantitative methods: Triangulation in action. *Administrative Sciences Quarterly* 24 (1979):601–11.

Jones, E.E., and R.E. Nisbett. The actor and the observer: Divergent perceptions of the causes of behavior. In E.E. Jones, D.E. Kanouse, H.H. Kelley, R.E. Nisbett, S. Valins, and B. Weiner (eds.), *Attribution: Perceiving the causes of behavior*. Morristown, N.J.: General Learning Press, 1972.

Kahneman, D., and A. Tversky. On the psychology of prediction. *Psychogicial Review* 80 (1973):237–51.

Kazdin, A.E. Drawing valid inferences from case studies. *Journal of Consulting and Clinical Psychology* 49 (1981):183–92.

Kazdin, A.E. The influence of behavior preceding a reinforced response on behavior change in the classroom. *Journal of Applied Behavior Analysis* 10 (1977):299–310.

Kerlinger, F.N. *Behavioral research: A conceptual approach*. New York: Holt, Rinehart & Winston, 1979.

Koch, S. The nature and limits of psychological knowledge: Lessons of a century qua 'science.' *American Psychologist* 36 (1981):257–69.

Krippendorff, K. *Content analysis: An introduction to its methodology*. Beverly Hills: Sage, 1980.

Lancy, D.F. The classroom as phenomenon. In D. Bar-tal and L. Saxe (eds.) *Social psychology of education*. Washington, D.C.: Hemisphere, 1978.

Laws, J.L. Patriarchy as paradigm: The challenge from feminist scholarship. Paper presented at the annual meeting of the American Sociological Association, New York, 1976.

Leinhardt, G. Coming out of the laboratory closet. In D. Bar-tal and L. Saxe (eds.) *Social psychology of education*. Washington, D.C.: Hemisphere, 1978.

Levy, R.L., and D.G. Olson. The single-subject methodology in clinical practice: An overview. *Journal of Social Service Research* 3 (1979):25–49.

Lewis, A. Minority Education in Sharonia, Israel, and Stockton, California: A comparative analysis. *Anthropology and Education Quarterly* 12 (1981):30–50.

Light, R.J. Measures of response agreement for qualitative data, some generalizations and alternatives. *Psychological Bulletin* 76 (1971):365–77.

Lutz, F.W. Ethnography—the holistic approach to understanding schooling. In J.L. Green and C. Wallat (eds.), *Ethnography and language in educational settings*. Norwood, N.J.: Ablex, 1981.

Lytton, H. Observation studies of parent-child interaction: A methodological review. *Child Development* 42 (1971):651–84.

Macke, A.S., L.W. Richardson, and J. Cook. Sex-typed teaching styles of university professors and student reactions. Final Report, NIE (Grant NIE-G-78-0144), April 1980.

Maher, B.A. Stimulus sampling in clinical research: Representative design reviewed. *Journal of Consulting and Clinical Psychology* 46 (1978a):643–47.

Maher, B.A. (ed.). Special issue: Methodology in clinical research. *Journal of Consulting and Clinical Psychology*, 46(4), (1978b).

Mahoney, M.J. Experimental methods and outcome evaluation. *Journal of Consulting and Clinical Psychology* 46 (1978):660–72.

McCall, R.B. Challenges to a science of developmental psychology. *Child Development* 48 (1977):333–44.

McClintock, C.C., D. Brannon, and S. Maynard-Moody. Applying the logic of sample surveys to qualitative case studies: The case cluster method. *Administrative Science Quarterly* 24 (1979):612–29.

McGuire, W.J. The yin and yang of progress in social psychology: Seven koan. *Journal of Personality and Social Psychology* 26 (1973):446–56.

Mehan, H. *Learning lessons: Social organization in the classroom*. Cambridge: Harvard University Press, 1979.

Metz, M.H. *Classrooms and corridors. The crises of authority in desegregated secondary schools*. Berkeley: University of California Press, 1978.

Miles, M.B. Qualitative data as an attractive nuisance: The problem of analysis. *Administrative Science Quarterly* 24 (1979):590–601.

Monson, T.C., and M. Snyder. Actors, observers, and the attribution process: Toward a reconceptualization. *Journal of Experimental Social Psychology* 13 (1977):89–111.

Myers, V. Survey methods for minority populations. *Journal of Social Issues* 33(4), (1977):11–19.

Neisser, U. *Cognition and reality: Principles and implications of cognitive psychology*. San Francisco: Freeman, 1976.

Newfield, J. Accuracy of teacher reports: Reports and observations of specific classroom behaviors. *Journal of Educational Research* 74 (1980):78–82.

Ogbu, J. School ethnography: A multilevel approach. *Anthropology and Education Quarterly* 12 (1981):3–29.

Ogbu, J.U. *Minority education and caste: The American system in cross-cultural perspective.* New York: Academic Press, 1978.

Parlee, M.B. Appropriate control groups in feminist research. *Psychology of Women Quarterly* 5(4), (1981):637–44.

Patton, M.Q. *Qualitative evaluation methods.* Beverly Hills: Sage, 1980.

Pepper, S.C. *World hypotheses: A study of evidence.* Berkeley: University of California Press, 1942.

Petronovich, L. Probabilistic functionalism: A conception of research method. *American Psychologist* 34 (1979):373–90.

Reid, J.B. Reliability assessment of observational data: A possible methodological problem. *Child Development* 41 (1970):1143–50.

Rist, R. On the relations among educational research paradigms: From disdain to détente. *Anthropology and Education* 8 (1977):42–49.

Rosenblum, L.A. The creation of a behavioral taxonomy. In G.P. Sackett (ed.), *Observing behavior* (vol. 2). Baltimore: University Park Press, 1978.

Rosenfield, D., D.S. Sheehan, M.M. Marcus, and W.G. Stephan. Classroom structure and prejudice in desegregated schools. *Journal of Educational Psychology* 73 (1981):17–26.

Rosenfield, G. *Shut those thick lips: A study of slum failure.* New York: Holt, Rinehart & Winston, 1971.

Rosenthal, R., and R.L. Rosnow (eds.). *Artifact in behavioral research.* New York: Academic Press, 1969.

Saal, F.E., R.G. Downey, and M.A. Lahey. Rating the ratings: Assessing the psychometric quality of rating data. *Psychological Bulletin* 88 (1980):413–28.

Sackett, G.P. (ed.). *Observing behavior* (vol. 2). Baltimore: University Park Press, 1978.

Sanday, P.R. The ethnographic paradigms. *Administrative Science Quarterly* 24 (1979):527–38.

Sanders, W.B. (ed.). *The sociologist as detective: An introduction to research methods.* New York: Praeger, 1974.

Sarason, I.G., and V.J. Ganzer. Modeling and group discussion in the rehabilitation of juvenile delinquents. *Journal of Counseling Psychology* 20 (1973):442–49.

Schaeffer, N.C. Evaluating race-of-interviewer effects in a national survey. *Sociological Methods and Research* 8(4), (1980).

Schofield, J.W., and H.A. Sager. Peer interaction patterns in an integrated middle school. *Sociometry* 40 (1977):130–38.

Schuman, H., and S. Presser. The assessment of "no opinion" in attitude surveys. In K.F. Schuessler (ed.), *Sociological Methodology, 1979.* San Francisco: Jossey-Bass, 1978.

Seaver, W.B. Effects of naturally induced teacher expectancies. *Journal of Personality and Social Psychology* 28 (1973):333–42.

Serbin, L.A., D.K. O'Leary, R.N. Kent, and J.J. Tonick. A comparison of teacher response to the preacademic and problem behavior of boys and girls. *Child Development* 44 (1973):796–804.

Sevigny, M.J. Triangulated inquiry—A methodology for the analysis of classroom interaction. In J.L. Green and C. Wallat (eds.), *Ethnography and language in educational settings.* Norwood, N.J.: Ablex, 1981.

Sherif, C.W. Bias in psychology. In J.A. Sherman and E.T. Beck (eds.), *The prism of sex: Essays in the sociology of knowledge.* Madison: University of Wisconsin Press, 1979.

Sherman, J.A., and E.T. Beck (eds.). *The prism of sex: Essays in the sociology of knowledge.* Madison: University of Wisconsin Press, 1979.

Shields, S.A. Functionalism, Darwinism, and the psychology of women: A study in social myth. *American Psychologist* 10 (1975):739–54.

Simon, A., and E.G. Boyer. *Mirrors for behavior: An anthology of observation instruments.* Wincote, Pa.: Community Materials Center, 1974.

Smith, P.K., and A.M. Sluckin. Ethology, ethogeny, etics, emics, biology, culture: On the limitations of dichotomies. *European Journal of Social Psychology* 9 (1979):397–415.

Smith, R.L., C. McPhail, and R.G. Pickens. Reactivity to systematic observation with film: A field experiment. *Sociometry* 38 (1975):536–50.

Spencer, F.W., C.A. Corcoran, G.J. Allen, J.M. Chinsky, and S.W. Veit. Reliability and reactivity of the videotape technique on a ward for retarded children. *Journal of Community Psychology* 2 (1974):71–74.

Stephan, W.G. School desegregation: An evaluation of predictions made in Brown v. Board of Education. *Psychological Bulletin* 85 (1978):217–38.

Stephenson, W. Newton's fifth rule and Q methodology: Application to educational psychology. *American Psychologist* 35 (1980):882–89.

Sternglanz, S.H., and L.A. Serbin. Sex role stereotyping in children's television programs. *Developmental Psychology* 10 (1974):710–15.

Taplin, P.S., and J.B. Reid. Effects of instructional set and experimenter influence on observer reliability. *Child Development* 44 (1973):547–54.

Taylor, S.E., and S. Fiske. Salience, attention, and attribution: Top of the head phenomena. In L. Berkowitz (ed.), *Advances in experimental social psychology,* New York: Academic Press, 1978.

Tikunoff, W.J., and B.A. Ward, (eds.). Exploring qualitative/quantitative research methodologies in education. *Anthropology and Education Quarterly* 8(2), (1977).

Trend, M.G. On the reconciliation of qualitative and quantitative analysis: A case study. *Human Organization* 37 (1978):345–54.

Tripodi, T., and J. Harrington. Uses of time-series designs for formative program evaluation. *Journal of Social Service Research* 3 (1979):67–68.

Tsukashima, R.T. Merging field work and survey research in the study of a minority community. *Journal of Social Issues* 33(4), (1977):133–43.

Tunnell, G.B. Three dimensions of naturalness: An expanded definition of field research. *Psychological Bulletin* 84 (1977):426–37.

Tyler, L.E. More stately mansions—psychology extends its boundaries. In M.R. Rosenzweig and L.W. Porter (eds.) *Annual review of psychology* 32 (1981):1–20.

Unger, R.K. Sex as a social reality: Field and laboratory research. *Psychology of Women Quarterly* 5 (1981):645–53.

Van Maanen, J. The fact of fiction in organizational ethnography. *Administrative Science Quarterly,* 24 (1979a):539–50.

Van Maanen, J. (ed.) Reclaiming qualitative methods for organizational research. *Administrative Science Quarterly* 24 (1979b):519–671.
Veit, S.W. Naturalistic observation of interpersonal interaction. Methods and models. Appendix to Veit, S.W. Interpersonal interactions among mentally retarded group-home residents: The development of naturalistic observation procedure. Doctoral diss., George Peabody College, Nashville, Tenn., 1979.
Wallston, B.S. What are the questions in psychology of women? A feminist approach to research. *Psychology of Women Quarterly* 5(4), (1981):597–617.
Wallston, B.S. Values and social psychology. *Society for the Advancement of Social Psychology Newsletter* 5(3) (1979):7–8.
Wallston, B.S., S.W. Alagna, B.M. DeVellis, and R.F. DeVellis. Social support and physical health. Manuscript submitted for publication, 1983.
Wallston, B.S., M. Foster, and M. Berger. I will follow him: Myth, reality or forced choice: Job seeking experiences of dual career couples. *Psychology of Women Quarterly* 3 (1978):9–21.
Wallston, B.S., and K.E. Grady. Integrating the feminist critique and the crisis in social psychology: another look at research methods. In V.E. O'Leary, R.K. Unger, and B.S. Wallston (eds.), *Women, gender, and social psychology*. Hillsdale: N.J.: Lawrence Erlbaum, 1983.
Weick, K.E. Systematic observational methods. In G. Lindzey and E. Aronson (eds.), *The handbook of social psychology* (vol. 2). Reading, Mass.: Addison-Wesley, 1968.
Weiss, C.H. Survey researchers and minority communities. *Journal of Social Issues* 33(4), (1977):20–35.
Weiss, H.B. The contribution of qualitative methods to the feminist research process. Paper presented to Association for Women in Psychology, Boston, 1981.
Weiss, H.B.. Qualitative contributions to ecological research. Unpublished manuscript, Cornell University, 1980.
Weitzman, L.,. D. Eifler, E. Hokada, and C. Ross. Sex-role socialization in picture books for preschool children. *American Journal of Sociology* 77 (1972):1125–50.
Wicker, A.W. Ecological psychology: Some recent and prospective developments. *American Psychologist* 34 (1979):755–65.
Wicker, A.W. Cognitive complexity, school size, and participation in school behavior settings: A test of the frequency of interaction hypothesis. *Journal of Educational Psychology* 60 (1969):200–03.
Willems, E.P. Behavioral technology and behavioral ecology. *Journal of Applied Behavioral Analysis* 7 (1974):151–64.
Wohlwill, J.F. *The study of behavioral development*. New York: Academic Press, 1973.
Wolcott, H. Criteria for an ethnographic approach to research in schools. *Human Organization* 34 (1975):111–28.
Wrightsman, L.S., and K. Deaux. *Social psychology in the 80s* (3rd ed.) Monterey, Calif.: Brooks/Cole, 1981.
Wyner, G.A. Response errors in self-reported number of arrests. *Sociological Methods and Research* 9 (1980):161–77.
Zahavi, S., and R. Asher. The effect of verbal instructions on preschool children's

aggressive behavior. *Journal of School Psychology* 16 (1978):146–53.
Zelditch, M. Some methodological problems of field studies. *American Journal of Sociology* 67 (1962):566–76.
Zusman, M.E., and A.O. Olson. Gathering complete response from Mexican-Americans by personal interview. *Journal of Social Issues* 33(4), (1977):46–55.

5

Evaluation Issues in Women's Studies

Naida Tushnet Bagenstos and Mary Ann Millsap

INTRODUCTION

Any discussion of evaluation issues that surround women's studies should begin with a definition of women's studies and a sense of the scope of women's studies programs—both in terms of numbers of such programs across the nation and the breadth or depth of the goals. According to Howe and Lauter (1980), a distinction needs to be drawn between women's studies programs and individual courses. Not only is there a difference in numbers (330 programs vs. 3,000 campuses reporting courses (*Women's Studies Newsletter,* Fall 1978)), but a difference in intent. Howe and Lauter assert (1980, p. 4): "What distinguishes a program from an isolated course or even group of courses is the effort to develop a somewhat structured and organized academic experience for women's studies students." The first goal, like the goal of other curricular areas (e.g., science and history), is for students enrolled in the program to learn a distinctive curriculum. The second is to use women's studies as a means for altering the typical (male centered) curriculum. Although evaluation problems are inherent in both goals, it is the second that raises the tougher issues.

Evaluation is essentially a process of assigning value, of trying to determine the worth of some thing or some activity. For example, in assigning grades to students, one looks at whether the students learned as much as or

---

The views expressed in this paper are those of the authors. They do not necessarily reflect the views of the National Institute of Education or the U.S. Department of Education.

more than some expected average. One makes judgments using information about the meeting of a criterion (or of criteria) and then assigns grades. Such professional judgment has also been used in program evaluation. Program evaluation is different from other evaluations in that the judgment of a program involves statements about objectives, the measures to be used in determining whether the objectives have been met, and the factors that seem to be responsible for creating the effects. Evaluating innovative programs and particularly programs that have as a goal some measure of social change (e.g., compensatory education, women's studies) involves not only the technical issues but also frequently involves debates over the desirability of the goals themselves.

Unlike research, designed primarily for the advancement of knowledge, evaluation is designed for immediate use in decision making. Program directors, institutions within which programs are located, funding agencies, and program participants can all use evaluation to improve or scuttle a program or to alter their participation in it. Because of the salience of the decision-making context, people concerned with evaluating women's studies must be cognizant not only of methodological issues (i.e., conducting a technically sound evaluation) but also of political issues (i.e., recognizing the potentially different values held by policymakers and program directors). Because one goal of women's studies seeks at least to present an alternative curriculum, if not to alter the extant curriculum, political or value issues are especially important in evaluating such programs.

This chapter addresses the development of evaluation and the mystique surrounding evaluation (i.e., the view of evaluation as mysterious, inspiring both awe and fear), the uses of evaluation for women's studies, the types of evaluation available, and early efforts in evaluating women's studies.

THE DEVELOPMENT OF EVALUATION AND THE EVALUATION MYSTIQUE

Over the past few years, a mystique has developed about what evaluation is. We need to understand a little more about this mystique before we examine how evaluation can be used in social change programs. Twenty years ago, evaluations consisted of the review of a program or its personnel by a panel of experts, persons whose informed judgment was employed to examine whether the proper range of programs was offered, whether the work was organized in an efficient manner, and whether attitudes about a program were positive. The use of expert consultants in site reviews fulfills a needed function, and such consultants have been used in a number of change programs. These expert consultants are aware of what is going on in different programs and can provide a broader perspective than program personnel typically have. Their reports can offer recommendations for improvement and, in some cases, can provide a "seal of approval" for a program.

Within the past 15 years, evaluations have taken on a wider focus and incorporated a number of new mechanisms. The newness of the field, in fact, is partially responsible for the evaluation mystique. Many of the people currently in the field have no formal university training in evaluation but have academic training in the social sciences (such as in survey research in sociology or in experimental design in psychology). Furthermore, a language of evalution has been developed, borrowed from several disciplines, for which no lexicon is readily available. In addition, as courses and programs in evaluation have grown, people have developed models (such as formative evaluation, summative evaluation, the decision theoretic approach to evaluation, goal-free evaluation, discrepancy evaluation), and these models are not always clearly described.

In addition to confusion about models and terms of evaluation, other difficulties arise when one explores the ways in which evaluation is used or can be used. Evaluations designed to meet the specific information needs of sponsors may be quite narrowly focused. However, evaluations often are used by individuals or interest groups concerned with objectives that the evaluation may not have addressed. In some cases the absence of information is equated with negative information to the detriment of programs. For example, while evaluations are often assumed to be concerned only with a program's effects, evaluations also can look at the process of a program's development in order to provide diagnostic information to program managers. Such process evaluations need not address the impact of a program at all. Yet some audiences upon discovering that program effects were not addressed, may conclude that the program was unsuccessful. Also an evaluation focused entirely on the impacts of participating, such as measures of student achievement or attitude change, may not provide adequate information on program effectiveness—if no steps were taken to determine whether the results are directly attributable to the program and not to other factors. In this case, one would not know whether the program was even implemented as planned (Charters and Jones, 1973).

It is not surprising, then, that program personnel often perceive evaluation as a threat; they assume that if evaluations do not show programs doing all the things they want to do, the programs will be punished by having funds withdrawn. This concern is not without foundation, because evaluations have been used to limit or reduce funding. While some programs have legitimately lost funding when they were not successful in attaining many objectives, evaluations often have been too narrowly defined to fully explore what programs are doing. As a result, these evaluations have presented an incomplete picture of program accomplishments. For example, the early negative Westinghouse evaluation of Head Start continues to haunt the program despite later findings of success (Weikert, 1980).

The narrow focus of many evaluations, especially those restricted to program impact on participants, can be traced back to early assumptions about fostering social change. Systematic program evaluation—setting of objectives, defining measures to assess their attainment, designing and carrying out a data collection plan, analyzing and reporting results—began in the late 1960s during a period that can be characterized as the rationalization of social change. Many assumed the "Great Society" programs, including federal aid to education, would alter long-standing social problems through targeted funding and good intentions. One needed only to follow the funding trail to see that crime rates were reduced or educational attainment was increased. As a consequence, most early evaluation efforts focused exclusively on outcomes such as student achievement gains; these impacts seldom fulfilled the programs' promises. Few recognized the difficulties of changing extant institutions or their practices, the limited transferability of program approaches (what seemed to work in one context may not work in another), or even the need for the massive publicity efforts to inform people about which students and program approaches were eligible for funding. It took ten years for policymakers and others to realize the complexities and difficulties inherent in social-change efforts, by which time program developers' fears of evaluation had grown.

The potential or perceived threat of evaluation may also have a legitimate political base. Within much of elementary and secondary education, for example, innovative programs but not traditional curricula are evaluated. This also has been the case with women's studies programs in colleges and universities. The traditional liberal arts curricula seldom are required to state explicitly their objectives for students, yet women's studies programs not only are expected to do so but also are judged by whether they have met those objectives.

While one can argue with the decision-making process and about what is going to be evaluated, it seems likely in a period of retrenchment in higher education that women's studies programs and other interdisciplinary programs are going to be evaluated. It is no longer a question of whether women's studies are going to be evaluated, but how they are going to be evaluated. One important step in developing a useful and nonbiased evaluation plan is to involve the key decision makers and participants in the design.

USES OF EVALUATION IN WOMEN'S STUDIES

The conduct of evaluations can be useful to people directing women's studies programs or concerned with programs that foster such change in a broader way. They can provide information on the extent to which programs are attaining their objectives, on where strengths and weaknesses are, and on what areas require improvement. Moreover, evaluations can buttress other kinds of information. For example, while evaluations often are concerned with the impact of programs on students or faculty, the goals of women's studies also include the desire for impacts on the institution in which programs are housed. Therefore, additional questions such as the following should be posed:

- Has there been an increased demand for women's studies programs (e.g., has the number of people enrolled in women's studies programs increased; are more students anticipating enrolling?)?
- Have the programs increased the amount of external money coming into colleges and universities?
- Have more students been attracted to the college or university in part because of the women's studies program?
- Have students enrolled in women's studies programs had higher retention rates in colleges and universities than other students?

For women's studies programs to compete successfully for the allocation of resources and staff, such information could be extraordinarily useful since it would show how women's studies programs affect broader institutional goals. Women's studies directors should be encouraged to view evaluation in an active rather than a passive light. Programs frequently can be criticized for not having sufficient evaluation data, but if programs have solid, positive results, the data can be used not only in discussions with the institution, but also in securing funds from other public and private sources.

TYPES OF EVALUATION

There are a variety of approaches to program evaluation, each with a different purpose and methodology. Each is listed below with a brief description and some analyses of its use, particularly in areas relevant to sex roles and social change. We should keep in mind that while these approaches differ, it is possible and often desirable to combine them in evaluation programs.

Professional Judgment

The major purpose of this mode of evaluation is to certify the acceptability of a program as seen by external groups of colleagues using preestablished reference points. Examples of this type of evaluation include accreditation visits and other professional certification of educational programs. While peer or expert acceptance of a program provides useful data for judgment of its merit, there are two problems inherent in this approach for women's studies programs: consultants who are the most well-informed about the growth and development of women's studies programs may be viewed by administrative officials as advocates rather than as informed and critical experts (Reuben, 1982); and criteria used for judging a program or its faculty may rely on traditional measures, such as judging the merit of faculty by publications in "high prestige" journals that may see women's issues as illegitimate or not valuable arenas for research.

Decision-theoretic Approach

This form of evaluation attempts to involve all decision makers in the design of the evaluation. In women's studies, Marcia Guttentag pioneered the use of the decision-theoretic approach (Guttentag, 1977; Guttentag et al., 1978). All decision makers (e.g., students, faculty, administrators, funding agencies) are asked to list what they think are the objectives of the program, to rank the objectives numerically in order of importance (so one can say, for example, that some objectives are 2 or 10 times as important as others), and then to estimate the chances of the objectives being accomplished (these are called prior probabilities, and a score of 0.5 would be a 50–50 chance while 0.9 would mean virtual certainty). Data are then collected on each objective and analyzed through the use of Bayesian statistics—that is, a statistic that accounts for the prior probabilities. The most useful part of the decision-theoretic approach is the deliberate involvement of all decision makers prior to the conduct of the evaluation. Several other models, such as Provus's discrepancy evaluation, also rely heavily on the early involvement of potential decision makers (Provus 1969). While time-consuming and difficult, this early involvement can lead to the development and acceptance of more realistic objectives for a program, to a more sensitive evaluation design, and to greater use of the evaluation data in decision making. The major problem in the use of the decision-theoretic approach in women's studies has been the difficulty of moving beyond the earlier stages to measuring achievement of the goals identified. Provus's evaluation of a large, federally sponsored educational change program met resistance of project personnel because of the complexity and burden of the coding scheme used in defining the goals against which the program was to be evaluated.

Goal-free Evaluation

The important aspect of this form of evaluation is that it pays as much attention to the unintended consequences of a program as to intended outcomes—and every program has both. The intended results are those embodied in the goals and objectives. But unintended consequences can be equally important, and goal-free evaluation, not limited by program goals, searches for these effects. For example, the Career Facilitation workshops of the National Science Foundation's Women in Science Program are designed to provide information about potential careers in science to young women. However, one result found by evaluators was that the development of the workshops led to the creation of strong and supportive networks among women who were already scientists. An evaluation that searches for unintended consequences is called "goal-free" because it is not bound by the program's goals. Since many positive aspects of programs and some of the more troublesome, negative aspects are unintended, evaluation designs might, insofar as possible, look for all effects goal-related or not.

The methodology of goal-free evaluation is almost anthropological. One examines the artifacts of a program, talks with its living survivors, and reviews the records—while also checking to see what happened and why, rather than whether objectives were met. Major proponents of this approach are Michael Scriven and Malcolm Parlett (Scriven 1967; Parlett and Dearden 1977).

Objectives-based Evaluation

This form of evaluation is probably the approach that most innovative programs use. The purpose of the evaluation is to understand the extent to which the stated objectives of the program were achieved. Since this is the most common form of evaluation, it is useful to describe in some detail major features and problems with this form of evaluation. We will focus on issues involved with defining objectives and then with developing research designs. Issues of measurement (e.g., instrument construction) and data analysis are covered in greater detail by other authors in this volume.

To judge a program in terms of whether its goals and objectives are accomplished, they must be clearly stated. The process of making the goals and objectives explicit can do more than guide the evaluation. It can help faculty and students focus on what they want to accomplish and guide program development so that each component (e.g., course, special event) can contribute to the desired end.

Goals are generally long-term, fairly global aims. A goal statement concerning women's studies from the University of Massachusetts (cited in Rhodes, Note 2), for example, is:

> ... the development of frameworks and methodologies which integrate women's experience and scholarly disciplines, and which ultimately will provide the incentives and expertise necessary to effect change in the larger community.

Objectives are usually more specific and attainable. Some evaluations also describe them as measurable. At the very least, there must be a direct way to gather evidence about their achievement. Often the method for evaluation is included in the objective. Two types of objectives—impact and process—are important. As the names imply, the former looks at results while the latter looks at the ways used to achieve them. An example of an impact objective is:

> Students in pre-service teacher education courses shall apply an analytical scheme for assessing sexism in textbooks. (Method of evaluation: given a textbook, 75 percent of the students will select and use correctly an appropriate analytical scheme to assess sexism.)

And a related process objective would be:

> to develop and teach a section of the Foundations of Education course that presents methods of analyzing sexism in textbooks. (Method of evaluation: analysis of course syllabus)

An evaluation of the program logically might show that the process objective was achieved (the section of the course was developed and taught) but the impact objective was not (students couldn't analyze the textbooks for sexism). In that case, the staff and students would need to look further to discover why the course was not successful and, as a result, would probably want to make program adjustments.

There may be a dilemma involved in designing an evaluation around explicit statements of goals and objectives. For women's studies, for example, the long-range goal may be to infuse the entire curriculum with feminism. As a path toward that goal, some intermediate goals—developing specific feminist courses—and objectives may be both necessary and desirable. Faculty and staff are more able to control and measure the achievement of the latter goals but, in the long run, they may be more concerned with the former. If the evaluation looks only at the feminist courses, it will not present guideposts or ideas for improving the more general atmosphere for women on campus.

Porter and Eileenchild (1980, p. 2) define feminism as "... the desire to increase the power and autonomy of women as individuals and as a group (so that) they will be able to make informed and flexible choices in their education and their lives." If a women's studies program accepts this definition and sees itself as both catalytic for others and important in its own right, it must take care to be evaluated in terms of both long- and short-range goals.

The problem, of course, is that the achievement of the longer term goals are seldom under the control of feminists themselves. Since evaluation results may be used to determine program budgets, program directors may be tempted to omit questions that are neither controllable by the program nor apt to lead to positive answers. On the other hand, omitting such questions deprives feminists of what may be important information. The nature of the dilemma is that there are no easy answers. Program developers and staff must decide what they want and indicate that to the evaluators.

Research designs are built around specific objectives. Often the most difficult step in constructing a research design is the first one—deciding what objectives the evaluation is going to address. An initial list of objectives for a program is often long, cumbersome, and totally unwieldy. It may contain 15 or 20 objectives. An initial list of objectives for women's studies programs could be equally long and unwieldy, especially when one considers objectives for students and graduates, for faculty and administrators, and for the program and its impact on other efforts. The key, as discussed with the decision-theoretic model above, is to rank the objectives in order of priority on the basis of what objectives are the most important (and to whom) and what objectives must be addressed this year rather than next year.

Once a list of objectives has reached a manageable size, one examines each objective in turn to decide what evidence would be needed to ascertain the extent to which the objective was accomplished. The question to pose is what evidence would be the most technically sound to show that the program is doing what it is intended to do.

For example, assume that an initial objective of a women's studies program is the following: At the end of a one-year introductory course sequence in women's studies, students shall have equitable sex role perceptions of women's roles in society. While the concept may be difficult to measure, the immediately obvious design strategy is a simple *post-only design* in which students are queried only at the end of a program about sex-stereotypic views and only students in the program are asked questions. Such a strategy would be faulty because it leaves open the question of whether the students in the program had sex-stereotypic views when they entered it.

A *pre-post design* involving only the students in the program would deal with that question. The design is flawed, however, because the evaluation does not account for whether the students changed their views because of the program or from what they learned just by being on campus, or from their friends, or from the women's movement in general. To respond to this concern, a still more complex design is required since we now must involve other students, ones not in the women's studies program.

We need both the pre-post design (for the beginning and end of the year), and some kind of control or comparison group. A control group would consist of students who are identical in all respects to the students in the women's studies program but are not enrolled in it. In field experiments, a control group is usually obtained by overrecruiting for a program and then randomly assigning students from the pool to the program (experimental group) and to the control group. The research design that uses experimental and control groups is called an *experimental design*. Since control groups are almost impossible to isolate in real life, most evaluation work these days uses comparison groups. Examples of comparison groups for women's studies may be a random sample of students from the rest of the college or university; or a random sample of students within a given department (in the event that the women's studies program was open only to students within a given department). The research design that uses experimental (women's studies students) and comparison groups is called a *quasi-experimental design*. These are the strongest, yet most realistic, designs since they enable us not only to examine program effects over time but also to determine whether any changes are the result of the program itself or stem from other factors.

Only a few of the completed evaluations of women's studies programs have used quasi-experimental designs, and only recently have people gathered data on the impact (such as increased enrollments) of women's studies programs on institutional objectives (Howe and Lauter 1980). Yet the knowledge gained from all efforts contribute to a greater understanding of how such programs can aid in the intellectual and social development of students.

CRITIQUE OF WOMEN'S STUDIES EVALUATIONS

For a number of reasons, only some of which are explicit, it is difficult to find exemplary evaluations of women's studies programs. First, evaluations generally serve a local audience (the program, the department, or a dean), and therefore are not often published in sources that allow national access to them. Second, many women's studies programs do not receive the funding that allows a "perfect" evaluation—or even an evaluation at all. Finally, there are few standardized instruments that measure the objectives of women's studies programs.

Of those evaluations that have been published or selected by the Educational Resources Information Center (ERIC) system, some critical comments can be made. The largest number evaluate single programs in a single context. It is therefore extremely difficult to look across evaluation studies to separate the effects of context from the effects of the program itself. A related problem is that not all evaluations use a comparison group design. For example, of the 14 evaluations cited in *Women's Studies: Evaluation Handbook,* only seven included comparison groups (Millsap, Bagenstos, and Talburtt 1979). As a result, one cannot tell if the treatment (women's studies) was responsible for positive effects or if the participants entered the program because of their special qualifications or interests, which could account for the effects.

Finally, because of constraints of time and money, each evaluation focuses only on a few of the multiple goals and objectives of women's studies. DeBiasi and Rhodes (no date), for example, are concerned with the attitudes of students, faculty and administrators who were not involved with women's studies, toward women's studies, while Canty (no date) evaluated the effects of women's studies on the goals of participating women. As a result, it is impossible to determine which objectives are most easily obtained in any context or the processes required to obtain them.

However, there are indications that women's studies programs are judged as successful. Both the number of such programs and their size keep growing, indicating that faculty and administrators deem them worthy of time and money. In all the evaluations located, there were positive effects on the learning of content, on sex role awareness, and on the aspirations of the participants.

Margaret Talburtt's (1978) evaluation project (Project WELD [Women's Education Learning and Doing]) combined a number of positive features of an evaluation. Her evaluation looked across settings, used comparison groups, and measured a number of objectives. This project was undertaken to provide information about three types of educational options available to women undergraduates: internships, women's studies classes, and skills development classes (or workshops). Eight schools were chosen for participation in the study. Six of the eight schools were predominantly women's colleges. The other two were women's centers at large coeducational universities. The rationale behind this choice was to begin an assessment of women's educational progress in settings that had committed themselves almost exclusively to the full development of women students.

Students reported that the three types of programs achieved the goals that they promised. Internships promoted professional skills and career exposures. Women's studies classes fostered feminist perspectives and expanded concepts about what women can achieve. Skills classes led to increased self-understanding, assertiveness, and other skills related to personal effectiveness. Quantitative student data gathered from standardized forms also indicated that these programs achieved other important results that were not expected but were highly valued by students. Their programs accomplished most of these outcomes significantly better than the traditional (or general) curriculum at each school. Internships did more than provide career exposures; they increased self-confidence, openness, and assertiveness. Women's studies fostered self-confidence, independence, and feminist perspectives as well as interpersonal skills. In sum, each type of program accomplished different results and all programs resulted in some outcomes that traditional educational experiences did not produce. Innovative structures have impact on outcomes that students rate as important—they do make a difference, supplementing the traditional experience in some important ways.

Talburtt's study indicates that the projects achieved their goals in a number of settings and also had unintended effects on participants that they viewed as important. However, whether those unintended results are viewed as positive or negative depends on one's position on feminism in general. Increased self-confidence and assertiveness for women may not be seen as valuable by all. The worth of the study is in its demonstration that both program objectives and longer term social change goals can be achieved, documented and expressed clearly. It then becomes possible to debate the value of the change directly since the technical adequacy of the evaluation approach has been established.

SUMMARY

In this chapter, we have sought to highlight some of the major issues in evaluating women's studies. With the exception of review by peers (professional judgment), program evaluation is a recent development, stemming from concerted efforts initiated in the 1960s to provide social justice. Partly because it is a new field with a new vocabulary, evaluation is misunderstood. More importantly, because evaluation exists within a political context, it is feared and evaluation results can be misused. At the same time, evaluation can be overpowering, providing information for program redesign as well as information on how effective the program has been in attaining its objectives. Two evaluation issues dominate women's studies (and all other efforts at social change): the political and value context within which evaluations are commissioned and used; and the technical adequacy of evaluation studies.

Political and Value Context

Because evaluations are designed for use within a decision-making context, evaluations must deal with both the objectives of the program and issues that concern the institution within which the program is housed. While institutions may not be sympathetic to a program or its values, it may become more supportive if it sees a program serving or its values, it may become more supportive if it sees a program serving on its own institutional needs (e.g., in expanding enrollments or in reducing drop-out rates). In addition, women's studies directors and faculties must address their own dilemmas about program objectives: about long-term goals (e.g., infusing feminism in all courses); and short-term goals (e.g., establishing independent courses specifically addressing women's issues). Setting objectives and establishing priority rankings are important initial activities that can help prevent conflict later on. In all instances—within a program and outside—it is important to keep one's audiences in mind while designing an evaluation and to include them throughout the evaluation to the extent possible.

If an outside evaluator is hired to assess a women's studies program, that person has an ethical responsibility to report results to whoever did the hiring. The client is the first audience, and that is not always the women's studies program staff. It may be a dean or other administrator. In those cases in which someone has commissioned an evaluation with the intent of discontinuing the program, there is really no way that program staff can avoid that person's getting the results first. They can, however, try to be simultaneous recipients of the results so that they are able to present their own interpretations. Because the evaluator owes the client the first hearing, it is probably to the program's advantage to be the client.

Besides the legal client, others should be informed of the evaluation results. Anyone who participated in the evaluation has a right to some feedback about its results. Students and potential students have an interest in what is found about a program, as do staff and faculty in related fields. College and university administrators are another audience for the results. If the program was developed with federal, state, or foundation funds, these agencies are especially interested in the results of an evaluation even if it is not (and it frequently is) mandated.

The lessons learned from Marcia Guttentag's pioneering work in the decision-theoretic approach to evaluation apply in any discussion of audiences. The more decision makers (regardless of funding source) are involved in setting the questions the evaluation is to address and in following the ongoing evaluation activities, the greater the likelihood the results will be used. While there are dilemmas here (e.g., what happens if we involve everybody and the results are all negative—does that mean women's studies will be discontinued?), in the vast majority of cases it is always better to share some of the design responsibility with others.

Results can be reported in many ways, ranging from a full-blown monograph with statistical data and computer printouts to an interactive seminar. What is important is to present the results in ways that meet the needs of the various audiences. Given the number and roles of people who might be interested, developing different modes of presentation for each might prove prohibitively expensive. In that case, it might be good to develop three products—the full report, an executive summary, and a press release—and augment those with whatever special materials are affordable.

No matter how the results are reported, the following information should be included:

- a program description (this can be very abbreviated if the audience consists solely of people who know the program well);

- the evaluation design and analytic techniques (written in nontechnical language for nontechnical audiences);
- the results.

Further, whether presented in writing or orally, the report should be in clear, jargon-free English. Clarity of expression is a sign of clarity of thought, and jargon usually muddles issues, rather than clarifying them. As a physician warned a friend about other doctors: "If they can't tell you what's wrong in plain English, they probably don't understand themselves."

Technical Adequacy

Within the domain of technical issues are the adequacy of instruments and data analysis procedures and the use of appropriate research designs. In concentrating on research designs, we encourage the use of quasi-experimental designs and the use of multiple evaluation approaches that look not only at the intended objectives of a program but also at its unintended consequences. Through the use of quasi-experimental design, program directors can be relatively certain that the effects of a program are due to the program itself and not to other factors. Evaluations that include several programs (such as Talburtt's Project WELD) can provide additional information on how easy (see note 72) or difficult it is to accomplish similar goals in different programmatic contexts.

Women's studies programs (and all other programs designed to encourage social change) must be particularly attuned to technical issues in evaluation. Too often, audiences who disagree with the values of a program will search for a technical flaw to dismiss the validity of an entire study. The debate over the evaluation of the elementary school program, Follow Through, is a good example (*Harvard Educational Review* 1978). Technically adequate evaluations can thus be used not only to learn more about how to organize and run women's studies programs, but can also serve to reduce the possibility that persons hostile to program objectives can use methodological issues to dismiss positive findings.

We would hope that women's studies directors and others would use evaluation in a spirit of enlightened self-interest—to realize that no single approach to evaluation is sacrosanct and to see how evaluation can serve their decision-making needs.

REFERENCES

Charters, W.W., and D. Jones. On the possibility of evaluating a non-event. *Educational Researcher,* May 1973.

Guttentag, M. (ed.) *Evaluation Studies Review Annual*, vol. 2. Beverly Hills: Sage, 1977.

Guttentag, M., L.R. Brush, A.R. Gold, M.W. Mueller, S. Tobias, and M.G. White. Evaluating women's studies: A decision-theoretic approach. *Signs*, vol. 3, no. 4. Chicago: University of Chicago Press, Summer, 1978, pp. 884–90.

Canty, E.M. Effects of women's studies courses on women's attitudes and goals. ED150490, mimeographed, n.d.

DeBiasi, G.L., and C. Rhodes. Attitudes of students, faculty and administrators toward a women's studies program, Old Dominion University, mimeographed, n.d.

Harvard Educational Review, vol. 48, no. 2, May 1978.

Howe, F., and P. Lauter. *The Impact on the Institution of Women's Studies Courses and Programs*. Washington, D.C.: National Institute of Education, 1980.

Millsap, M.A., N.T. Bagenstos, and M. Talburtt. *Women's Studies: Evaluation Handbook*. Washington, D.C.: National Institute of Education, 1979.

Parlett, M., and G. Dearden (ed.). *Introduction to Illuminative Evaluation*. San Francisco: Pacific Soundings Press, 1977.

Porter, N.M., and M.T. Eileenchild. *The Effectiveness of Women's Studies Teaching*. Washington, D.C.: National Institute of Education, 1980.

Provus, M. Evaluation of ongoing programs in the public school system. *The 68th Yearbook of the National Society for the Study of Education,* part 2. Chicago: University of Chicago Press, 1969, pp. 242–83.

Reuben, E. Personal communication, July 1982.

Rhodes, C. *Undergraduate Women's Studies Program*. Norfolk, Va.: Old Dominion University Research Foundation, November 1978, p. 58.

Scriven, M. The methodology of evaluation. *Perspectives on Curriculum Evaluation*. R.W. Tyler (ed.). Chicago: Rand McNally, 1967, pp. 39–83.

Talburtt, M.A. *Evaluation of Project WELD: Women's Education Learning and Doing*. Ann Arbor, Mich.: Formative Evaluation Research Associates, 1978.

Weikert, D. *The Students Fifteen Years Later*. Ypsilanti, Mich.: HiScope Foundation, 1980.

Women's Studies Newsletter, vol. 4, no. 4, Fall 1978.

6

Methodological Issues in the Study of Sex-Related Differences

Carol Nagy Jacklin

A number of methodological issues arise in the study of sex-related differences, and indeed in the study of all group differences. These issues will be listed and then discussed more fully in the context of cognitive and social sex-related differences. Although substantive findings will be used to illustrate methodological points, a substantive review is not intended.

The methodological issues in the study of sex-related differences include: (1) conceptualization of the term "difference"; (2) failure to distinguish the significance of an effect from the size of an effect; (3) bias toward positive findings in the publishing, abstracting, indexing, citing, and reprinting of results; (4) confusion of within-sex differences with between-sex differences; (5) assuming that all sex-related differences are expressions of genetic or innate differences; (6) confusion of sex-of-stimuli effects with sex-of-subject effects; (7) interaction of sex-of-experimenter effects with sex-of-subject effects; (8) disregard of systematic differences in self-report of males and females; (9) reliance upon a narrow data base in terms of subject characteristics from which most sex-related differences are generalized; and (10) the number of variables confounded with sex that make comparisons of sex difficult.

(1) The conceptualization of "difference" poses an immediate problem. A "difference" implies a contrast, something that distinguishes individuals or groups. However, when group differences are described in the social sciences, the characteristics usually do not distinguish most of the members of one

---

This chapter is reprinted with permission from Academic Press, Inc. It originally appeared in *Developmental Review* 1 (1981), pp. 266–73.

group from most of the members of the comparison group. Typically, only a few subjects of one group are different from the subjects of the other group. Rough-and-tumble play is a case in point.

One of the largest sex-related differences reported is rough-and-tumble play. In one study (DiPietro 1981), 15 to 20 percent of the boys scored higher than any of the girls. Although this is an unusually large group difference, it is concurrently the case that 80 to 85 percent of the boys are indistinguishable from 80 to 85 percent of the girls. One would certainly conclude that rough-and-tumble play is a sex-related difference. Nonetheless, focusing on 80 percent of the two populations seems as sensible as focusing on 20 percent which the word "difference" demands.

(2) A related methodological issue is the lack of information given in research articles on the size of group difference effects. The significance of an effect and the size of the significance statistic are still the coin of the social science realm. However, if a group difference is a significance difference, it is largely a function of sample size. With large enough samples, any group mean difference will be significant (some published examples are tabled in Jacklin 1979). What we need to determine and emphasize is how large a sex-related difference is. The size of a sex-related effect tells what can be predicted about an individual's behavior if one knows that individual's gender. Unless one has a measure of the size of the difference as well as its significance, very little is gained in predictive ability.

In an attempt to measure just how much predictive power is gained by sex in some established sex-related differences, Plomin and Foch (1981) did a large-scale measurement of the size of effect for verbal and quantitative abilities. Using the Maccoby and Jacklin (1974) tables on verbal abilities, they computed point biserial correlations for 26 studies representing 85,619 scores over 67,000 children. They found that the sex difference in verbal ability accounted for only 1 percent of the variance. Plomin and Foch succinctly state: "If all we know about a child is the child's sex, we know next to nothing about the child's verbal ability." Similarly, for the 292,574 children's scores listed in Maccoby and Jacklin's tables on quantitative ability, sex accounts for only 4 percent of the variance. Clearly, effect size must be distinguished from statistical significance. Recently, some attention has been given to detailed descriptions of distributions in sex-related differences (Favreau and Lepine 1981; Kail, Carter, and Pellegrino 1979) and size-of-effect discussions are increasing (Hyde 1981). However, until journal editors strongly encourage size-of-effect statistics, their use is unlikely to become widespread.

(3) A third serious issue in studies of sex-related differences is the bias toward publishing, abstracting, indexing, citing, and reprinting positive findings. If a positive instance is found, it is much easier to publish; it is more likely to be reprinted; it gets into the abstracts. In short, it becomes a part of the literature. Although it is possible to get negative results (or sex similarities)

into the literature, it is very difficult. The institutionalizing of a rubric like "sex similarities" or "sex-unrelated characteristics" would go a long way in rectifying this problem. If one could easily publish findings of similarities and if they were abstracted and indexed, these nondifferences would also become the material for summaries of sex-related differences. However, highlighting a nondifference or null finding is contrary to the traditional approach to science. Rejection of the null hypothesis is used to determine whether we actually have done the study correctly. A finding of no difference can always be attributed to problems in the study and often should be so attributed. Unfortunately, negative instances, particularly nonreplications, are as important in sorting out true group differences as positive instances. Rosenthal (1979) has called this the "file drawer problem" and has tried to quantify it. Actively retrieving negative results is difficult but necessary even before one can determine how big the "file drawer problem" really is.

(4) A glaring, but common, error is generalizing from a *within-sex*-difference finding to a *between-sex*-difference conclusion. One example is overgeneralization of current laterality data. Witelson (1977) found male dyslexics less lateralized than males who are not dyslexic. However, a recent study has not replicated this work (Cioffi and Kondels 1979). The Witelson work did not demonstrate a sex-related difference; only boy dyslexics were studied. Yet that study has been used to explain sex-related differences (e.g., see McGee 1979). Boys who were not dyslexic, it is argued, have an advantage over girls, because boys, in general, are more lateralized than girls. We have no evidence to date relating laterality and cognitive abilities in girls. And since there are very few dyslexic girls, the argument from general laterality differences seems prima facie absurd. Various sources do seem to indicate that girls and women, on the average, are less lateralized for a number of tasks than boys and men. If a female has massive brain damage, she is much more likely to recover than a male who has the same damage (e.g., Bryden 1979; McGlone and Davidson 1972). If females are somewhat more robust in surviving brain damage, it may be (as McGlone and others have argued) that females are more likely to have the same functions on both sides of the brain. What has not yet been demonstrated, but continues to be alleged, is a relationship between laterality and cognitive ability for males *and* females.

Another example of an erroneous generalization from a within-sex to a between-sex difference comes from studies using the menstrual cycle as a response measure. Certainly it is not possible to demonstrate a sex-related difference (or similarity) if the menstrual cycle is the response measure or if any response measure is used with only subjects of one sex. However, conclusions are often drawn about women's (as opposed to men's) hormone/mood relationships, or pheromone sensitivity, or cycle shift. If some other response measure is used the same questions can and have been studied in males. For example, some work has found roughly a 28-day cycle length (Doering et al. 1974; Doering et al. 1975) in male testosterone measured from plasma. In half the males hormone and mood covary.

This methodological problem is fairly obvious when studies using only one gender are used as explanations of sex-related differences. More subtle variants of the same problem exist for studies which do have data on both males and females. Inappropriate conclusions from some statistical procedures make the same within-sex/between-sex confusion. For example, in studies of intellectual performance, many current researchers (Leibowitz 1974/ Engle et al. 1979; Howell and Frese 1979) use multivariate regression analysis on data of both boys and girls. However, all of these investigations use separate regressions for each gender. And when they obtain a significant beta weight for one sex but not the other, they erroneously conclude they have found sex differences. When a variable is found to be significantly related to the intellectual performance in the regression equation of one sex but not the other, a sex-related difference has *not* been established. In order to establish a sex-related difference, one must show that two variables (as an example, parental education and intellectual performance) have a *significantly different relation* for boys than they do for girls. This can only be established if both sexes are included in the same regression equation.

There is a simpler version of this error: demonstrating a significant correlation between two variables for one sex but not the other and then concluding that a sex-related difference has been found. For example, finding mother's behavior is significantly correlated with son's behavior but not with daughter's. Only when significant differences *between* correlations of males and females are found, can one conclude rightly that a sex-related difference has been established.

(5) A striking logical error is assuming the *cause* of a sex-related difference is genetic once the existence of a sex-related difference is established. A recent example is a study of the mathematical ability of seventh-grade boys and girls (Benbow and Stanley 1980). In this study of children who volunteered to take an advanced math test, boys were found to have the highest scores. (The problem of sampling boys and girls from volunteers will be discussed below.) The authors state that "sex differences in achievement in and attitude toward mathematics result from superior male mathematical ability." Although the definition of "ability" is not given, the context suggests a genetic component. This is particularly surprising since no genetic evidence has been found to be related to math and math-related abilities in direct tests of the genetic hypothesis (see Vandenberg and Kuse 1979, for a review). Moreover, although the seventh-grade boys and girls had had the same number of mathematics classes, there is considerable work showing differences in classroom feedback to boys and girls from nursery school through grade school (e.g., Serbin et al. 1973; Dweck and Bush 1976; Dweck et al. 1978). Finding out whether some characteristic is or is not a

sex-related difference is the first step before trying to understand the cause of the difference. However, too often the documentation of a difference is seen as evidence that a natural, genetic, unchangeable sex-related difference has been established.

(6) Sex-of-stimuli effects have often been confused with sex-of-subject effects. Blatant examples are the use of "male" and "female" versions of a test. Some versions of the Thematic Apperception Test (TAT) give stories or pictures of girls to girl subjects and stories or pictures of boys to boy subjects. A famous example using a modified TAT test is the Horner (1968) "Fear of Success" study. In that study, men are asked to complete a story that starts "John is the top of his medical school class," and women are asked to complete a story starting "Ann is the top of her medical school class." In these cases, different stimuli are presented to the sexes, yet conclusions are made about sex-related differences. If the sexes are to be compared, both stories must be given to both sexes. When this is done, there are no sex-of-subject differences, although consistent sex-of-stimuli differences are found (Monahan, Kuhn, and Shaver 1974).

(7) The sex of the experimenter may be another confound in the design of a study. If the experimenter's sex produces an effect that happens to interact with the sex of the subject but that interaction is not measured, then there will appear to be a sex-of-subject effect when none actually exists. Classical conditioning of the eye-blink response is a case in point. A sex difference has been reported in eye-blink conditioning. However, being highly anxious produces faster eye-blink conditioning (see Spence and Spence 1966 for a review). Eye-blink conditioning is often carried out with elaborate equipment in dark rooms with male experimenters. Some anxiety is probably produced in all subjects. If the anxiety level is raised differently for male and female subjects, a sex-related difference will be found. Attributing the difference to a conditioning difference will be a mistake.

(8) Another methodological confound exists with data obtained by self-report. In general, males are more defensive when filling out self-reports than females (e.g., Lekarcyzk and Hill 1969; Williams and Byars 1968). For example, boys do not disclose their thoughts and personal feelings either to parents or peers as much as do girls (Riverbark 1971). Since there is a sex-related difference in the willingness and/or ability to be candid on self-report measures, their use must be suspect in trying to establish sex-related differences in personal attributes. Self-report may be the only possible way to study many aspects of adult feelings and behavior, but concern for the bias that this type of data collection produces must be taken into account. We should either attempt to estimate the defensiveness of subjects or attempt to validate the self-report measures more extensively than has been done.

(9) As in other areas of psychological research, there is a clear restrictedness of the subject characteristics used in sex-related research.

White, upper-middle-class, educated, largely Anglo-Saxon populations are disproportionately used, while generalizations are erroneously made to all. The availability of college students as subjects in psychological research will probably continue the practice of nonrepresentativeness of the research population to the general population. Still, sex-related differences found for this population may not be found generally.

(10) Probably the most pervasive problem in sex-related research is the number of variables that are confounded with sex. It is difficult to find populations on which sex-only comparisons can be made. As an extreme example, if army generals and their wives were used as subjects in a study and sex comparisons were made, they would match on many characteristics but would be unmatched on many others.

One longitudinal study of males and females, The Terman Genius Study, has been unusual in that the researchers were aware of the confounds with sex and wrote about them. In the initial identification of the gifted children, Miles (1954) notes two problems: teachers nominated more boys than girls for the tests, and gifted boys were more likely to volunteer to take tests than gifted girls. The researchers compensated for this tendency since when all boys and girls are tested equal numbers of genii-range scores are found. (Surprisingly, Bendow and Stanley [1980] used volunteers as their subject pool and then made sex-differences comparisons.) In the Terman sample, disproportionate numbers of males received college and graduate school education and in adulthood had higher-paying and higher-prestige jobs than females. However, Bayley and Oden (1955) were able to demonstrate that in the Terman data, occupation not sex accounted for IQ changes over the life span.

Problems of sampling appropriately matched males and females may be less obvious in cross-sectional studies. College students, for example, are likely to have had different numbers of high school math classes and are therefore suspect for cognitive sex difference comparisons.

With fewer variables confounded with sex, sex will account for smaller percentages of variance. Thus, paradoxically the better the sex-related research, the less useful sex is as an explanatory variable. In the best controlled sex-related research, sex may account for no variance at all. This may force researchers to stop focusing upon and trying to explain the trivially small amounts of variance accounted for by group differences, and start trying to explain the vast variance between individuals within the groups.

There are psychological dimensions on which one can find statistically significant differences between males and females. And findings of sex differences and interest in sex-related research may have helped change the tradition in psychology of considering individual differences as error variance. However, from all indications thus far, there are many more psychologically interesting ways in which males and females differ from other males and females. It may be time to turn our scientific attention to the search for these variables.

REFERENCES

Bayley, N., and M. Oden. The maintenance of intellectual ability in gifted adults. *Journal of Gerontology* 10 (1955): 91–107.
Benbow, C.P., and J.C. Stanley. Sex differences in mathematical ability: Fact or artifact? *Science* 210 (1980): 1262–64.
Bryden, P. Evidence for sex differences in cerebral organization. In M.A. Witting and A.C. Petersen (eds.), *Sex-related differences in cognitive functioning: Developmental issues.* New York: Academic Press, 1979.
Cioffi, J., and G. Kondels. Laterality of stereognostic accuracy of children for words, shapes, and bigrams: A sex difference for bigrams. *Science* 204 (1979): 1432–34.
DiPietro, J.A. Rough and tumble play: A function of gender. *Developmental Psychology* 17 (1981): 50–58.
Doering, C.H., H.K.H. Brodie, H.C. Kraemer, H.B. Becker, and D.A. Hamburg. Plasma testosterone levels and psychologic measures in men over a 2-month period. In R.C. Friedman, R.M. Richart, and R.L. Vande Wiele (eds.), *Sex differences in behavior.* New York: Wiley, 1974.
Doering, C.H., H.K.H. Brodie, H.C. Kraemer, R.H. Moos, H.B. Becker, and D.A. Hamburg. Negative affect and plasma testosterone: A longitudinal human study. *Psychosomatic Medicine* 37 (1975): 484–91.
Dweck, C.S., and E.S. Bush. Sex differences in learned helplessness. I. Differential debilitation with peer and adult evaluators. *Developmental Psychology* 12 (1976): 147–56.
Dweck, C.S., W. Davidson, S. Nelson, and B. Enna. Sex differences in learned helplessness. II. The contingencies of evaluative feedback in the classroom. III. An experimental analysis. *Developmental Psychology* 14 (1978): 268–76.
Engle, P.L., C. Yarbrough, J. Townsend, R.E. Klein, and M. Irwin. *Sex differences in the effects of nutrition and social class on mental development in rural Guatemala.* Guatemala: INCAP, 1979.
Favreau, O.E., and L. Lepine. *Spatial abilities: What is a sex difference?* Submitted for publication, 1981.
Horner, M.S. *Sex differences in achievement motivation and performance in competitive and noncompetitive situations.* Unpublished doctoral diss. University of Michigan, 1968.
Howell, F.M., and W. Frese. Race, sex, and aspirations: Evidence for the "Race Convergence" hypothesis. *Sociology of Education* 52 (1979): 34–46.
Hyde, J.S. How large are cognitive gender differences? A meta-analysis using ω^2 and d. *American Psychologist* 36 (1981): 892–901.
Jacklin, C.N. Epilogue. In M. Wittig and A.C. Petersen (eds.), *Sex-related differences in cognitive functioning: Developmental issues.* New York: Academic Press, 1979.
Kail, R., P. Carter, and J. Pellegrino. The locus of sex differences in spatial ability. *Perception and Psychophysics* 26 (1979): 182–86.
Leibowitz, A. Home investments in children. In T.W. Schultz (ed.), *Economics of the family.* Chicago: University of Chicago Press, 1974.
Lekarczyk, D.T., and K.T. Hill. Self-esteem, test anxiety, stress, and verbal learning. *Developmental Psychology* 1 (1969): 147–54.

Maccoby, E.E., and C.N. Jacklin. *The psychology of sex differences.* Stanford, Calif.: Stanford University Press, 1974.

McGee, M.G. Human spatial abilities: Psychometric studies and environmental, genetic, hormonal and neurological influences. *Psychological Bulletin* 86 (1979): 889–918.

McGlone, J., and W. Davidson. The relationship between cerebral speech laterally and spatial ability with special reference to sex and hand preference. *Neuropsychologia* 11 (1972): 105–13.

Miles, C.C. Gifted children. In L. Carmichael (ed.), *Manual of child psychology* (2nd ed.). New York: Wiley, 1954.

Monahan, L., D. Kuhn, and P. Shaver. Intrapsychic versus cultural explanations of the "Fear of success" motive. *Journal of Personality and Social Psychology* 29 (1974): 60–64.

Plomin, R., and T.T. Foch. Sex differences and individual differences. *Child Development* 52 (1981): 383–85.

Riverbark, W.H. Self-disclosure among adolescents. *Psychological Reports* 28 (1971): 35–42.

Rosenthal, R. The "file drawer problem" and tolerance for null results. *Psychological Bulletin* 86 (1979): 638–40.

Serbin, L.A., K.D. O'Leary, R.N. Kent, and I.J. Tonick. A comparison of teacher response to the preacademic and problem behavior of boys and girls. *Child Development* 44 (1973): 796–804.

Spence, K.W., and J.T. Spence. Sex and anxiety differences in eyelid conditioning. *Psychological Bulletin* 65 (1966): 137–42.

Vandenberg, S.G., and A.R. Kuse. Spatial ability: A critical review of the sex-linked major gene hypothesis. In M.A. Wittig and A.C. Petersen (eds.), *Sex-related differences in cognitive functioning: Developmental issues.* New York: Academic Press, 1979.

Williams, T.M., and H. Byars. Negro self-esteem in a transitional society. *Personnel and Guidance Journal* 47 (1968): 120–25.

Witelson, S.F. Neural and cognitive correlates of developmental dyslexia: age and sex differences. In C. Shagass, S. Gershon, and A.J. Friedhoff (eds.), *Psychopathology and brain dysfunction.* New York: Raven Press, 1977.

PART IV

SAMPLING AND MEASUREMENT

7

Sampling: Issues and Problems in Sex Role and Social Change Research

Charol Shakeshaft and David W. Gardner

The four sampling issues discussed in this chapter all relate to the problem of generalizability of the sample to a larger population and reflect four particular weaknesses found in the sampling designs of social change research. The sampling problems are: (1) noncoverage of the population by the sample; (2) the use of accidental or volunteer samples; (3) inappropriate sample size; and (4) nonresponse by a large portion of the sample. It is interesting to note that these issues identified as sampling problems in equity research are similar to those found by Borg and Gall (1979) in social science research in general and are, thus, not specific to social change research. Nevertheless, even though these are general sampling problems encountered in research on a variety of subjects, the issues highlighted here are important ones for social change researchers.

TYPES OF SAMPLE DESIGNS

When carried out correctly, probability sampling is "the most respected and useful method" of sampling (Babbie 1973, p. 76). Types of probability samples include the simple random sample, the systematic sample, the stratified sample, and the cluster sample. The basic principle of probability sampling is that "a sample will be representative of the population from which it is selected, if all members of the population have an equal chance of being selected in the sample" (Babbie 1973, p. 78). This is accomplished through random selection. Thus, a carefully drawn probability sample will allow the researcher to select from population elements that are representative in proportion to their existence in the general population so that generalizations about that population can be made. However, probability sampling alone does not insure representativeness. Thus, even when probability sampling was used in the equity research analyzed, the issues of noncoverage of the population by the sample, inappropriate sample size, and nonresponse by a large portion of the sample still threatened generalizability.

Unfortunately, probability sampling is often difficult to accomplish, particularly in schools, and thus is often not used in social change research. For instance, in a study of 114 dissertations investigating women educators (Shakeshaft 1979), it was found that fewer than 15 percent of the researchers used probability samples when conducting research. Bailar and Lanphier (1978) in a pilot study of surveys, found that probability sampling was not implemented in nearly two-thirds of the federally funded samples and over two-thirds of the nonfederally funded samples. The most often used substitutes for probability samples are the nonprobability techniques which include purposive or judgment, quota, volunteer, snowball, dense, and saturation samples. Since these methods do not rely on randomization, the result is a sample that may not be representative of the population to which the researcher wishes to generalize. In addition to the problems surrounding nonrandom selection, nonprobability samples, like probability samples, are also weakened by noncoverage of the population of the sample, inappropriate sample size, and nonresponse.

A frequently used type of nonprobability sampling is that which Kerlinger (1973) calls "accidental" sampling, also referred to as opportunistic or haphazard sampling:

> So-called *"accidental" sampling*, the weakest form of sampling, is probably also the most frequent. In effect, one takes available samples at hand: classes of seniors in high school, sophomores in college, a convenient PTA, and the like. (p. 129)

An often-used accidental sample in psychological and social change research consists of college students enrolled in introductory psychology classes. This presents problems when making comparisons between females and males because:

> different social and economic conditions for men and women introduce serious sampling biases. Colleges and universities may have different admissions policies, procedures, and standards of evaluation on a formal or informal level for female and male applicants. Families and funding sources may be more willing to financially support the education of boys and men.

> Men may be distributed over a wider range of sciences, including natural and physical sciences while women are concentrated in the behavioral sciences. (Grady 1981, p. 635)

Accidental sampling differs from probability sampling and the other examples of nonprobability sampling in that it lacks a theoretical foundation but is similar in that some of the same kinds of errors occur in accidental designs as occur in probability and other kinds of nonprobability designs. Which is to say that usually accidental sampling not only has its own flaws but shares those one might find in more rigorous sampling designs. As a general rule, accidental sampling is useful in the piloting of studies but seriously limited for other uses.

GENERAL GUIDELINES IN SAMPLE SELECTION

Regardless of the approach, general guidelines for the selection of a good sample have been identified by a number of researchers. Kish (1965) advises that goal orientation, measurability, practicality, and economy should guide the formulation of the sample design. Many researchers (for instance: Borg and Gall 1979; Kish 1965; Sudman 1976) stress that no sample will be perfect and that a number of factors including degree of generalizability, cost, and purpose of the study need to be considered in designing a sample. Sudman (1976) points out that:

> The quality of the sample depends entirely on the stage of the research and how the information will be used. At one extreme, there is exploratory data gathering used in the process of generating hypotheses for later study. At the other extreme are large-scale continuing studies used to supply the input for major policy decisions of the federal government. Obviously, the levels of accuracy required differ in these two extreme cases. Thus, one of the earliest decisions that must be made in planning a study is how good the sample must be. (p. 2)

Sudman (p. 27) offers a credibility scale for judging "how good" the sample is and which can serve as a useful guide for analyzing important factors in drawing a sample. Factors considered include generalizability, sample size, sample execution, and use of resources.

NONCOVERAGE OF THE POPULATION BY THE SAMPLE

Perhaps one of the most obvious, and yet most pervasive, threats to the utility of the sampling process is noncoverage, or the failure to include individuals essential to the achievement of the stated objectives of the inquiry. Noncoverage is distinct from nonresponse bias in which individuals are not at home, refuse to participate, or do not return questionnaires. These and similar problems which will be discussed later in this chapter result even though the necessary types of elements have been selected and included in the sample. Nor does noncoverage include the deliberate exclusion of certain types of individuals. Instead, noncoverage refers to the exclusion of elements due to the unlikelihood that all desired elements will be selected (Kish 1965, p. 528). That is, due to some limitation in the sampling frame, elements have little or no chance of being selected. Problems resulting from noncoverage appear particularly acute in social change research as it, by its very nature, requires the identification of often less accessible types of elements. While one can, with relative ease, select a simple probability sample, it becomes considerably more difficult when one hopes to address the needs of specialized populations. As this is a domain of particular importance to social-change researchers, it is essential that the potential for noncoverage be examined carefully in the preparation and subsequent implementation of the sampling design. Particular attention should be focused upon the sampling frame or list utilized in the inquiry. Simply, does it include the types of individuals one is interested in and does it include them in sufficient numbers to yield an adequate sample size?

Dillman (1978) notes six areas in which sampling frames have shortcomings. Frequently, individuals desired for the sample are excluded from a seemingly appropriate list because they do not possess the attributes required for inclusion. For example, one might assume that a membership list for a local teachers' union would include a comparable group of female and male teachers. However, differing abilities among males and females who enter teaching as well as differing perceptions of unionization among females and males would make such a list an inaccurate sampling frame from which to draw comparable female/male teachers for study. Other failings noted by Dillman include the ability of some individuals to keep their names off lists, as in the case of unlisted telephone numbers, and the inevitable fact that many lists are out-of-date or incorrect.

Probably the most written about noncoverage problem is the use of the telephone in surveys. For many years, the use of telephone surveys was deprecated for its alleged systematic exclusion of individuals who could not afford or otherwise chose not to possess a phone. More recently, however, telephones have been a more acceptable means of access since census data began to report that a very high percentage of the households in most communities have telephones. This enthusiasm is tempered when it is realized that such access does not cut equally across all races or socioeconomic classes. For instance, fewer than 50 percent of minority families with a father-in-residence and living in urban areas have a telephone available, while 95 percent of white families with a father-in-residence above the poverty level have a telephone available (Dillman 1978, p. 42). Further, many people choose not to list their telephone numbers, particularly females and high-visibility persons, thus injecting bias into telephone lists. Additionally, married females are seldom listed in telephone books, and thus efforts to locate female respondents are hampered by using telephone directories. Random digit dialing can overcome the latter problem (see, for example, Glasser and Metzger 1972), but poses its own unique problems for the social change researcher.

Noncoverage must also be watched for in area sampling. Transportation problems and bad weather can result in the exclusion of elements in less accessible areas (Cochran 1977). If area sampling is the method of choice, the implementation design must consider the hours at which the desired respondents are most likely to be at home. An interesting example of noncoverage occurs in the Gallup polls. A well-thought-out sampling technique, designed to represent the entire population of the United States, ends with interviewers being instructed to interview women from 4:00 P.M. and men from 6:00 P.M. on weekdays. Thus, the woman who is not at home at 4:00, but instead returns home at 6:00 from her job, may not be selected for the Gallup sample (Gallup 1980).

For some specialized populations, no lists are available. The principal means of identifying such populations is by screening populations or through the secondary analyses of existing surveys. Screening requires the examination of a probability sample of the population. From this screening of a large general sample, the specialized population can be identified. Secondary analysis of existing surveys is an inexpensive, but sometimes deceptive, means of locating specialized populations (Reed 1975). In this approach, national samples drawn for other purposes are examined in the hopes of identifying the desired population, or questions are added to periodic surveys until enough of the rare population is identified. Unfortunately, this process makes it difficult to estimate the size of the group with precision (see Reed 1975, p. 516). A detailed examination of this process is provided by Reed (1975) and the identification of rare populations is discussed more fully by Kish (1965), as well as by Hansen, Hurwitz, and Madow (1953), and Sudman (1972).

USE OF VOLUNTEER SAMPLES

Volunteer samples very often cannot be avoided in social-change research. Because volunteers may differ significantly from nonvolunteers, volunteer samples can confound the results of the study so that the findings become meaningless. An example of the hazards of volunteer sampling is the Benbow and Stanley (1980) study of sex differences in mathematical ability of the gifted. Jacklin (1981) points out that Benbow and Stanley used volunteers even though studies of volunteers find that highly gifted boys are more likely to volunteer to take such tests than are highly gifted girls (Miles 1954; Rosenthal and Rosnow 1975). In this case, not only did use of volunteers confound the results of the study, it was unnecessary to use volunteers since alternate arrangements could have been made to draw a more reliable sample (see the Terman Genius Study, for example, as an alternative approach to this problem).

Rosenthal and Rosnow (1975) have assembled a review of the research on the characteristics of volunteers so that the researcher using volunteers may attempt to control or test for these differences in her/his particular sample. These characteristics should be taken into account when using volunteer samples.

INAPPROPRIATE SAMPLE SIZE

Since most research efforts are restricted by limited personnel, time, and finances, decisions about sample size are often made on practical, rather than on theoretical grounds. While these are certainly realistic as well as important considerations, the statements one wishes to be able to make, and the precision with which one wishes to make these statements, must not be overlooked. Unfortunately, weak samples in social change research can be rather simplistically described: they are either too large or too small. Specifically, samples are drawn larger than necessary for the desired precision, thus wasting financial and human resources; or samples are drawn that are too small for statistical analysis of major and minor subgroups, either because the original sample was too small or because problems of attrition were not taken into account.

Borg and Gall (1979, pp. 195-97) identify a number of conditions for which larger samples are necessary:

- when many uncontrollable variables are present
- when small differences or small relationships are present
- when groups must be broken into subgroups
- when populations are highly heterogeneous on the variables being studied
- when reliable measures of the dependent variables are not available

One should keep in mind, however, that the larger the sample, the more likely will be the chance of finding statistical significance (Hayes 1973). Thus, practical significance (McNamara and Gill 1978) as well as statistical significance of findings need to be calculated. The question that is usually asked is how small may the sample be and still be appropriate. Because of human, financial, and time constraints, samples must have parameters. If this were not the case, populations, rather than samples would be investigated. Therefore, tables have been computed to help researchers calculate the minimum sample needed (Krejcie and Morgan 1970).

Even when the original sample size drawn is of adequate size, problems often arise because researchers have not taken into account the sample size needed for interesting subgroups in order to allow statistical analyses, nor do they plan for attrition or nonresponse (this is particularly a problem in longitudinal studies). Thus, the researcher should be careful to draw a sample large enough to allow for statistical analysis despite attrition or nonresponse.

The discussion of sample size up to this point has been primarily concerned with either probability or large samples. What about case studies? The number of cases chosen for observational and case-study research depends on a number of factors—time, access, economics, and generalizability. Most often judgment sampling is used to select the particular elements for case studies. However, even with the very small samples, some form of random sampling may be used (Lawton 1980). For a more thorough approach to sample size, the reader is urged to consult Cochran (1977).

REDUCING NONRESPONSE BIAS

Discussion of sample size must necessarily include consideration of the problems that accrue when all elements selected in a probability sample are not available. This problem is particularly acute in mail surveys in which returns are often less than 50 percent. Thus, we often read reports of survey research in which generalizations are made to the population as a whole based upon a response rate of 20 percent. We neither know how the other 80 percent would respond, nor what are the implications of those who did respond (e.g., by age/sex/race). Similarly, longitudinal research suffers greatly from nonresponse due to attrition; thus, comparisons over time are often erroneous. Furthermore, the increase in the width of the confidence intervals can be quite dramatic as nonresponse rate increases in size. Fuller (1974) has demonstrated that even small variations in response rate have a major effect on the range of the confidence interval.

While some reduction in range of the confidence interval can be achieved through an increase in sample size, the minimal gains achieved quickly diminish as the level of nonresponse increases. The increased costs required to gain but a small reduction in the range of the confidence interval would likely prove prohibitive, except in unusually well-funded studies. Moreover, any gain achieved through increased sample size must be balanced with the realization that trivial associations may be revealed as significant when the sample size becomes large (Hayes 1973). Thus, it behooves the researcher to take appropriate action to reduce nonresponse (Cochran 1977; Fuller 1974; United States Bureau of Census 1967).

Several procedures are offered for consideration to reduce nonresponse problems, including weighting for over and underrepresentativeness, estimating the effects of nonresponse, substituting for nonresponses, developing replacement procedures, and the Politz-Simmons procedure (Fuller 1974; Kish 1965). The substitution for nonresponses, though frequently proposed, is not useful and can actually create more problems (Kish 1965, p. 558). A variation of the substitution scheme is that proposed by the United States Bureau of the Census (1967) to adjust weights for interviewed households to account for those not interviewed.

The Politz-Simmons weighting method is a procedure to adjust for bias resulting when individuals cannot be reached for inclusion in the sample (Politz and Simmons, 1949; Simmons 1954). Designed with the telephone survey in mind, the procedure eliminates callbacks using a weighting procedure which acknowledges that those who are home most frequently are more likely to be included in the sample.

Researchers considering the Politz-Simmons procedure should examine commentary on its utility provided in the texts of Kish (1965), Cochran (1977), and Sudman (1976) as well as articles comparing studies using the procedure with those using callbacks (Durbin and Stuart 1954; Simmons 1954; Deming 1950). Sudman (1976) notes the scheme suffers from its dependence on the respondent's memory of her/his availability, a substantial increase in the sampling variability, and diligent supervision to insure proper weighting of the data.

Another tack is the formal examination of nonresponse bias in order to estimate the size of its effect. On mail surveys, Borg and Gall (1979) and Sudman (1976) provide a rule of thumb that requires testing for nonresponse bias on an 80 percent-or-less return rate. Such information can be then employed in the analysis of the data. In his review of the area, Kish (1965) recommends the reviews of Houseman (1953) and Zarkovich (1963). Although the test of nonresponse bias is particularly important in survey research, such procedures should not serve as an excuse for failing to encourage the maximum response through the use of follow-up mailings and reminders.

The definition of a replacement procedure prior to the actual implementation of the study is another possibility to correct for nonresponse bias. Such prior definition is designed to help insure the replacement of missing elements with those of similar background. The formalization of the procedure is particularly important in those surveys which rely upon field interviewers to replace missing elements. If, for example, dwellings in a residential area are serving as elements, the interviewer has a prepared plan of action to replace dwellings for which there is no one at home. It has been suggested in such cases (Kish 1965) that nonresponse from former surveys in the area serve as replacements for nonresponses in the current survey. Of course, in many surveys one does not have such information from surveys with similar objectives. In these cases, one must consider whether the differences in the objectives might have led to differences in the types of individuals responding.

SUMMARY

This chapter touches briefly on four common mistakes which have been found in the sampling designs of social-change research. We suggest that the reader use this discussion as a springboard for further investigation of these issues, consulting the sources listed in the attached bibliography.

REFERENCES

Babbie, E. *Survey research methods.* Belmont, Ca.: Wadsworth, 1973.

Bailar, B.A., and C.M. Lanphier. *Development of Survey Methods to Assess Survey Practices.* Washington, D.C.: American Statistical Association, 1978.

Benbow, C.P., and J.C. Stanley. Sex differences in mathematical ability. Fact or artifact? *Science* 210 (1980): 1262–64.

Borg, W., and M. Gall. *Educational research: An introduction.* New York: Longman, 1979.

Chein, I. An introduction to sampling. In C. Selltiz et al., *Research methods in social relations.* New York: Holt, Rinehart, Winston, 1959.

Cochran, W. *Sampling techniques.* New York: Wiley, 1977.

Deming, W.E. *Some theory of sampling.* New York: Wiley, 1950.

Denzin, N. *Sociological methods: A source book.* Chicago: Aldine Publishing, 1970.

Dillman, D. *Mail and telephone surveys: The total design method.* New York: Wiley, 1978.

Durbin, J., and A. Stuart. Call-backs and clustering in sample surveys. *Journal of the Royal Statistical Association* 19 (A) (1954): 54–66.

Fuller, C.H. Weighting to adjust for survey non-response. *Public Opinion Quarterly* 37 (1974): 239–46.

Gallup, G. *The Gallup Poll: Public Opinion, 1979.* Princeton, N.J.: Scholarly Research, 1980.

Glasser, G., and G. Metzger. Random-digit dialing as a method of telephone sampling. *Journal of Marketing Research* 9 (1972): 59–64.

Grady, K.E. Sex bias in research design. *Psychology of Women Quarterly* 5 (4) (1981): 628–36.

Hansen, M., W. Hurwitz, and W. Madow. *Sample survey methods and theory.* New York: Wiley, 1953.

Hayes, W. *Statistics for the social sciences.* New York: Holt, Rinehart, Winston, 1973.

Houseman, E. Statistical treatment of the nonresponse problem. *Agricultural Economics Research* 5 (1953): 12–18.

Jacklin, C. Methodological issues in the study of sex-related differences. Paper read at the meeting of the American Psychological Association, New York, September 1981.

Kerlinger, F. *Foundations of behavioral research.* New York: Holt, Rinehart, Winston, 1973.

Kish, L. *Survey sampling.* New York: 1965.

Krejcie, R.V., and D.W. Morgan. Determining sample size for research activities. *Educational and Psychological Measurement* 30 (1970): 607–10.

Lawton, S. *Myth III: Judgmental sampling is better than random sampling when sample sizes are small.* A paper presented at the annual meeting of the American Educational Research Association, Boston, April 1980.

McNamara, J., and D. Gill. Practical significance in vocational education research. *Journal of Vocational Education Research* 3 (1978): 27–48.

Miles, C.C. Gifted children. In L. Carmichael (ed.), *Manual of child psychology* (2d ed.). New York: Wiley, 1954.

Reed, J. Needles in haystacks: Studying rare populations by secondary analysis of national sample surveys. *Public Opinion Quarterly* 39 (1975): 514–22.

Rosenthal, R., and R.L. Rosnow. *The Volunteer Subject.* New York: Wiley, 1975.

Shakeshaft, C. *Dissertation research on women in academic administration: A synthesis of findings and paradigm for future research.* Unpublished doctoral diss., Texas A&M University, 1979.

Shakeshaft, C. Women in public school administration: A descriptive analysis of dissertation research and paradigm for future research. In P.A. Schmuck, W.W. Charters, and R.O. Carlson (eds.), *Educational Policy and Management: Sex Differentials.* New York: Academic Press, 1981.

Simmons, W. A plan to account for "not at homes" by combining weighting and callbacks. *Journal of Marketing* 19 (1954): 42–53.

Stephan, F., and P. McCarthy. *Sampling opinions.* New York: Wiley, 1963.

Sudman, S. *Applied sampling.* New York: Academic Press, 1976.

Sudman, S. The uses of telephone directories for survey sampling. *Journal of Marketing Research* 10 (1973): 204–7.

Sudman, S. On sampling of very rare human populations. *Journal of the American Statistical Association* 67 (1972): 335–39.

U.S. Bureau of the Census. *The current population survey—a report on methodology: technical paper #7.* Washington, D.C.: Government Printing Office, 1967.

Zarkovich, S. *Sampling methods and censuses; vol. II, quality of statistical data.* Rome: FAO, 1963.

8

Instruments and Measures in a Changing, Diverse Society

Carole A. Beere

It is indisputable that good measures are fundamental to quality research. Just as physical scientists should not use a rubber band (unreliable) to measure length nor a ruler (invalid) to measure weight, social scientists must be careful to use reliable and valid measures in their research. Unfortunately for the social scientist, developing and/or locating reliable, valid measures is often very difficult. Nevertheless, the quality of the measures is crucial if we are to have confidence in the conclusions derived from our research. Furthermore, the comparability of research results from different studies, and hence the development and testing of relevant theory is directly related to the measures used.

The purpose of this chapter is to increase the likelihood that researchers pursuing gender-related research will rely on psychometrically sound measures. This goal is being pursued by acquainting present and potential researchers with the issues and problems regarding measures used in certain areas of gender-related research. Hopefully, by sensitizing researchers to the relevant issues, they will be able and motivated to avoid the more common pitfalls—and they will strive to rely only on good quality measures.

The goal, as just described, is rather formidable and so it was necessary to limit the coverage. Thus the discussion in this chapter is confined to two areas not covered elsewhere in this book: the measurement of sex roles in adults and children and the measurement of sex stereotypes. The overwhelming emphasis is on paper-and-pencil measures.

Extensive reviews of gender-related research have demonstrated that reliability and validity are frequently ignored by researchers investigating gender-related issues. In her literature search, Beere (1979) found that the authors of over 70 percent of gender-related studies failed to provide any information regarding the reliability and validity of their measures, and they did not describe how their measures were developed. Though it is possible that the researchers had evidence of their measure's reliability and validity and simply did not report that data in their publications, it seems more likely that the researchers failed to consider reliability and validity before using the measure.

Since the issues described in the chapter frequently pertain to the reliability and validity of measures, it seems appropriate at the outset to provide a brief review of these two concepts.

RELIABILITY

There are several types of reliability and each one provides different information about the measure. *Internal consistency* or *homogeneity* indicates whether the various items on the test are measuring the same thing. "If a test has substantial internal consistency, it is psychologically interpretable" (Cronbach 1951, p. 320). Computing the internal consistency or homogeneity of a multi-item measure is generally rather simple as the computation relies on a single administration of the measure. *Stability* indicates whether a measure yields similar results when administered to the same persons on two different occasions and thus indicates whether scores can be generalized over time. If the stability coefficient is low, results obtained from the measure are virtually useless. *Equivalence* indicates whether two measures yield similar results and should be calculated when two forms of the same measure are being developed. If the two forms are administered on different occasions, a coefficient of equivalence and stability may be determined, indicating whether scores can be generalized over time and across content.

When there is an element of subjectivity in scoring, it is crucial that *interrater reliability* also be computed. Interrater reliability indicates whether different raters or scorers obtain the same results from the same set of responses. If interrater reliability is low, the scores on the measure will vary depending on who does the scoring, and the same set of responses are subject to more than one interpretation. Though interrater reliability is important for some measures, it is never a substitute for other types of reliability.

VALIDITY

As with reliability, there are several types of validity.

Content validity pertains to whether test items are representative of the domain to which the scores should generalize. It should be built into the test by carefully defining and sampling from the domain of interest. It is difficult to interpret test scores without knowing the content domain from which the items were sampled and the extent to which the domain was represented on the measure. For example, if one wishes to measure sex stereotypes of occupations, one must carefully define the domain of occupations which should be sampled. Should it include blue-collar jobs? White-collar jobs? Professional jobs? Low-paying jobs? High-paying jobs? Etc. Ignoring the issue of content validity allows one to overload the measure with one or two types of occupations and yet erroneously draw inferences to all occupations. If one included primarily low-paying social service jobs on the measure, one might conclude that sex stereotyping of occupations favors women. Clearly this conclusion would be incorrect. Content validity is not sufficient evidence of validity for the types of measures to be discussed here, but it should not be ignored.

Construct validity pertains to whether a test measures the theoretical construct or trait it is designed to measure. Clearly the construct being measured (e.g., femininity) must be adequately defined before its construct validity can be assessed. If we are uncertain of what we are trying to measure, how can we ever know if we have succeeded?

Criterion-related validity indicates whether test scores are related to some independently obtained criterion. Careful selection of the criterion is imperative as it, too, must be a reliable and valid measure, uncontaminated by the results of the test it is validating.

Face validity is not validity in the technical sense. Rather it is someone's subjective judgment of whether the test *looks valid.* Though face validity is often desirable, it is not always so: The presence of face validity may mean the test is rather transparent and hence easily fakeable. Regardless of whether the researcher decides that face validity is or is not important in a particular study, face validity should never be considered as a substitute for other types of validity.

With the concepts of reliability and validity in mind, attention can now be given to specific areas of gender-related research.

ADULT SEX ROLE SCALES

Adult sex role measures, historically called masculinity-femininity scales, have been used by psychologists for almost 50 years. Despite the long history of their use, they continue to generate considerable criticism largely questioning whether they meet the standards of good psychological scales. For example, Thomas (1978) reviewed 96 articles involving a measure of sex role and concluded that there was "little concern... evident for the reliability or validity of the instruments used, whether published, unpublished, or devised especially for that research project" (p. 4). She was particularly critical of specially constructed scales since she found a "lack of concern with validation, or what exactly, was being measured.... The tacit assumption was that the instrument was valid and measured what the researcher intended ... a concept that could be termed 'declarative validity'" (p. 10). Of course, many sex role researchers do not construct new measures of sex role; rather they use one of the sex role scales in common use at the time they are conducting their study. However, the commonly used sex role scales have also been the focus of extensive criticism.

A careful review of the commonly used sex role measures suggests they fall into two general categories: The *older scales* were published prior to 1960 with the oldest scale published in 1936; the *newer scales* have been published since 1970. The older and newer scales differ in the ways in which they were developed, the types of items included on the scales, and the assumptions made about the relationship between masculinity and femininity.

The Past: Older Scales

A variety of sex role scales were developed prior to 1960—e.g., the Attitude Interest Analysis Test (Terman and Miles 1936), the Gough Femininity Scale (Gough 1952), the mf scale of the MMPI (Hathaway and McKinley 1942)—and were used in a large number of research studies spanning several decades. However, by the early 1970s, they were the focus of considerable criticism.

The scales were strongly criticized because the constraints they were measuring—i.e., masculinity and femininity—were not defined theoretically. Test developers simply administered an item pool to a group of respondents and selected items which successfully differentiated between the sexes. Thus, which items were included on a particular scale depended on what groups were used for scale development. One cannot presume that differences between one group of men and women (e.g., white, middle-class college students) would also be found among a different group of men and women (e.g., black factory workers). Similarly, one cannot presume that sex differences obtained in one decade would still be found in another decade.

Questions can be raised about what the older scales are actually measuring. An examination of item content suggests that some items which supposedly reflect femininity—e.g., Sometimes I feel I am about to go to pieces (Gough 1952)—are really reflecting neuroticism. This criticism is supported by the results of a factor analytic study of several of the older sex-role scales: One of the factors was labeled neuroticism (Lunneborg 1972). Pleck (1975) has pointed out that generally the traits differentiating males and females are the ones which "are relatively secondary rather than dominant in the personality" (p. 165).

An examination of item content on the older sex role scales suggests they were sampling a variety of areas. This diversity of item content was true within a single measure as well as across various measures. It is thus not surprising that studies examining the intercorrelations among the older sex role scales have failed to demonstrate the convergent validity of the scales. After reviewing numerous correlational studies, Constantinople (1973) concluded: "Although the tests have something in common, a considerable proportion of the variance associated with any two tests is not held in common" (p. 398). It follows then that factor analytic studies (e.g., Engel 1966; Lunneborg 1972; Lunneborg and Lunneborg 1970) have demonstrated that the items did not load on a single factor.

One of the most strongly criticized aspects of the older sex role scales is that they were developed on the assumption that masculinity and femininity are the opposite ends of a single continuum; they were treated as bipolar. A respondent could score high on masculinity or high on femininity, but it was impossible to score high on both. Given the nature of the older sex role scales, it is impossible to determine whether the assumption of bipolarity was valid, or whether the two constructs would be more accurately represented on two separate continua. This debate between the bipolar versus dualistic nature of masculinity and femininity led to the development of the newer sex-role scales.

The Present: Newer Scales

The term "newer scales" is being used to refer to three measures: the Bem Sex Role Inventory (BSRI); the Personal Attributes Questionnaire (PAQ); and the PRF ANDRO.* These newer scales differ from the old scales in that all three treat masculinity and femininity as falling along separate continua and thus allow for a person to score high on both traits, low on both traits, or high on just one trait. They also differ from the older scales in that their development did not rely on actual sex differences for item selection.

Bem Sex Role Inventory

The BSRI (Bem 1974) consists of 60 adjectives or descriptive phrases with 20 representing each of three subscales: masculinity, femininity, and social desirability. Respondents use a seven-point scale to indicate the extent to which each item is true of them. Item selection was based on college students' ratings of the desirability of each of 400 traits in a man and the desirability of

---

*The Adjective Check List (Heilbrun 1976) will not be discussed since it appears less often in the literature and differs in some significant ways from the other three measures, though it is not exempt from the criticism directed at the newer scales.

each trait in a woman. Desirability of items was rated independently in that no student rated the items for both men and women. Twenty items that were judged as significantly more desirable in a man than in a woman comprise the masculinity scale, and 20 items judged significantly more desirable in a woman than in a man comprise the femininity scale. The social desirability scale includes ten positive and ten negative characteristics, all of which were judged to be no more desirable for one sex than the other. Bem (1974) reported high test-retest reliability using a 4-week interval between administrations: masculinity = .90; femininity = 90; androgyny = .93; and social desirability = .89. She also reported high internal consistency estimates (coefficient alpha) for two samples: masculinity = .86 and .86; femininity = .80 and .82; androgyny = .85 and .86; and social desirability = .75 and .70.

A few years ago, Bem (1979) announced the development of a short form of the BSRI that includes half of the original items. The short form supposedly corrects some of the deficiencies revealed by factor analytic studies and eliminates some feminine items which were judged to be of low social desirability. Thus the short form of the BSRI has been modified in response to some of the criticisms described below.

Personal Attributes Questionnaire

The original PAQ (Spence, Helmreich, and Stapp 1974) consisted of 55 sets of bipolar self-descriptive phrases with each set placed at the end of a 5-point scale. Respondents are to rate themselves on each of the 55 scales. The items were selected based on sex-stereotype research conducted by Rosenkrantz et al. (1968). For 23 of the 55 items, males were believed to possess the trait more than females, but the trait was judged as socially desirable for both males and females. These items comprise the masculinity scale. For 18 items, the trait was believed to be characteristic of females more than males, but these traits were also judged as socially desirable for both sexes. These items comprise the femininity scale. For 13 items, ratings of the ideal man fell at the opposite pole from ratings of ideal woman and the presence of the trait was judged to differ in men and women. One item was not classified on these three scales. Based on early studies using the PAQ, Spence, Helmreich, and Stapp (1974) report test-retest reliabilities, with a 13-week interval, varying from .65 to .91. They also report internal consistency estimates (alpha) of .73 for men and .91 for women. More recently, Spence and Helmreich (1979b) recommend using a short form of the PAQ which includes eight instrumental and/or expressive items from each subscale.

PRF ANDRO

The PRF ANDRO (Berzins, Welling, and Wetter 1978) is a true-false measure with 29 items on the masculine scale and 27 items on the feminine scale. Items were selected from the 400 items on the PRF (Personality Research Form) if they were judged by the scale authors to be more desirable in one sex than in the other, and if they were related to content themes on the BSRI. Berzins, Welling, and Wetter (1978) described those themes as "social-intellectual ascendancy, autonomy and orientation toward risk" on the masculinity scale, and "nurturance, affiliative-expressive concerns, and self-subordination" (p. 128) on the femininity scale. The authors' judgment that the desirability of the items was different for the ideal man and ideal woman was verified by college students who indicated how desirable it was for a man (or a woman) to mark "true" to each item. Berzins, Welling, and Wetter (1977) reported test-retest reliabilities, based on a 3-week interval, of .81 for both the masculinity and femininity scales. Internal consistency coefficients (alpha) for seven different samples, ranged from .68 to .79 for the masculinity scale and .65 to .70 for the femininity scale.

Scoring

There has been considerable discussion in the relevant literature regarding the appropriate procedure for interpreting scores from the newer scales. (See, for example, Harrington and Anderson 1981; Spence and Helmreich 1979a). One method of scoring involves using a t score which is "the difference between an individual's masculinity and femininity normalized with respect to the standard deviations of his or her masculinity and femininity scores" (Bem 1974, p. 158). This procedure was rather cumbersome and Strahan (1975) recommended using the simple difference between the masculinity and femininity scores. If the difference was small, the person would be labeled androgynous; if the difference was large, the person would be labeled either masculine or feminine depending on which score was greater. Strahan found a correlation of .98 between the two procedures. By these scoring procedures, persons are considered androgynous if they endorse equal or similar numbers of masculine- and feminine-typed items, regardless of whether they endorse few or many of those characteristics. Furthermore, persons are sex-typed if they endorse far more items on one subscale than on the other, even though they may be endorsing a greater than average number of traits from both subscales.

In the median split method of scoring, persons are classified as: (1) androgynous, if they are above the median on both masculinity and femininity; (2) masculine or feminine, if they are above the median on one of the two scales; and (3) undifferentiated, if they are below the median on both scales. This method also raises questions: What median should be used for determining the median split? If the sample median is used, then a person's classification is largely a function of the sample they are part of. This could be particularly problematic if the sample is a homogeneous group, such as truck drivers, since it is impossible for all respondents to be categorized the same. If another group other than the sample is used, who should that group be? At this time, there appear to be no national norms from which one could identify a median. Should people be compared with a median based only on their own sex? If they are, scoring categories are defined differently for males and females. A question can also be raised regarding whether it is appropriate to classify as sex-typed someone who is just barely above the median on one scale and just barely below the median on the other scale. The difference method would obviously classify that person as androgynous.

A third method has been proposed: the difference/median split method (Orlofsky, Aslin, and Ginsburg 1977), which takes account of the difference between the masculinity and femininity scores and also where the scores lie relative to the medians.

In summarizing studies comparing the various methods of interpreting scores from the newer scales, Kaplan and Sedney (1980) report that between 25 percent and 50 percent of respondents are classified differently depending on the scoring procedure used. What is the best method to use? Clearly the answer depends on the definitions of "androgynous" and "sex-typed" that one is using, and on the research question that one is posing. All three methods can be criticized on the ground that a category system precludes within-group comparisons and is not useful for predicting individuals' scores on other variables.

Bem (1974) originally recommended the difference method and also has suggested using regression analysis (1977). However, in 1977 she conceded that the median split method is preferable to the difference method. Spence and Helmreich (1978) have always used the median split method and suggest that regression analysis is not useful. Berzins, Welling, and Wetter (1978) use the median split method. Though the authors of the scales now agree on the use of the median split method, Jones, Chernovetz, and Hansson (1978), based on their research using the BSRI, recommend against the median split method claiming it "obscures relative differences between masculinity and femininity that...were consistently related to important behaviors and dispositions for both males and females" (p. 312). Kelly, Furman, and Young (1978) concurred with Jones, Chernovetz, and Hansson (1978) when they stated "the current data indicate that there is little empirical basis for configurally combining these scores into broad typological categories based on median splits" (p. 1576).

Criticisms

Of the newer scales, the one that has attracted the most attention, been used the most in published research studies, and hence has been the focus of most criticism, is the BSRI. However, much of the criticism directed at the BSRI applies to the other scales as well.

The older sex role scales were criticized because they were not based on theoretical definitions of the constructs. Though scale authors may disagree, the newer scales suffer the same deficit and the problem is exacerbated by the introduction of an additional construct: androgyny.

There seems to be general agreement that an androgynous person is one who scores high on both masculinity and femininity (Bem 1977; Berzins, Welling, and Wetter 1978; Spence and Helmreich 1978). However, Spence and Helmreich (1978) differ with Bem on the underlying meaning of androgyny. They state that, unlike Bem,

> We do not *define* the individual who is androgynous on the PAQ or the BSRI...as a person who is "flexible"(i.e., who exhibits both masculine and feminine behaviors) across the general category of sex role behaviors. Nor do we *predict* that these androgynous individuals are less likely to differ markedly from others in sex role behaviors that do not directly involve expressive or instrumental skills (p. 1039).

As stated above, the definition of androgyny hinges on the definitions of masculinity and femininity. Bem (1974) and Berzins, Wellington, and Wetter (1978) see masculinity and femininity as endorsement of those personality traits which are differentially desirable in males and females; i.e., femininity is endorsement of those traits judged to be significantly more desirable in females, and masculinity is endorsement of those traits which are judged to be significantly more desirable in males. Spence and Helmreich (1978) see masculinity and femininity as endorsement of characteristics which are socially desirable for both males and females, but which are believed to characterize one sex more than the other. Endorsement of those socially desirable traits which are believed to be more characteristic of females is femininity; endorsement of those socially desirable traits which are believed to be more characteristic of males is masculinity. These definitions are not identical (Heerboth and Ramanaiah 1981), but they are both normatively based. Bem (1979) acknowledges the normative basis of the constructs when she states: "The theory underlying the BSRI asserts that sex-typed individuals will conform to whatever definitions of femininity and masculinity the culture happens to provide" (p. 1049). Who is to decide what the "cultural prescriptions" are? The United States, to say nothing of the world, is composed of many subcultures and they may well differ in their definitions of masculinity and femininity.

As was the case with the older sex role scales, one cannot assume that norms are constant across different populations and at different times. Since there is every reason to believe that the cultural prescriptions will change over time, existing measures of sex role are doomed to obsolescence. Spence and Helmreich (1978) have shown that the PAQ is presently quite consistent across people of varying ages and demographic characteristics within the United States, and they have shown that it is somewhat consistent cross-culturally. However, it is premature to test whether the PAQ yields consistent results across long time spans. Data on the consistency of the BSRI across subgroups, cultures, and time has not been published. One must avoid *assuming* that the normatively defined scales apply to anyone other than the group on which they were developed.

The outstanding distinction between the older and newer sex role scales is that the former assume that masculinity and femininity are bipolar and the latter treat them as dualistic.* Do the data obtained with the newer scales support the dualistic notion? The evidence is mixed. Both positive and negative correlations have been obtained between masculinity and femininity scores (Bem 1974; Berzins, Welling, and Wetter 1978; Edwards and Norcross 1980; Kelly and Worell 1977; Spence and Helmreich 1978; Whetton and Swindells 1977), and though they are usually low, the correlations are often significantly different from zero. A startling contrast to the generally low correlations was reported by LaTorre and Piper (1978) who obtained a correlation of −.90 for noncollege females. Spence and Helmreich (1978) conclude that their correlations between M and F provide "striking disconfirmation of a bipolar conception of masculinity and femininity..." but their M−F scale provides "some support for the bipolar model" (p. 20).

In discussing the BSRI, Jackson and Paunomen (1980) suggest that independence of masculinity and femininity is an artifact of the scale's development and not necessarily a reflection of reality. Although the evidence regarding the relationship between the constructs masculinity and femininity is ambiguous, the relationship between the self-descriptive adjectives "masculine" and "feminine" is unequivocal. In factor analytic studies (Berzins, Welling, and Wetter 1978; Gaudreau 1977; Moreland et al. 1978; Pedhazur and Tetenbaum 1979; Whetton and Swindells 1977), these two adjectives were found not to load with other adjectives and to be strongly, negatively correlated.† Thus, in describing themselves, respondents consider masculinity and femininity to be bipolar.

Another significant difference between the older and newer scales concerns the way in which they were developed. Older scales include both positive and negative items for which there were actual sex differences. For example, the Gough Femininity Scale (Gough 1952) includes positive items such as "I always tried to make the best school grades that I could," and negative items such as "A windstorm terrifies me." These items showed actual sex differences. Newer scales include only positive traits for which there were

---

*It seems somewhat paradoxical that the PAQ items are themselves bipolar.

†When sex of subject was included as a variable in the factor analysis, it was found to load on the same factor with "masculine" and "feminine" (Gaudreau 1977).

stereotyped differences. For example, the BSRI (Bem 1974) includes the positive trait "affectionate" which was stereotyped as feminine and the positive trait "acts as a leader" which was stereotyped masculine.

Bem (1974) developed the BSRI by asking respondents how *desirable* various traits were. However, the term desirable is itself ambiguous. Is it prescriptive or descriptive? Pedhazur and Tetenbaum (1978) report that "Overall, the mean ratings for traits designated as feminine tend to be lower than those designated as masculine, even when the former are applied to a woman.... Some of the feminine items are perceived as relatively undesirable or negative"(p. 999) even in comparison to neutral items that were intended to be negative. In reporting results of factor analytic studies, Silvern and Ryan (1979) report that items of questionable desirability on the femininity scale of the BSRI, such as gullible and childlike, do not load on the same factors as other items. Bem (1979) reports that these weaknesses have been corrected on the short form of the BSRI.

One might also question whether the same traits are seen as desirable for all men or all women. It is known that different traits are seen as *characteristic* of women depending on the type of women being described (e.g., housewife, career woman, woman athlete) (Clifton, McGrath, and Wick 1976). Isn't it also possible that different traits are *desirable* in different types of women or men? And different traits may be desirable depending on the situation or circumstance the man or woman is facing. Locklsey and Colten (1979) suggest that the adjectives that Clifton, McGrath, and Wick (1976) found to describe the typical housewife are similar to the adjectives on the BSRI and PAQ.

A study by Lowell (1981) raises additional questions regarding scale development procedures. She asked respondents to indicate the extent to which particular adjectives were characteristic of masculine males, masculine females, feminine females and feminine males. Her results showed that almost half of the adjectives from the BSRI "were found to be differentially descriptive of masculinity or femininity depending on whether they were used to describe males or females" (p. 8). Locksley and Colten (1979) question whether the adjectives are interpreted similarly by males and females who, they point out, may perceive the items in different contexts. Men may think of *loyalty* to their employer; women may think of *loyalty* to their family. Are these equivalent? Or women might consider themselves *aggressive* in defending their children's rights in schools; men may consider themselves *aggressive* in business negotiation. Are these equivalent?

Since the newer sex role scales are intended to include only positive attributes, questions can be raised about the implications of omitting negative traits since "negative attributes may be a functional part of some or all sex role orientations" (Kelly and Worell 1977). Kelly et al. (1977) and Spence, Helmreich, and Holahan (1979) have reported some research results comparing BSRI and PAQ scores with responses to negative sex-typed traits.

Pedhazur and Tetenbaum (1979) criticize Bem's scale development on the grounds that using 400 t tests, as she did, is bound to yield some significant differences due to chance alone, and statistical significance does not guarantee practical significance. Bem (1979) countered their criticism by indicating that each item was judged by four independent samples and the probability of all four groups agreeing on any one item, by chance alone, was 1/160,000. Furthermore, although Edwards and Ashworth (1977) obtained different results when replicating the development of the BSRI, Heerboth and Ramanaiah (1981) and Walkup and Abbott (1978) obtained confirmatory results.

Spence and Helmreich (1979b) report that their research supports the unidimensionality of the PAQ scales. However, factor analytic studies of the BSRI and PRF ANDRO have consistently shown that these scales are not unidimensional (Berzins, Welling, and Wetter 1978; Feather 1978; Gaudreau 1977; Moreland et al. 1978; Pedhazur and Tetenbaum 1979; Tetenbaum 1977; Whetton and Swindells 1977). As a result of these findings, two suggestions have emerged: Avoid the use of a summated score (Pedhazur and Tetenbaum 1979), and score the scales consistent with their factor structure (Gaudreau 1977; Moreland et al. 1978; Silvern and Ryan 1979). It was found that when the latter suggestion is followed, item analysis results and alpha coefficients improve (Moreland et al. 1978; Tetenbaum 1977). Bem (1979) used the results of factor analytic studies in developing the short form of the BSRI.

The older sex role scales were criticized for lack of high correlations between them. How do the newer scales fare on this issue? Positive correlations have been found among the newer scales with coefficients generally above .5 and often above .6 (Berzins, Welling, and Wetter 1978; Edwards and Norcross 1980; Gayton et al. 1977; Kelly, Furman, and Young 1978; Spence and Helmreich 1978; Wiggins and Holzmuller 1978). However, when scores are used to categorize respondents into four groups (as described in the Scoring section above), there tends to be considerable inconsistency in category assignment (Edwards and Norcross 1980; Gayton et al. 1977; Kelly, Furman, and Young 1978). When the newer and older sex role scales have been compared, the correlations are generally low, though there are occasional exceptions (Bem 1974; Berzins, Welling, and Wetter 1978; LaTorre and Piper 1978; Spence and Helmreich 1978).

Significant sex differences have been found on all three scales (Berzins, Welling, and Wetter 1978; Deutsch and Gilbert 1976; Minnigerode 1976; Spence and Helmreich 1978, 1979b). However, Tetenbaum (1977) reports that when the traits "masculine" and "feminine" are deleted from analysis of BSRI scores, the obtained sex difference is greatly reduced.

Questions can be raised about the transparency or fakeability of the scales, particularly since the newer scales are supposed to include only positive items. In discussing the PAQ, Spence and Helmreich (1978) contend that "individuals' perceptions of themselves are not distorted by their perceptions of modal differences between the sexes on these attributes" (p. 20). However, data collected using the newer scales indicate that sex role scores are positively and often significantly correlated with social desirability scores (Bem 1974; Berzins, Welling, and Wetter 1978; Jordan-Viola, Fassberg, and Viola 1976; Spence and Helmreich 1978; Whetton and Swindells 1977). Based on their own research, Hinrichson and Stone (1978) concluded "The BSRI is an extremely obvious measure which is highly susceptible to faking" (p. 512).

Scores from the newer sex role scales have been related to a variety of other paper-and-pencil measures and to behavioral measures. (See Beere 1979; Spence and Helmreich 1978.) The results are frequently in the predicted direction (Bem 1975, 1977; Bem and Lenney 1976; Bem, Martyna, and Watson 1976; Berzins, Welling, and Wetter 1978; Spence and Helmreich 1978). However, taken together, the studies lead to the following conclusions and questions. First, the particular findings may vary depending upon which sex-role scale is administered and which scoring procedure is used (Bem 1977; Edwards and Norcross 1980; Spence and Helmreich 1979b). Second, the pattern of results is not always identical for male and female respondents (Bem 1975, 1977; Spence and Helmreich 1978). Third, it is unclear whether androgyny or masculinity is the better predictor of other paper-and-pencil and behavioral measures (Silvern and Ryan 1979). For example, Jones, Chernovetz, and Hansson (1978, p. 298) related BSRI scores to a variety of other measures and concluded:

> Contrary to expectation a pattern of findings replicated across measures of attitudes toward women's issues, gender identification, neurosis, introversion-extraversion, locus of control, self-esteem, problems with alcohol, creativity, political awareness, confidence in one's own ability, helplessness, and sexual maturity indicated that flexibility and adjustment were generally associated with masculinity rather than androgyny for both males and females.

Fourth, since androgynous persons are describing themselves with positive traits and undifferentiated persons are not, are the obtained results merely a function of the sex role relatedness of the traits? On the BSRI, the masculine traits are consistently judged as positive while some of the feminine traits have been identified as negative. (See earlier discussion.) Could this be accounting for the results obtained from studies such as Jones, Chernovetz, and Hansson (1978)? Fifth, though Bem (1974, 1975) contends that androgynous persons should be more flexible, there is evidence to suggest that the possession of masculine and feminine traits does not guarantee that the traits are integrated, equally accessible across situations, nor indicative of mental health (Kaplan 1979).

The Future

Given what has been presented about both the older and newer sex-role scales, what conclusions can be drawn? Anyone wishing to compare data collected today with data previously collected must, of course, rely on the same instruments used previously. Similarly, anyone wishing to build upon what has already been learned is likely to use instruments previously used. However, in the long run pursuing the study of "masculinity," "femininity," and "androgyny" may be counterproductive.

For both the older and newer sex role scales, masculinity and femininity are essentially undefined terms—except in a normative sense. Hence, a sex role scale may only be appropriate for persons similar to those on whom it was developed. How useful can the concepts "masculinity" and "femininity" be if they are defined differently for different groups or at different times? True, sex role scales might be useful to determine the extent to which people adhere to the sex role norms as defined by a particular group at a particular time, but it is questionable whether they are useful for much more than that.

Since androgyny denotes simultaneously scoring high on masculinity and femininity, the construct can be expected to self-destruct. As Bem (1978) points out:

> The concept of androgyny necessarily presupposes that the concepts of masculinity and femininity themselves have distinct and substantive content. ... As the androgynous message is absorbed by the culture, the concepts of masculinity and femininity will cease to have such content, and the distinctions to which they refer will blur into invisibility. Thus, when androgyny becomes a reality, the *concept* of androgyny will have been transcended. (p. 19)

Stated differently, the construct will become obsolete if androgyny becomes the norm.

It can be argued that there are no such things as masculinity, femininity or androgyny apart from the measuring instruments used to assess them. "There are many masculinities and femininities, and androgyny has many identities" (Spence and Helmreich 1979b, p. 1045). It is also generally acknowledged that masculinity and femininity are not unitary traits: "The search for global measures of masculinity and femininity or sex role identity—measures that allow individuals to be placed along a quantitative dimension—is a snare and a delusion" (Spence and Helmreich 1979b, p. 1045); "the notion of two sex dimensions, masculinity and femininity, may be as simplistic as the traditional assumption of only one" (Whetton and Swindells 1977, p. 153). Thus Constantinople's (1973) criticism made prior to the publication of the newer sex role scales, still stands today:

> It seems quite clear from the available evidence that none of the existing tests is measuring a unitary trait and that one will derive different estimates of a person's relative M–F level depending on the kinds of behaviors sampled. If the M–F characteristic is multidimensional, a single summary score that ignores variations in what could be designated as subtraits would seem to be less appropriate than a profile of scores on the various subtraits measured. (p. 391)

Basically then, the newer sex role scales do not overcome many of the criticisms directed toward the older sex role scales.

It seems important to repeat another observation offered by Constantinople (1973): "Society attaches value statements, implicity or explicitly, to the results of psychological testing" (p. 390). Social scientists might be encouraging sex stereotyping by focusing on masculinity and femininity.

Given all these criticisms, social science researchers might consider replacing the sex role scales with measures of other variables, such as measures of personality attributes, which can be defined across groups and across time. Since the PAQ is acknowledged to measure instrumental and expressive traits, it could be identified as a measure of those traits—not a measure of masculinity and femininity. Based on their research, Moreland et al. (1978) concluded that the BSRI includes two factor analytically derived scales: instrumentality and emotional expressiveness. Perhaps those two scales should be used in future research and labeled instrumentality and emotional expressiveness. Social scientists ought to consider whether the concepts "masculinity" and "femininity" really add anything to our understanding of human behavior.

CHILDREN'S SEX ROLE SCALES

The sex role measures intended for use with children are plagued with many of the same problems intended for adults, and they suffer from some unique problems as well. Only the unique problems will be highlighted here.

The literature on children's sex roles includes some terminology not typically encountered in adult sex role literature. Those terms include sex role preference, sex role adoption, sex role orientation, and sex role identity. (For definitions, see Lynn 1966; Biller and Borstelmann 1967.) Unfortunately, the relationship between the various sex role measures and the terminology is often unclear. The same instrument is often used to measure more than one construct. For example, the author of the It Scale for Children (Brown 1956) claimed that the scale measured sex role preference, but Biller (1968) used it as a measure of sex role orientation.

A common method for assessing children's sex roles focuses on their preference for, or actual play behavior with, particular sex-typed toys and/or games (Anastasiow 1965; Bates and Bentler 1973; Biller 1968; DeLucia 1963; Fauls and Smith 1956; Laosa and Brophy 1972; Lefkovitz 1962; Rabban 1950; Sears, Rau, and Alpert 1965). Some significant issues have been overlooked by the developers of some of these measures. It is important that the masculine-typed and feminine-typed toys be matched in terms of color, attractiveness, size, and number of moving parts. If a large, bright-red fire engine with a working bell and siren, detachable extension ladder, and functional hoses were compared with a small stuffed animal, it is unlikely that the sex-typing of the toys would be the crucial variable affecting a child's preference. In a study of 13-month-old babies, Goldberg and Lewis (1969) found that "the toys which received the most attention were those that offered the most varied possibilities for manipulation" (p. 27). Clearly, extraneous variables must be controlled for in these measures of toy and game preference.

Measures of toy and game preference can easily become outdated, not only in terms of the sex typing or normative information regarding the items, but also in terms of the child's familiarity with the items. On self-report measures, children cannot be expected to report their preference for a particular game if they have never heard of the game. Children are frequently passive recipients of toys rather than active participants in their selection. Therefore, when children were asked to report their toy preference or parents are asked to describe the play behavior of their children, the data obtained may say more about the adults who purchased the children's toys than about the children themselves.

Of the various sex role measures for children, the one that has been used most often is the It Scale for Children (ITSC) (Brown 1956). Its continued use is most unfortunate as there is little to recommend it: some items on the scale are outdated; some of the pictures used appear rather bizarre; the projective nature of the scale is questionable; the It figure looks rather masculine although it is supposed to be neutral; and the various modifications in administration lead to different results. Though there are many alternatives to the It Scale, they are all subject to varying degrees of criticisms. (For information regarding other specific sex role measures for children, see Beere 1979.)

SEX STEREOTYPES

The measurement problems encountered in measuring attitudes toward gender-related issues are discussed in Chapters 6 and 8. However measures of sex stereotypes can be considered a special subset of attitude measures and pose some additional problems that warrant consideration. Sex stereotypes have commonly been measured by presenting respondents with a set of personality traits (e.g., logical, talkative), activities (e.g., mending clothes, reading a book), objects (e.g., screwdriver, dustpan, butterfly), or occupations (e.g., miner, nurse), and asking the respondents to associate each element of the set with males, females, both or neither. Depending on the particular scale, stimuli are presented orally, in writing, through pictures, or with actual objects; and responses are communicated through writing, by pointing, or orally. Scores are sometimes assigned to individuals to indicate either the respondent's agreement with commonly held stereotypes or the extent to which the respondent's perceptions are based on stereotypes. At other times, responses are summed across respondents to indicate the extent to which personality traits, activities, or objects are perceived as sex-typed.

Another common method for assessing sex stereotypes has been to use a semantic differential scale with terms denoting males and females as the concepts, and personality descriptors as the bipolar scales. The most frequently used semantic differential has been the Sex Role Stereotype Questionnaire (Rosenkrantz et al. 1968), but it has been modified so often that it is probably more accurately described as a technique rather than as a unique scale. Recently, researchers (Ashmore and Tumia 1980; Del Boca and Ashmore 1980) have related sex stereotypes to implicit personality theory (see Ashmore and Del Boca 1979) and thus have investigated sex stereotyping using the two basic methods for studying implicit personality theory: "personality description, where subjects ascribe traits to other people, and trait inference, where subjects are presented with a list of traits that are said to characterize a particular person and asked to make inferences about the presence of other attributes in the person" (Del Boca and Ashmore 1980, p. 520).

In general, the instruments used to measure sex stereotypes have been weak. Based on an extensive literature review, Beere (1979) concluded:

> The measuring instruments to assess sex stereotypes are not well developed. Researchers rarely use an empirical procedure for developing the instruments; and if there is a theoretical basis for their development, it is not communicated in the report of the research study. The reliability and validity of the instruments are rarely considered. (p. 164)

For example, content validity is generally ignored in the development of sex-stereotype measures. There appears to be no attempt to define a domain and then sample from it to determine which items should be included on the scale. As a result, it is difficult to know how to interpret the results obtained.

The directions on sex-stereotype measures are often ambiguous. It is important to communicate to respondents whether they are being asked to respond in terms of their own perceptions, their beliefs regarding society's perceptions, or their beliefs regarding how things ought to be. This problem is underscored by the finding (Spence, Helmreich, and Stapp 1974) that ratings differ depending on whether the referent is labeled as "ideal" or "typical."

A related problem pertains to the assumption made by many researchers that persons hold stereotypes of males and females that apply equally to all males and to all females. Researchers have shown that different stereotypes are held of women depending on the type of woman who is the referent (e.g., typical housewife, clubwoman, bunny, career woman, or woman athlete) (Clifton, McGrath, and Wick 1976). It has also been shown that respondents react differently if the referent is a college student or an adult (Spence, Helmreich, and Stapp 1974).

Sex-stereotype measures often force, or at least encourage, the expression of stereotypes even for respondents whose perceptions may not be very stereotyped. When respondents are given only two response options—one denoting male and one denoting female—it is impossible for them to avoid stereotyping their responses unless they are able to resist the demand characteristics of the situation. The options "both" and "neither" should be available to the respondent. Even better would be the use of independent measures to obtain stereotypes of males and females; it is not necessary for the scale to explicitly compare the sexes. Similarly, when the semantic differential uses sex-stereotyped adjectives as the endpoints of a scale (e.g., passive-active), it may encourage stereotyping. The use of the adjectives "active" and "not active" as the endpoints of one continuum, and "passive" and "not passive" as the endpoints of the other may lead to different results. Of course, empirical verification is necessary to determine whether the results would really differ. But the issues suggested here are analogous to the bipolar versus dualistic assumptions in measures of sex role. It seems reasonable that the measuring instruments should at least allow for females or males to be stereotyped as both active and passive. It is important that sex-stereotype measures include only items familiar to the respondents. This is more likely to pose a problem when the measure is used with children. Children are unable to respond meaningfully to words descriptive of occupations, personality traits, or objects that are totally unknown to them.

Sex-stereotype measures are generally very obvious measures in that respondents can easily tell what is being assessed. As a result, these measures are generally very easy to fake and social desirability may be a major factor affecting responses. With the expression of sex stereotypes being less fashionable today, this is a serious drawback to the measures. When using a sex-stereotype measure to ascertain whether respondents agree with prevailing stereotypes, researchers must be aware that stereotypes have been changing rapidly—at least, self-reported stereotypes have been changing (Kravetz 1976; Petro and Putnam 1979). Thus, a stereotype measure developed ten years ago may already be obsolete.

Caution should be exercised in comparing results from sex-stereotype studies which used different measures and in generalizing the results from sex-stereotype studies. Cowan and Stewart (1977) demonstrated that different results are obtained when different methods are used to measure stereotypes. It is not known which yields the most accurate reflection of persons' stereotypes.

One method used to avoid some of the problems discussed here is to use what might be termed a simulated behavior measure. This procedure, which has been used to assess sex stereotypes and attitudes toward gender-related issues, involves developing two sets of stimulus materials that are identical in all respects except the sex of the stimulus persons. Each set of materials is given to a different group of subjects who are asked to independently evaluate the stimulus persons on some criteria (e.g., appropriateness for a particular job). A similar procedure, which involves actual behaviors, has been used to study responses toward infants or toddlers of different sexes. The subject is given a certain amount of time to interact with an infant and the subject's behaviors are observed. Half of the subjects are told that the infant is a boy and the other half are told that the infant is a girl—though the same infant is used with both groups. (See, for example, Frisch 1977.) In both of these types of studies, mean scores from the two groups of subjects are compared. If differences exist, they are attributed to sex bias since the stimulus differs on only one variable: perceived gender. (For abstracts of over 150 studies using simulated or actual behavior measures, see Beere and King 1980.) A major drawback to this method is that it does not yield scores for individuals: "These methods are useful to the researcher who is interested in the phenomenon of sexism, but not to the psychologist who is interested in knowing whether a particular person is sexist" (Beere and King 1980, p. 2). The major concern in designing studies of this type is that the gender of the stimulus person must be communicated subtly. Otherwise, subjects are likely to suspect which variable is at issue, and faking and social desirability can again be problems.

OVERVIEW

A myriad of problems have been presented here, with the major problems pertaining to lack of adequate or consistent construct definition, lack of adequate reliability, and lack of demonstrated validity. Most of the constructs discussed here have normatively-based definitions which means their definitions will change over time. Although adequate reliability has been established for many measures, the reliability of many other measures is undetermined. Furthermore, internal consistency, which is easier to assess, is reported more often than test stability. Validity, which is often difficult to demonstrate, is frequently presumed. Face validity or "declarative validity" (Thomas 1978) is substituted for construct or criterion-related validity. Campbell and Fiske's (1959) multitrait-multimethod model for establishing validity has rarely been applied. Since the model provides for establishing both convergent and discriminant validity, it is strongly recommended.

Scales which are multidimensional have been presumed unidimensional. Content domains have been inadequately defined prior to scale construction. Problems of faking or social desirability bias are frequently ignored. This is particularly problematic given the transparent nature of many of the measures, combined with people's heightened sensitivity to gender-related issues. People are very much aware of what the "right" answers are. This may account for part of the discrepancy between what researchers are finding and what people experience in the "real world."

Unfortunately the problems do not stop here. Even when a measure is shown to have adequate reliability and validity, it may not be appropriate to use; a measure that was reliable and valid at one time may no longer be reliable or valid. The items may now be obsolete; the scale responses may now be largely a function of social desirability bias. Similarly normative data in this rapidly changing area must be regularly updated.

A measure that is reliable and valid for one population (e.g., white college students) may not be reliable or valid for another population (e.g., inner-city sixth graders or senior citizens). Most measures are developed using the responses of college students. Similarly, reliability and validity data are frequently obtained from college populations. One should not generalize the data to other populations. The reliability and validity of the measure should be empirically demonstrated for each population for which the measure will be used. A measure that is valid for one purpose may not be valid for another purpose. A measure is not simply valid or invalid; it is valid or invalid for a particular purpose.

A common, but inexcusable error, is for a researcher to modify an existing measure and presume that the reliability and validity of the modified measure is equivalent to that of the original measure. The modified measure must be considered a new measure and its reliability and validity must be established anew. Even when nothing more than the directions accompanying the measure are changed, there is the possibility that the reliability and validity of the measure change.

Another problem occurs when researchers ignore the potential effects of situational variables on responses given. DeLucia (1963) showed that the reliability of a toy preference test to measure children's sex role identification varied considerably as a function of the examiner's sex. Shomer and Centers (1970) have shown that the results obtained on the scale were substantially affected by the sex composition of the group responding to the scale, while Hough and Allen (1975) showed that responses can be affected by the conditions of administration. More needs to be known about the effects of these and other situational variables.

The issues and problems raised in this paper are not unique to the measures described here. They apply equally to other measures which are likely to be used in gender-related research including, for example, measures of attitudes, personality variables, interests, anxiety, and fear-of-success (which has some unique problems associated with it as well). The researcher must carefully review and evaluate measures before using them in a study.

Because research results are more comparable when they are based on the same measures, researchers are advised to try to locate an existing measure for their study. In addition to consulting the relevant periodical literature, there are two books which should prove useful: Beere's (1979) *Women and Women's Issues: A Handbook of Tests and Measures* describes 235 scales used in gender-related research; the *Sourcebook of Measures of Women's Educational Equity* (Parks et al. 1982) describes 198 research instruments useful for evaluating educational equity programs. There is only slight overlap between the two publications.

In selecting an existing measure, one must insure that the measure is reliable and valid at the time it is to be used and for the group of subjects with whom it will be used. When an appropriate measure is not already available, researchers are forced to construct their own scales. However, this task should be undertaken only with the full realization of its scope. The process of scale development is an involved, time-consuming, and costly project in itself.

Perhaps it is time to slow the collection of data pertaining to gender-related issues, to concentrate instead on the development of adequate measures. Some would argue that the issues being studied are too important *today* to postpone their study. Brannon (1978) makes some excellent points relevant to this argument. In discussing the literature regarding racial prejudice, he states: "Quite literally, mountains of data about prejudice have been collected... but the net result of all this time and effort seems, to me at least, extremely meager" (p. 648). He blames this dismal state of affairs, at least in part, on measurement problems and he states: "I see strong indications that the same mistakes—both conceptual and methodological—are being made in the rapidly developing area of measuring attitudes and other dispositions toward and about women"(p. 649). It seems a shame to repeat the mistakes of the past!

REFERENCES

Anastasiow, N.J. Success in school and boys' sex role patterns. *Child Development* 36 (1965): 1053–66.

Ashmore, R.D., and F.K. Del Boca. Sex stereotypes and implicit personality theory:

Toward a cognitive-social psychological conceptualization. *Sex Roles* 5 (1979): 219-48.

Ashmore, R.D., and M.L. Tumia. Sex stereotypes and implicit personality theory I. A personality description approach to the assessment of sex stereotypes. *Sex Roles* 6 (1980): 501-18.

Bates, J.E., and P.M. Bentler. Play activities in normal and effeminate boys. *Developmental Psychology* 9 (1973): 20-27.

Beere, C.A. *Women and women's issues: A handbook of tests and measures.* San Francisco: Jossey-Bass, 1979.

Beere, C.A., and L.A. King. Sexism: Abstracts of studies using disguised or unobtrusive measures. JSAS *Catalog of Selected Documents in Psychology* 10 (39) (Ms. no. 2043), (1980).

Bem, S.L. The measurement of psychological androgyny. *Journal of Consulting and Clinical Psychology* 42 (1974): 155-62.

Bem, S.L. Sex role adaptability: One consequence of psychological androgyny. *Journal of Personality and Social Psychology* 31 (1975): 634-43.

Bem, S.L. On the utility of alternative procedures for assessing psychological androgyny. *Journal of Consulting and Clinical Psychology* 45 (1977): 196-205.

Bem, S.L. Beyond androgyny: Some presumptuous prescriptions for a liberated sexual identity. In J.A. Sherman and F.L. Denmark (eds.), *The psychology of women: Future directions in research.* New York: Psychological Dimensions, 1978.

Bem, S.L. Theory and measurement of androgyny: A reply to the Pedhazur-Tetenbaum and Locksley-Colten critiques. *Journal of Personality and Social Psychology* 37 (1979): 1047-54.

Bem, S., and E. Lenney. Sex-typing and avoidance of cross-sex behavior. *Journal of Personality and Social Psychology* 33 (1976): 48-54.

Bem, S.L., W. Martyna, and C. Watson. Sex typing and androgyny: Further explorations of the expressive domain. *Journal of Personality and Social Psychology* 34 (1976): 1016-23.

Berzins, J.I., M.A. Welling, and R.E. Wetter. A new measure of psychological androgyny based on the Personality Research Form. *Journal of Consulting and Clinical Psychology* 46 (1978): 126-38.

Berzins, J.I., M.A. Welling, and R.E. Wetter. *The PRF ANDRO Scale: User's manual* (revised). Unpublished manuscript, University of Kentucky, 1977.

Biller, H.B. A multiaspect investigation of masculine development in kindergarten-age boys. *Genetic Psychology Monographs* 78 (1968): 89-138.

Biller, H.B., and L.J. Borstelmann. Masculine development: An integrative review. *Merrill-Palmer Quarterly* 13 (1967): 253-94.

Brannon, R. Measuring attitudes toward women (and otherwise): A methodological critique. In J.A. Sherman and F.L. Denmark (eds.), *The psychology of women: Future directions in research.* New York: Psychological Dimensions, 1978.

Brown, D.G. Sex role preference in young children. *Psychological Monographs* 70 (no. 421), (1956).

Campbell, D.T., and D.W. Fiske. Convergent and discriminant validation by the multitrait-multimethod matrix. *Psychological Bulletin* 56 (1959): 81-105.

Clifton, A.K., D. McGrath, and B. Wick. Stereotypes of woman: A single category?

Sex Roles 2 (1976): 135–48.

Constantinople, A. Masculinity-femininity: An exception to a famous dictum? *Psychological Bulletin* 80 (1973): 389–407.

Cowan, M.L., and B.J. Stewart. A methodological study of sex stereotypes. *Sex Roles* 3 (1977): 205–16.

Cronbach, L.J. Coefficient alpha and the internal structure of tests. *Psychometrika* 16 (1951): 297–334.

Del Boca, F.K., and R.D. Ashmore. Sex stereotypes and implicit personality theory. II. A trait-inference approach to the assessment of sex stereotypes. *Sex Roles* 6 (1980): 519–35.

DeLucia, L.A. The Toy Preference Test: A measure of sex role identification. *Child Development* 34 (1963): 107–17.

Deutsch, C.J., and L.A. Gilbert. Sex role stereotypes: Effect on perceptions of self and others and on personal adjustment. *Journal of Counseling Psychology* 23 (1976): 373–79.

Edwards, A.L., and C.D. Ashworth. A replication study of item selection for the Bem Sex Role Inventory. *Applied Psychological Measurement* 1 (1977): 501–7.

Edwards, K.J., and B.N. Norcross. A comparison of two sex-role androgyny measures in a study of sex-role identity for incarcerated delinquent and non-delinquent females. *Sex Roles* 6 (1980): 859–70.

Engel, I.M. A factor-analytic study of items from five masculinity-femininity tests. *Journal of Consulting Psychology* 30 (1966): 565.

Fauls, L.B., and W.D. Smith. Sex role learning of five-year-olds. *Journal of Genetic Psychology* 89 (1956): 105–17.

Feather, N.T. Factor structure of the Bem Sex Role Inventory: Implications for the study of masculinity, femininity, and androgyny. *Australian Journal of Psychology* 30 (1978): 241–54.

Frisch, H.L. Sex stereotypes in adult-infant play. *Child Development* 48 (1977): 1671–75.

Gaudreau, P. Factor analysis of the Bem Sex-Role Inventory. *Journal of Consulting and Clinical Psychology* 45 (1977): 299–302.

Gayton, W.F., G.F. Hauv, K.L. Ozmon, and J. Tavormina. A comparison of the Bem Sex Role Inventory and the PRF ANDRO Scale. *Journal of Personality Assessment* 41 (1977): 619–21.

Goldberg, S., and M. Lewis. Play behavior in the year-old infant: Early sex differences. *Child Development* 40 (1969): 21–32.

Gough, H.G. Identifying psychological femininity. *Educational and Psychological Measurement* 12 (1952): 427–39.

Harrington, D.M., and S.M. Andersen. Creativity, masculinity, femininity, and three models of psychological androgyny. *Journal of Personality and Social Psychology* 41 (1981): 744–57.

Hathaway, S.R., and J.C. McKinley. *Minnesota Multiphasic Personality Inventory.* New York: Psychological Corp., 1942.

Heerboth, J.R., and N.V. Ramanaiah. *Evaluation of BSRI masculinity and femininity scale items using stereotype instructions.* Paper presented at the meeting of the Midwestern Psychological Association, Detroit, May 1981.

Heilbrun, A.B., Jr. Measurement of masculine and feminine sex role identities as independent dimensions. *Journal of Consulting and Clinical Psychology* 44 (1976): 183–90.

Hinrichsen, J.J., and L. Stone. Effects of three conditions of administration on Bem Sex Role Inventory scores. *Journal of Personality Assessment* 42 (1978): 512.

Hough, K.S., and B.P. Allen. Is the "women's movement" erasing the mark of oppression from the female psyche? *Journal of Psychology* 89 (1975): 249–58.

Jackson, D.N., and S.V. Paunonen. Personality structure and assessment. *Annual Review of Psychology* 31 (1980): 503–51.

Jones, W.H., M.E. Chernovetz, and R.O. Hansson. The enigma of androgyny: Differential implications for males and females? *Journal of Consulting and Clinical Psychology* 46 (1978): 298–313.

Jordan-Viola, E., S. Fassberg, and M.T. Viola. Feminism, androgyny, and anxiety. *Journal of Consulting and Clinical Psychology* 44 (1976): 870–71.

Kaplan, A.G., and M.A. Sedney. *Psychology and sex roles: An androgynous perspective.* Boston: Little, Brown, 1980.

Kaplan, A.G. Clarifying the concept of androgyny: Implications for therapy. *Psychology of Women Quarterly* 3 (1979): 223–30.

Kelly, J.A., M.S. Caudill, S. Hawthorn, and C.G. O'Brien. Socially undesirable sex-correlated characteristics: Implications for androgyny and adjustment. *Journal of Consulting and Clinical Psychology* 45 (1977): 1185–86.

Kelly, J.A., W. Furman, and V. Young. Problems associated with the typological measurement of sex roles and androgyny. *Journal of Consulting and Clinical Psychology* 46 (1978): 1574–76.

Kelly, J.A., and J. Worell. New formulations of sex roles and androgyny: A critical review. *Journal of Consulting and Clinical Psychology* 45 (1977): 1101–15.

Kravetz, D.F. Sex role concepts of women. *Journal of Consulting and Clinical Psychology* 44 (1976): 437–43.

Laosa, L.M., and J.E. Brophy. Effects of sex and birth order on sex-role development and intelligence among kindergarten children. *Developmental Psychology* 6 (1972): 409–15.

LaTorre, R.A., and W.E. Piper. The Terman-Miles M–F Test: An Examination of Exercises 1, 2, and 3 forty years later. *Sex Roles* 4 (1978): 141–55.

Lefkovitz, M.M. Some relationships between sex role preference of children and other parent and child variables. *Psychological Reports* 10 (1962): 43–53.

Locksley, A., and M.E. Colten. Psychological androgyny: A case of mistaken identity? *Journal of Personality and Social Psychology* 37 (1979): 1017–31.

Lowell, N. *Masculinity and femininity: Are we measuring them correctly?* Paper presented at the meeting of the American Educational Research Association, Los Angeles, April 1981.

Lunneborg, P.W. Dimensionality of MF. *Journal of Clinical Psychology* 28 (1972): 313–17.

Lunneborg, P.W., and C.E. Lunneborg. Factor structure of MF scales and items. *Journal of Clinical Psychology* 26 (1970): 360–66.

Lynn, D.B. The process of learning parental and sex role identification. *Journal of Marriage and the Family* 28 (1966): 466–70.

Minnigerode, F.A. Attitudes toward women, sex role stereotyping and locus of control. *Psychological Reports* 38 (1976): 1301–2.

Moreland, J.R., N. Gulanick, E.K. Montague, and V.A. Harren. Some psychometric properties of the Bem Sex-Role Inventory. *Applied Psychological Measurement* 2 (1978): 249–56.

Orlofsky, J.L., A. Aslin, and S.D. Ginsburg. Differential effectiveness of two classification procedures on the Bem Sex-Role Inventory. *Journal of Personality Assessment* 41 (1977): 414–16.

Parks, B.J., K. Bogart, D.F. Reynolds, M. Hamilton, and C.J. Finley. *Sourcebook of measures of women's educational equity.* Newton, Mass.: Women's Educational Equity Act Publishing Center, 1982.

Pedhazur, E.J., and T.J. Tetenbaum. Bem Sex Role Inventory: A theoretical and methodological critique. *Journal of Personality and Social Psychology* 37 (1979): 996–1016.

Petro, C.S., and B.A. Putnam. Sex-role stereotypes: Issues of attitudinal changes. *Sex Roles* 5 (1979): 29–39.

Pleck, J.H. Masculinity-femininity: Current and alternative paradigms. *Sex Roles* 1 (1975): 161–178.

Rabban, M. Sex role identification in young children in two diverse social groups. *Genetic Psychology Monographs* 42 (1950): 81–158.

Rosenkrantz, P., S. Vogel, H. Bee, I. Broverman, and D.M. Broverman. Sex role stereotypes and self-concepts in college students. *Journal of Consulting and Clinical Psychology* 32 (1968): 287–95.

Sears, R.R., L. Rau, and R. Alpert. *Identification and Child Rearing.* Stanford: Stanford University Press, 1965.

Shomer, R.W., and R. Centers. Differences in attitudinal responses under conditions of implicitly manipulated group salience. *Journal of Personality and Social Psychology* 15 (1970): 125–32.

Silvern, L.E., and V.L. Ryan. Self-rated adjustment and sex-typing on the Bem Sex Role Inventory: Is masculinity the primary predictor of adjustment? *Sex Roles* 5 (1979): 739–63.

Spence, J.T., and R.L. Helmreich. On assessing "androgyny." *Sex Roles* 5 (1979a): 721–38.

Spence, J.T., and R.L. Helmreich. The many faces of androgyny: A reply to Locksley and Colten. *Journal of Personality and Social Psychology* 37 (1979b): 1032–46.

Spence, J.T., and R.L. Helmreich. *Masculinity and femininity: Their psychological dimensions, correlates, and antecedents.* Austin: University of Texas Press, 1978.

Spence, J.T., R.L. Helmreich, and C.K. Holahan. Negative and positive components of psychological masculinity and femininity and their relationships to self-reports of neurotic and acting out behaviors. *Journal of Personality and Social Psychology* 37 (1979): 1673–82.

Spence, J.T., R. Helmreich, and J. Stapp. The personal attributes questionnaire: A measure of sex role stereotypes and masculinity-femininity. JSAS *Catalog of Selected Documents in Psychology* 4 (1974): 43–44.

Strahan, R.F. Remarks on Bem's measurement of psychological androgyny: Alternative methods and a supplementary analysis. *Journal of Consulting and Clinical Psychology* 43 (1975): 568–71.

Terman, L.M., and C.C. Miles. *Sex and personality.* New York: McGraw-Hill, 1936.

Tetenbaum, T. *Masculinity and femininity: Separate but equal?* Paper presented at the meeting of the American Psychological Association, San Francisco, August 1977.

Thomas, S. *Measurement of sex roles: What are we really measuring?* Paper presented at the meeting of the National Council of Measurement in Education, Toronto, March 1978.

Walkup, H., and R.D. Abbott. Cross-validation of item selection on the Bem Sex Role Inventory. *Applied Psychological Measurement* 2 (1978): 63–81.

Whetton, C., and T. Swindells. A factor analysis of the Bem Sex-Role Inventory. *Journal of Clinical Psychology* 33 (1977): 150–53.

Wiggins, J.S., and A. Holzmuller. Psychological androgyny and interpersonal behavior. *Journal of Consulting and Clinical Psychology* 46 (1978): 40–52.

9

All Things Being Equal, a Behavior Is Superior to an Attitude: Studies of Sex-Typed and Sex-Biased Attitudes and Behaviors

Reesa M. Vaughter

The aim of this chapter is to provoke critical thinking with respect to attitudinal and behavioral measurement of social processes in women's research, in the hope of clarifying some of the salient methodological and theoretical issues. The central concern is to understand the extent to which attitude-questionnaire data correlate with, or are predictive of, observed behaviors.

The analyses and inferences drawn herein are based upon two presumptions. First, it is presumed that an expected or observed relationship between an expressed attitude and an observed behavior is absolutely determined by the domains of attitudes and behaviors under consideration; no attempt will be made to generalize about the relationship between attitudes and behaviors in general. The present summary is confined to the domains of sex-typed and sexist attitudes and behaviors; and only three types of attitudinal measures have been selected for study: measures of gender identity, measures of sex-stereotypes, and measures of beliefs about the appropriate social roles for women and men. Second, it is presumed that: "Prediction of relevant behaviors toward the attitude object is not the only acceptable evidence of (a scale's) validity, but it is certainly the best" (Brannon 1979). Surely, then, a

---

*The author wishes to express her sincere appreciation to the editors of this volume for their suggestions, contributions, and patient helpfulness in completing the manuscript, a revised version of a paper of the same title, presented for the Conference on Attitudinal and Behavioral Measurement in Social Processes/ Women's Research, National Institute of Education, Washington, D.C., December 1980.

behavior* *is* superior to an attitude. Thus, the present chapter focuses specifically upon the question: To what extent do attitude-questionnaire data predict, or lend understanding to, sex-typed and sex-biased (i.e., sexist) behaviors, and expand earlier reviews (Vaughter 1976; Vaughter 1979)?

Before examining some of the empiricial findings in the area, it may be anticipated that apparent empirical contradictions may reflect methodological failures to be precise. Careful reading of the literature suggests that the absence of empirical distinctions between attitudes may reflect the absence of theoretical definitions that distinguish the attitude the investigator is attempting to employ in order to predict some type of behavior. For example, sex-typed behavior—that is, a person's acting in a manner that is typical of his/ her sex—is not the same as sex-ist (sex-biased) behavior; that is, a person's acting in a manner that discriminates against another person on the basis of her/ his sex. Attitudinal measures of gender identity attempt to measure the person's description of herself/ himself as possessing feminine- and masculine-typed characteristics (Vaughter 1976). And the most widely used measures of gender identity are Bem's Sex Role Inventory (BSRI) (Bem 1974) and Spence, Helmreich, and Stapp's (1975a) Personal Attributes Questionnaire (PAQ), developed from Rosenkrantz et al. (1968). Complicating the empirical findings, the PAQ has also been used to measure stereotypes. Measures of sex stereotypes attempt to measure a person's affirmation of and adherence to the culture's definitions of the femininity and masculinity of women and men. The stereotype measured may be one of two types: (1) prescriptive stereotypes, i.e., the respondent provides a description of the personality characteristics she/ he believes that women and men *should* have; (2) descriptive stereotypes, i.e., the respondent provides a description of the personality characteristics he/she believes that men and women do, in fact, possess. Still distinguishable are a very large number of scales, most developed within the past decade (Vaughter 1979), that measure attitudes about the "appropriate" social roles of men and women: roles in the family, in the labor force, in politics, and in interpersonal and sexual domains. These are the measures of sexism (i.e., sex bias); the most widely used measure of sexist attitudes has been Spence and Helmreich's (1972a) Attitudes Toward Women Scale (AWS).

In sum, clear theoretical distinctions of the constructs and types of attitudes referred to above have not always been drawn or been made explicit, but such efforts would seem necessary in planning and in evaluating empirical inquiries. The present summary, then, attempts to draw some tentative conclusions about the attitude-behavior relationship with a view toward clarifying the theoretical structures of: (1) attitudes of gender identity and sex bias (sexism); and (2) sexist/sex-biased behaviors and sex-typed behaviors.

---

*Brannon (1979) defines a behavior as an action which people perceive as likely to have definitive consequences to them personally, or to those they care about.

GENDER IDENTITY AND SEX-TYPED BEHAVIORS

Sandra Bem and colleagues have demonstrated a functional, predictive relationship between gender identity and sex-typed behavior. That is, a substantial number of studies have demonstrated a functional relationship between a person's describing herself/himself as masculine and behaving in a manner typical of the male/masculine stereotype, or describing oneself as feminine and behaving in a manner typical of the female/feminine stereotype, and describing oneself as androgynous and behaving "masculine" in one situation and "feminine" in another (Bem 1975; Bem and Lenny 1976; Bem, Martyna, and Watson 1976). Lively and astute criticisms of the theoretical properties of the concept of androgyny (e.g., Jones, Chernovetz, and Hansson 1978; Kaplan and Sedney 1980), as well as of the psychometric properties of the BSRI (Pedhazur and Tetenbaum 1979), will, presumably, have a progressive impact upon attitudinal scaling and interpretations of data derived from such scales. Nonetheless, when it comes to predicting sex-typed behavior, the BSRI has had a most impressive record. Brannon (1979) concluded that "the studies taken together...provide ample behavioral evidence for the construct validity of the BSRI...the only gender-related instrument of which this statement may currently be made" (p. 53).

GENDER IDENTITY AND SEXIST BEHAVIORS

For several years, reviewers (e.g., Mednick 1976) have noted researchers' interest in the relatedness of a person's gender identity and her/his sexist attitudes and behaviors; however, the precise nature of the supposed relationship has not been clearly explicated in research design or theory. The popular hypothesis is that one who is sex-typed (i.e., the feminine female and the masculine male) is likely to be sexist; and a person who is not sex-typed, who is androgynous, is likely to be egalitarian, if not feminist (e.g., Trilling 1975). Bem (1975) had argued that the androgynous person should display flexibility in thought, feelings, and behaviors. Thus, it was reasoned, the androgynous person's cognitive flexibility should facilitate the development of egalitarian attitudes and behaviors.

Although such a relationship between gender identity and sex-biases may exist, we do not have convincing empirical support for it. Spence and Helmreich (1972b), for example, found no relationship between respondents' femininity-masculinity and sex biases in the evaluations of a female job applicant. Calway-Fagen, Wallston, and Gabel (1979) found no significant relationship between the gender identities (measured with the BSRI) of parents-to-be and their preference that their firstborn be a boy or girl. On the other hand, recently, a study did obtain the expected relationship between gender identities and sex-biases, or lack of them. Arkin and Johnson (1980) found that sex-typed individuals (feminine females, masculine males) devalued high-prestige occupations that expected to show an increase in women practitioners, while androgynous college students rated the high-prestige occupations more attractive if they were expected to show an increase in the proportion of women. Thus, in the absence of a clear theoretical base upon which to anchor the contradictory findings, one may be left with explanatory ambiguity. Nonetheless, gender identity measures appear to be quite useful as indices of the degree of impact of the sexist and sex-typed socialization process. The more influential a sexist, sex-typed socialization has been, the more likely the male will describe himself with masculine-typed characteristics and will display masculine-typed behaviors, and the more likely the female will describe herself with feminine-typed characteristics and will display feminine-typed behaviors.

ATTITUDES TOWARD SOCIAL ROLES OF WOMEN AND MEN AND SEX-TYPED BEHAVIORS

Compared to the attitude-behavior studies of gender identity, many more studies have been completed which relate a person's attitudes about the social roles of men and women to the person's sex-typed behaviors. Interestingly, the studies of the early 1970s were concerned with the question: Is the woman a woman of her word? Typically, the behavior of women expressing traditional, sexist attitudes was compared with the behavior of women espousing egalitarian or feminist attitudes in situations in which women have tended to respond in a sex-typed manner. The question was whether or not women with egalitarian attitudes behaved in a "male-like" manner in "stereotypic dilemmas" (e.g., is the woman with egalitarian ideas more likely to race sports cars?). The theoretical rationale for proposing the relationship between expressing egalitarian attitudes toward the social roles and behaving in ways contradictory to one's socialization in sex-typed behaviors has been imprecise, but nonetheless practical.

Goldberg (1975) found that college students with nonegalitarian attitudes toward women's and men's roles were more likely to conform to majority opinion than were students holding egalitarian attitudes. Ditmar, Mueller, and Mitchell (1975) also found that proliberationist women conformed less than antiliberationist women to false evaluations of ambiguous and nonambiguous stimuli in a mixed-sex situation. However, a later study has indicated that personality variables might be better predictors of conformity behavior. Fitzgerald and Huston (1976) obtained measures of self-esteem, fear of negative evaluation, social anxiety, and attitudes toward women from a group of college women (the sample was small, but a number of observations were made of each participant). Participants were assigned a group task to determine the equipment needed by a space crew lost on the moon; there was a money prize for the best solution. It was arranged that the women could easily infer the best solution because of the type of information contained in their instruction booklets. Male confederates participated in the groups and were "trained" to display sexist behaviors throughout the decision-making process. Analyses revealed that self-esteem, rather than the Attitudes Toward Women Scale score, was the best predictor of the college women's verbal competency (e.g., standing up for one's rights, stating one's opinion, persisting throughout the task, etc.). The researchers concluded that a woman's self-esteem—the confidence and belief she has in her own worth—is a better predictor of the woman's ability to engage in traditionally sex-inappropriate, but situationally-appropriate and self-enhancing behavior.

The reader is urged to consult Eagly's (1978) review and critique of sex differences in conformity. Nonetheless, the point to be summarized here is that in this case, as may often be the case in social processes research, variables like social desirability and intervening personality variables pose challenging measurement and design problems.

More egalitarian attitudes toward the social roles of women and men do appear to signal career commitment, and behaviors consistent with career commitment in women (Alper 1973; Brogan and Kutner 1976; Gump 1972; Lipman-Blumen 1972). Since most of the attitudinal scales are loaded with items tapping the respondent's beliefs about women's right to work in the paid labor force and equities in work compensation, perhaps it is not surprising, but it is nonetheless reassuring, to those who believe in the attitude-behavior connection, to find an apparent congruent relationship between her attitudes about women working in the paid labor force and her plans for a career.

ATTITUDES TOWARD THE SOCIAL ROLES AND SEXIST/SEX-BIASED BEHAVIORS

Intuitively, sex-stereotyping would seem to be a self-defined measure of sex bias or sexism. Although research has verified the pervasiveness of sex stereotypes and the prevalence in the belief of the male's "all-around superiority" (Neufield, Langmeyer and Seeman 1975), the author found only a couple of studies that investigated directly the relationship between the tendency to stereotype and the expression of discriminatory behavior against women; and both studies demonstrated a logical, positive correlation between stereotyped attitudes and discriminatory behavior. Ellis and Bentler (1973) obtained an index of stereotyping with the SRQ and measured college students' attitudes toward the traditional roles of women. For females, the greater the perceived difference between males and females, in general, the more she tended to endorse women and men's traditional social roles. For men, the greater the difference between his self-description and that of females in general, the more he favored traditional roles. In a study of personnel administrators, Sharp and Post (1980) also found a significant, positive relationship between stereotyping (measured with the PAQ) and differential evaluations of job applicants. Those endorsing sex stereotypes showed discrimination against women applying for the male-typed position of "sports reporter" and showed no discrimination against men applying for the female-typed position of "fashion reporter."

An impressive number of studies, all in the 1970s, and most all measuring attitudes with the Attitudes Toward Women Scale, have attempted to relate attitudes toward the social roles to sexist/sex-biased behavior; however, the findings have not been particularly impressive from the perspective of behavioral validation. Spence and Helmreich (1972b) conducted one of the earliest studies of this type: college students' AWS scores were related to their ratings of a female stimulus person (SP) being interviewed for a job. Complicated relationships were obtained; but, generally, proegalitarian and feminist, as well as students with sexist attitudes, of both sexes, liked the masculine more than the feminine SP and liked the competent more than the incompetent SP. Gomes and Abramowitz (1976) found that AWS scores were not predictive of male and female therapists' sex-biased ratings of the social adjustment of women and men clients. And Goldberg, Katz, and Rapport (1979) found that college students' AWS scores were not indicative of their responses to a letter asking for students to volunteer time and money to a feminist cause.

There seems to be a trend emerging in recent studies that indicates that measures of sexist attitudes are predictive of the sexist behaviors of women, but not of men. In a study of the emotional responses of students to profeminist literature (Gackenback and Auerback 1975), females who expressed egalitarian attitudes on the AWS had significantly different, more sympathetic reactions to a profeminist film than did women espousing antiliberationist attitudes. The responses of men espousing egalitarian attitudes were similar to those of men espousing sexist attitudes. Pines (1979) also found that females' (college students') perceptions of stimulus persons were consistent with their expressed egalitarian attitudes (as measured by the AWS) while the males' perceptions were not. Males did more stereotyping; and while the female SP who planned to pursue a career was liked more by profeminist females, profeminist males preferred the women who intended "to stay home and raise her son." And in a replication of the Broverman study, Brooks-Gunn and Fisch (1980) asked college students to describe the healthy man, woman, or "adult" (sex unspecified) using the adjectives of the BSRI. Female students did less stereotyping. Male, but not female, students described the healthy man to be similar to the healthy adult, but described the healthy woman to be different from the healthy adult. And finally, Ghaffaradli-Doty and Carson (1979) observed that college women with more egalitarian attitudes reported themselves to act more feminist in their everyday lives. Compared to women expressing traditional sexist attitudes on the AWS, the proliberationists more frequently checked such items as: "I have spoken up in class to state a pro-women's rights position," and "I have turned off a TV program because it annoyed me for its sexist view of women."

In sum, then, the empirical ambiguities of the behavioral validity of the AWS and other such measures of sexist attitudes are highly visible but not clearly attributable to methodological or to theoretical deficiencies.

FURTHER THEORETICAL CONSIDERATIONS

A few tentative conclusions about measurement in the domains of sex-typed and sexist attitudes and behaviors have been drawn by the author. The attitudinal measures of gender identity (e.g., BSRI) appear to be significantly predictive of sex-typed behaviors. Gender identity, methodological considerations aside, is probably not significantly related to sexist (sex-biased) attitudes and behaviors. The utility of the psychometric scales attempting to measure stereotyping and sexism appears to be highly questionable. Surely, sexist behaviors are related to sexist attitudes, but this relation may not be verifiable with conventional methods of measurement due to the social desirability factors that plague these types of questionnaires (e.g., AWS).

Certainly, methodological refinements in scaling techniques can be made to increase the power of attitudinal scales to predict behavior (e.g., making the attitude measure more congruent with the target behavior to be predicted, making salient the basic value conflict underlying the attitudes about the issue, etc.) (Brannon 1979); and current trends in attitudinal, demographic scaling (Anastasi 1982) are encouraging. However, it is suggested here that we need to reach beyond psychometric improvements if we are going to adequately assess the various components of sexism and offer specific recommendations for social policy changes.

First, it is recommended that we link our concern for measurement with a concern for theory development to ensure that we have some means to understand and interpret empirical results. It is not uncommon, for scales of gender roles and of attitudes toward the social roles of men and women, to lack a theoretical definition of what it is they attempt to measure; and the inadequacies of our theoretical definitions are bound to be translated into the measuring instruments. More succinctly, when the a priori theoretical account of why certain variables are likely to be related to the dependent variable is missing, "then obtained findings are left in a sort of explanatory

146 • SEX ROLE RESEARCH

ambiguity" (Ryff 1982, p. 210). Thus, we need theoretical models to specify which attitudes we want to measure, which behaviors we want to monitor or predict, and how these variables are mediated and linked together.

Kutner and Brogan (1976) have offered a model of sexism in the education system, and their model was expanded in the present review (Fig. 9.1) in order to recognize two additional systems, that is, a definition of sexism and the mediating variables of sex-typed and sexist behaviors.

FIGURE 9.1   A Model of Sexism

Sexism: An Ideology
(Belief in the superiority of male/masculine)

- Nonconscious and conscious rules
- Descriptive and prescriptive definitions

Independent Variables[1]
(Prescribed structure)

- Psychological-cognitive structures of individuals participating in the system
  - Gender identity, attitudes toward social roles, stereotypes
  - Sex-typed attitudes and skills
  - Self-socialization
- Socialization processes
- Structures of the system
- Other factors (structure of related systems such as the economy, occupational structure, etc.)

Intervening Variables[1]
(Prescribed structure)

- Sex discrimination and devaluation of female/feminine

Mediating Variable:
Behavioral consequences of Discrimination
(Prescribed function)

- Sexist behavior/sex-biased behavior
- Sex-typed behavior

Dependent Variables (Consequences)[1]
(Prescribed function)

- Sex inequalities

[1] Variables identified in Brogan and Kutner's (1976) model.

Sexism is defined as an ideology that prescribes both the structure (the "independent" and "intervening" variables) and the function (the "mediating" and "dependent" variables) of a system. Of course, this is a "feedback" system and directionality is characteristically obscured; sex differences (sex-typed attitudes and behaviors) may result from, as well as contribute to, sex discrimination. Stereotypes are reinforced by, as well as reinforce, the consequences of sex inequalities. Behavior, sex-typed behavior and sexist behavior, is seen as a critical link in the sequence toward and in the maintenance of inequalities.

Clarifications provided by this, admittedly rudimentary, model indicate why attitudinal-behavioral issues go beyond challenges in psychometric sophistication and lie in the conceptualization of the domains of attitudes and behaviors being studied. For example, if sexism is an ideology, a world view which has both "conscious" and "nonconscious" components, which most researchers believe it has (e.g., Bem and Bem 1972), then the "nonconscious" aspect of sexism must receive more attention in scale development and in research designs. Furthermore, the model states that all attitudes and behaviors occur and develop within the context of social exchange within a changing social climate. Because of the impact of the feminist movement, it may be becoming less socially acceptable to verbalize one's sex-biased and stereotypic attitudes, at least in public, at least in publically scrutinized situations (e.g., "this is a psychological test"). Indeed, as reference to stereotypic traits are abandoned, discrimination against women may be justified more often on other grounds. Whatever the process, the result is that verbal reports are not likely to predict sexist behavior accurately.

Furthermore, the present model encourages the researcher to focus on behavior; it encourages us to focus upon monitoring and understanding *when* sexist behavior is likely to occur, upon *how* intense it is likely to be (Mednick 1976), and upon *what* circumstances the negative consequences of sexist behavior might outweigh the positive and reinforcing consequences for the person emitting the behavior. The "all things being equal" evaluative bias paradigm (wherein the single independent variable of sex is allowed to vary while all other variables are held constant) has been quite effectively employed to identify the nature of the sex-biases of groups of students, mental health practitioners, and psychology department chairpersons. The paradigm is easily adaptable to measure individual differences, and the consequences of the behavior are immediately perceptible. Such behavioral analyses are not only direct and powerful; they circumvent or minimize many of the problems associated with attitudinal scaling, such as social desirability response bias.

To summarize, working from a theoretical base and focusing on behavior may encourage diagnostic analyses of sexism that would provide an evaluation of the interchange between the stimulus situation, the characteristics of the interacting persons, the sexist behaviors, and the consequences of sexist behavior. Such diagnostic profiles should clearly delineate the targets for structural and policy change. Theoretical guidance fosters the application, as well as the generation, of knowledge (Ryff 1982). For example, the study of communication patterns within an institution could illuminate the decision-making processes that regulate women's entry into and progression through educational and occupational structures. Such analyses would clarify the barriers to implementing affirmative action programs which, if enforced, would go a long way toward eliminating sexism in our society.*

The recommendation to move away from our investment in the attitudinal measurement of sexism and toward the behavioral measurement of sexism may not be greeted with enthusiasm by many. Attitudinal scaling has been the "apple pie" of American psychology; but, the author suspects that persons of power are far more likely to rely upon behavioral evaluations, and there does seem to be a convergence of opinion (e.g., Brannon 1979) that diagnostic profiles of sex-typed and sex-biased attitudes and behaviors may yield more accurate assessments and more definitive recommendations for social policy change.

REFERENCES

Alper, T.G. The relationship between role orientation and achievement motivation in college women. *Journal of Personality* 41 (1973).

Anastasi, A. *Psychological Testing, 5th Ed.* New York: Macmillan, 1982.

Arkin, R.M., and K.S. Johnson. Effects on increased occupational participation by women on androgynous and nonandrogynous individuals ratings of occupational attractiveness. *Sex Roles* 6(4), (1980):593–605.

Bem, S.L. Sex-role adaptability: One consequence of psychological androgyny. *Journal of Personality and Social Psychology* 31 (1975):634–43.

Bem, S.L. The measurement of psychological androgyny. *Journal of Consulting and Clinical Psychology* 42 (1974):155–62.

Bem, S.L., and D.J. Bem. Homogenizing the American woman: The power of annonconscious ideology. In D.J. Bem (ed.), *Beliefs, Attitudes, and Human Affairs.* Belmont, Cal.: Brooks/Cole, 1972.

Bem, S.L., and E. Lenny. Sex-typing and the avoidance of cross-sex behavior. *Journal of Personality and Social Psychology* 33 (1976):48–54.

Bem, S.L., W. Martyna, and C. Watson. Sex-typing and androgyny: Further explorations of the expressive domain. *Journal of Personality and Social Psychology* 3 (1976):1016–23.

Block, J., A. Von der Lippe, and J.H. Block. Sex-role and socialization patterns: Some personality concomitants and environmental antecedents. *Journal of Consulting and Clinical Psychology* 41 (1973):321–41.

---

*Shomers and Centers (1970) found that simply increasing the number of women in a college classroom significantly decreased the expression of antifemale attitudes of the class members.

Brannon, R. Measuring attitudes (toward women, and otherwise): A methodological critique. In J. Sherman & F. Denmark (eds.), *Psychology of Women: Future Directions of Research.* New York: Psychological Dimensions, 1979.

Brogan, D., and N.G. Kutner. Measuring sex-role orientation: A normative approach. *Journal of Marriage and the Family,* (February 1976):31–40.

Brooks-Gunn, J., and M. Fisch. Psychological androgyny and college students' judgments of mental health. *Sex Roles* 6(4), (1980):575–80.

Calway-Fagen, N., B.S. Wallston, and H. Gabel. The relationship between attitudinal and behavioral measures of sex preference. *Psychology of Women Quarterly* 4 (1979):274–80.

Constantinople, A. Masculinity-Femininity: An exception to a famous dictum? *Psychological Bulletin* 80 (1973):389–407.

Ditmar, F., N. Mueller, and J. Mitchell. Females' attitudes toward feminism and their conformity in heterosexual groups. Paper presented at the American Psychological Association, Chicago, August, 1975.

Eagly, A.H. Sex differences in influencibility. *Psychological Bulletin* 85 (1978):86–116.

Ellis, L.J., and P.M. Bentler. Traditional sex-determined role standards and sex stereotypes. *Journal of Personality and Social Psychology* 25 (1973):28–34.

Fitzgerald, N.M., and T.L. Huston. Verbal competency in a sex-stereotyping dilemma. Paper presented at the American Psychological Association, Washington D.C., September 1976.

Gackenback, J.I., and S.M. Auerback. Empirical evidence for the phenomenon of the "well-meaning liberal male." *Journal of Clinical Psychology* 31 (1975):632–35.

Ghaffaradli-Doty, P., and E.R. Carlson. Consistency in attitude and behavior of women with a liberal attitude toward the rights and roles of women. *Sex Roles* 5(4), (1979):395–404.

Ginorio, A.B. A comparison of Puerto Ricans in New York with native Puerto Ricans and native Americans on two measures of acculturation: Gender role and racial identification. Doctoral Diss., Fordham University, 1978.

Goldberg, C. Conformity to majority as a function of task and acceptance of sex-related stereotypes. *Journal of Psychology* 89 (1975):25–37.

Goldberg, P.A., J.F. Katz, and S. Rapport. Posture and prediction on the attitudes toward women scale. *Psychology of Women Quarterly* 3 (1979):403–06.

Gomes, B., and S.I. Abramowitz. Sex-related patient and therapist effects on clinical judgment. *Sex Roles* 2 (1976):1–14.

Gump, J.P. Sex-role attitudes and psychological well-being. *Journal of Social Issues* 28 (1972):79–92.

Jones, W.H., M.E. Chernovetz, and R.O. Hansson. The enigma of androgyny: Differential implications for males and females? *Journal of Consulting and Clinical Psychology* 46(2), (1978):298–313.

Kaplan, A.G., and M.A. Sedney. *Psychology and Sex Roles.* Boston: Little, Brown, 1980.

Kulik, J.A., and J. Harackiewiez. Opposite-sex interpersonal attraction as a function of the sex roles of the perceiver and the perceived. *Sex Roles* 5(4), (1979):443–52.

Kutner, N.G., and D. Brogan. Sources of sex discrimination in educational systems: A conceptual model. *Psychology of Women Quarterly* 1 (1976):50–69.

Lipman-Blumen, J. How ideology shapes women's lives. *Scientific American* 226 (1972):34–42.

Mason, K.O., and L.L. Bumpass. U.S. women's sex-role ideology, 1970. *The American Journal of Sociology* 80 (1975):1212–19.

Mednick, M.T.S. Psychology of women: Research issues and trends. Presentation to the New York Academy of Sciences, New York, May 1976.

Neufield, E., D. Langmeyer, and W. Seeman. Some sex-role stereotypes and personal preferences, 1950–1970. *Journal of Personality Assessment* 39 (1975):110–13.

O'Leary, V.E., and A.O. Harrison. Sex role stereotypes as a function of race and sex. Paper presented at the American Psychological Association, Chicago, August 1975.

Pedhazur, E.J., and T.J. Tetenbaum. Bem sex role inventory: A theoretical and methodological critique. *Journal of Personality and Social Psychology* 37(6), (1979):996–1016.

Pines, A. The influence of goals on people's perceptions of a competent woman. *Sex Roles* 5(1), (1979):71–76.

Richardson, D., A. Vinsel, and S.P. Taylor. Female aggression as a function of attitudes toward women. *Sex Roles* 6(2), (1980):395–404.

Rosenkrantz, P.S., S.R. Vogel, H. Bee, I.K. Broverman, and D.M. Broverman. Sex-role stereotypes and self concepts in college students. *Journal of Consulting and Clinical Psychology* 32 (1968):287–95.

Ryff, C.D. Successful aging: A developmental approach. *Gerontologist* 22(2), (1982):209–14.

Sharp, C., and R. Post. Evaluation of male and female applicants for sex-congruent and sex-incongruent jobs. *Sex Roles* 6(3),(1980):391–402.

Shomer, R.W., and R. Centers. Differences in attitudinal responses under conditions of implicity manipulated group salience. *Journal of Personality and Social Psychology* 15 (1970):125–32.

Spence, J.T., and R. Helmreich. The attitudes toward women scale: An objectivie instrument to measure attitudes toward the rights and roles of women in contemporary society. JSAS *Catalog of Selected Documents in Psychology* 2 (1972a):2–66.

Spence, J.T., and R. Helmreich. Who likes competent women? *Journal of Applied Psycology* 2 (1972b):197–213.

Spence, J.T., R. Helmreich, and J. Stapp. The personal attributes questionnaire: JSAS *Catalogue of Selected Documents in Psychology* 4 (1975a):127.

Spence, J.T., R. Helmreich, and J. Stapp. Ratings of self and peers on sex-role attributes and their relation to self-esteem and conceptions of masculinity and femininity. *Journal of Personality and Social Psychology* 32 (1975b):29–39.

Trilling, B.A. Factors related to women's prejudice against women. Doctoral diss., Fordham University, 1975.

Vaughter, R.M. Psychology. *Signs* 2 (1976):120–46.

Vaughter, R.M. Evaluating Measures of Sexism. JSAS *Catalog of Selected Documents* 9 (1979):1–62 (ms. 1915).

Vaughter, R.M., D. Horber, and S.L. Vedovato. Demographic characteristics and attitudes toward women. Paper presented at the American Psychological Association, Toronto, August, 1978.

Vogel, S.R., I.K. Broverman, D.M. Broverman, F.E. Clarkson, and P.S. Rosenkrantz. Maternal employment and perception of sex roles among college students. *Developmental Psychology* 3 (1970):384–90.

PART V

ANALYSIS AND INFERENCE

10

Statistical Analysis in Sex Roles and Social Change

Evelyn R. Rosenthal

Empirical investigation of social processes often entails the statistical analysis of relatively large numbers of variables. With wide availability of electronic data processing to ease the computational drudgery of manipulating data matrices, problems in the analysis of large numbers of variables have shifted from computation to conceptualization. It is not unreasonable now to demand of researchers as much care in the conceptualization of a data analysis strategy as in the conceptualization of a research problem. In quantitative empirical research, a data analysis plan links a substantive theory to a statistical model, and a well-conceptualized data analysis strategy minimizes the distance between them.

Too often, we fail to match our statistical analysis to our research questions. This failing is certainly not unique to sex-roles researchers, but it seems particularly unfortunate when creative and flexible thought, yielding exciting new research questions or reconceptualization of old questions, is not matched with equally creative and flexible data analysis. Just as our theories set limits to the kinds of questions we ask, so too do our choices of statistical techniques set limits on the kinds of questions we actually answer. Taking as my theme the gap between the questions we pose and the questions we actually answer, I focus on the possibilities of data analysis for narrowing the gap. I will argue for more complex data analysis strategies to confront our complex research questions. I realize the double difficulties of making my argument persuasive: the reward structure of social science favors theorizers not data analysts, and complex data analysis may arouse suspicion of obscuring more than clarifying.

I can't do much to surmount the first difficulty, but for the second I offer as refutation the seeming paradox that more complex data analysis strategies often permit the use of simpler statistical models whose clarity and ease of interpretation serve us well. The remainder of this essay attempts to explain and illustrate the seeming paradox.

My argument for more complex data analysis strategies entails three suggestions for sex-roles researchers: (1) develop research questions and data analysis plans concurrently and interactively; (2) explore the data fully to learn its structure and its limitations before applying it to any multivariate statistical techniques; and (3) try more than one multivariate statistical technique—because there is seldom one technique that emerges unambiguously optimal for addressing a particular research question with a particular set of data. Each of these suggestions adds complexity to our plans. I will expand on each of them, outline some common difficulties that arise as a data analysis plan is developed, review the major statistical techniques appropriate for analyzing large numbers of variables, and present two extended examples to illustrate the simplifying possibilities of a complex plan to link theory and data.

Throughout the essay, I cite published research articles and statistical textbooks as suggestions for further study. The articles illustrate problematic issues and provide good models; the textbooks provide details to supplement my brief, nontechnical review. My presentation is aimed at a middle ground between polished, edited articles that reveal little of the mess and complexity of preliminary analyses, and statistical texts whose technical discussions sometimes intimidate the unprepared reader.

I. DEVELOPING A DATA ANALYSIS PLAN

Preplanning is an essential step in developing a data analysis strategy. To match statistical analysis to research questions, we need to develop both together and recognize their interdependence. This mutual development preceeds and guides the collection of new data or the search for existing data. Despite careful preplanning efforts, however, the data we locate are invariably more or less a mess: incomplete, error-laden loose approximations to social reality. The next essential steps, therefore, are exploration of the data to reveal the nature of the messiness and adjustment of the data to clean it up in preparation for multivariate statistical analysis.

I hesitate to outline a standard series of steps to be followed in all data analysis plans since I wish to emphasize flexibility and multiple strategies for the analysis of multivariate data. However, there are a few preliminary steps basic to any data analysis plan that should not be neglected. Before the data are collected, the prudent researcher will, in outlining a general data analysis strategy, conform to the conceptualization of the research problem. Variables must be conceptualized clearly and operationalized concretely. The form of the social process to be investigated must guide the researcher in blocking out the data analysis strategy. This is the time to consult with a statistician to help solve problems in visualizing statistical techniques appropriate for the research problem.

Commonly used statistical techniques for the analysis of multivariate data are based on (more or less well-developed) theoretical models; consultation with a statistician prior to data collection will alert the researcher to the inevitably less-than-perfect fit among the abstract mathematical model underlying a given statistical procedure, the concrete data the researcher plans to generate, and the questions about social process the researcher seeks to answer. Such consultation may suggest to the researcher ways of modifying data collection plans to allow for a more flexible approach to data analysis. For example, modifying plans to include several additional indicators of a key variable may encourage the researcher's including in the exploratory phase of data analysis an explicit examination of assumptions about measurement errors, and thereby facilitate better informed decisions about the use of statistical procedures. Although as researchers we cannot expect a statistical consultant to deal directly with the problems inherent in employing error-laden and incomplete data to test or illustrate our conceptualization of a social process, we often gain insight into these problems as we examine the assumptions we must make in joining social theory to mathematical models via statistical procedures applied to these same untidy data.

After the data are collected, the researcher begins exploratory data analysis by examining the distribution of each variable to note its form, range, variation and central tendency. This is an important step for secondary analyses as well as for the analysis of newly collected data. Special attention should be paid to examining the characteristics of dependent variables since most multivariate statistical techniques require carefully measured, often normally distributed dependent variables.

If the dependent variables have a restricted range because of floor or ceiling effects, or because the subject pool was fairly homogeneous, the researcher must consider applying appropriate transformations to the data before proceeding with more complex analysis techniques.

Expressing the data in more than one way through mathematical transformations allows the researcher greater flexibility and often greater simplicity in data analysis. In some cases, we transform data so it conforms more closely to the underlying mathematical model of a particular statistical technique. For example, use of the F-distribution in tests of significance requires sampled populations to be normally distributed with a common variance. Although F-tests are quite robust under some violations of these assumptions, we sometimes avoid gross violation of assumptions by applying to the raw data a transformation such as square root or logarithmic. More commonly, transformations are used to facilitate interpretation of data by converting two or more variables to comparable scales such as centile ranks or standard scores. A good introduction to common transformations and examples of their uses to either facilitate interpretation or simplify statistical analysis is Schuessler's (1971) final chapter in *Analyzing Social Data*.

In addition to examination of univariate distributions, the exploratory phase of statistical analysis includes examination of bivariate relationships of interest. Graphic techniques are usually helpful here in highlighting non-linearities that may not be apparent from inspection of correlation coefficients and other linear measures of assosciation. Leinhardt and Wasserman's (1979) essay, "Exploratory Data Analysis: An Introduction to Selected Methods" is a concise and readable introduction to Tukey's paper-and-pencil techniques for exploratory data analysis; the essay may be read with profit by researchers with minimal statistical preparation.

There is no need for the researcher to limit exploration of the data to only those statistical procedures whose underlying assumptions are fully met by the data. Especially for the analysis of ordinal variables, where no standard techniques are without drawbacks, the researcher needs to use several techniques and compare results. Usually in the analysis of ordinal data the trade-off is between treating the ordinal variables as categorical and losing information inherent in the hierarchical ordering of the categories, and treating the ordinal variables as continuously distributed interval measures and risking the violation of assumptions demanded by powerful parametric techniques. Exploring the data in several different ways allows the researcher to assess the effects such trade-offs entail for a particular research problem, and perhaps develop new insights into the social process under investigation. At the very least, through extending the exploratory phase of data analysis the researcher's increased familiarity with the data may yield a heightened alertness in the later, confirmatory phase of analysis to procedures or interpretations that distort either the data's statistical structure or substantive meaning.

Special data analysis problems that add complexity to exploratory analysis may arise in using available data originally collected for other purposes. The variables in a secondary analysis often do not correspond very closely to the concepts in the researcher's theoretical model, a serious problem for secondary analysis. If this is the case, an appropriate strategy is to develop auxiliary theories relating the unmeasured constructs to their measured indicators from the existing data. Existing data sets may contain more than one measured variable to include as multiple indicators of the unobserved constructs.

Although formulating auxiliary theories relating unmeasured constructs of interest to the measured indicators in a set of available data adds complexity to the data analysis, the alternative strategy of ignoring the conceptual gap between the research hypothesis and the data used to test it can yield confusion. The researcher claims to be testing one hypothesis while actually testing another; better to restate the hypothesis in terms of the measured variables. For example, a recent secondary analysis of the 1970 National Fertility Survey data proposes to estimate the relationship of high relative economic status to the fertility of married women (Bean and Swicewood 1979). Relative economic status is conceptually defined as the ratio of lifetime income to consumption preferences formed in the parental household. With no available measure of either lifetime income or pre-established consumption preferences, the researchers use an occupational-status score (Duncan Socioeconomic Index [SEI]) of the respondent's husband's current occupation (for lifetime income) and that of the respondent's father-in-law's occupation (for preestablished consumption patterns) as imperfect indicators. If the difference between the respondent's husband's SEI and her father-in-law's SEI exceeds 40 points, the respondent is classified as upwardly mobile. I chose this example not to add one more case to support Joan Acker's (1978) analysis of how "intellectual sexism" creates conceptual confusion in the sociological study of women, but to illustrate a common problem in the secondary analysis of existing data, especially for research on women. A sex-roles researcher using existing data may face tough decisions in attempting to recast into a feminist analysis variables whose measurement was guided by a different view of social life. The decisions are likely to involve weighing the trade-offs among four options: (1) reformulating hypotheses to fit existing indicators; (2) developing new indicators from the existing data; (3) collecting new data; or (4) abandoning the project. The first option has the virtue of adding no new statistical complexity to the analysis and contains the obvious drawback of forcing the researcher to abandon her own conceptualization of a problem in favor of one compatible with the paradigm underlying the original plan for collecting the data. The second option inevitably adds complexity to the analysis as the researcher develops a statistical model to link a well-conceptualized but unmeasured variable with its measured but far-from-perfect indicator. The third option may be too expensive, or impossible in the case of historical research. The final option's effects must be identified by each researcher individually.

In the illustration summarized above, the researchers explicitly recognize the problem of imperfect indicators and choose to restate the hypothesis in more general terms of upward mobility rather than in specific terms of high relative economic status; statistical analysis proceeds straightforwardly with the estimation of parameters for a regression equation. Alternatively, they could have attempted the strategy I am suggesting here of contructing an auxiliary theory expressing the relationship between the measured variables (SEI scores) and the unmeasured variables (lifetime income and consumption patterns). To do this, a researcher must first define the unmeasured variables as clearly as possible before constructing the measurement-error model; the model itself is constructed on substantive, not statistical, grounds. An excellent introduction to the estimation of parameters in simple measurement-error models is Namboodiri, Carter, and Blalock's (1975) *Applied Multivariate Analysis and Experimental Design,* Part Four.

Many large data sets are now available for secondary analysis by social researchers, such as the National Longitudinal Surveys of Labor Market Experience, the Public Use Samples from the U.S. Census, and the Quality of Employment Surveys. Secondary analyses of these national-level data sets may be incorporated into a data analysis strategy along with results obtained from the analysis of primary data. Often, parts of theories and limited hypotheses documented by case studies or explored with the analysis of data from small restricted samples may be supplemented with the secondary analysis of large social surveys. The strengths and limitations of case studies and restricted samples are then complemented by the strengths and weaknesses of the large survey, providing greater credibility or suggesting necessary cautions to interpretations of the smaller studies.

Statistical analysis in social research seldom involves nothing more than the automatic application of one or the other unambiguously appropriate and preferable data analysis technique. Developing a data analysis plan and performing exploratory analyses challenge us as researchers to approach our data with the same flexibility and creativity we employ in developing our conceptual frameworks.

II. STATISTICAL TECHNIQUES FOR ANALYZING LARGE NUMBERS OF VARIABLES

A creative approach to strategies of data analysis may encourage more creative theorizing and a good fit of data analysis to research questions. To enhance the likelihood of fitting data analysis to research questions, investigators need a functional awareness of a variety of statistical techniques for analyzing multivariate data. Toward that end, I will describe several multivariate statistical methods, indicate research situations where each method may be most usefully employed, note the necessary assumptions made for each case, and cite an example of the method in use. Throughout this section, I assume the reader's familiarity with the contents of an introductory statistics text.

Several multivariate data analysis techniques are variations of the General Linear Model, as are bivariate regression and analysis of variance. *Multiple Correlation* is a model for estimating the linear correlation between a dependent variable (Y) and the weighted sum of two or more independent variables (X_i). The squared multiple correlation coefficient (R^2) is a measure of the influence of the set of predictors on the dependent variable expressed as the proportion of the total variance of Y accounted for by the independent variables taken together. Multiple correlation is useful for prediction problems, where R^2 is interpreted as the degree to which a set of variables predicts the values of Y. Of wider interest than prediction problems may be problems of replication or generalization: Are the independent variables related to the dependent variable in the same manner today compared to some past time, or for one social group compared to another, or under one set of specified conditions compared to others? To answer these questions the researcher compares the weights (partial regression coefficients) of independent variables across two or more multiple correlation models.

Multiple correlation analysis may be employed to test theory that requires nonlinear terms as well as nonlinear forms by creating new variables or forms via transformations in the preliminary analysis stage. Patricia Taylor's (1979) "Income Inequality in the Federal Civilian Government" illustrates the introduction of nonlinear terms in multiple correlation equations. In her analysis, which compares the structure of earnings determination across race and sex groups within a single labor market, years of work experience is one predictor of earnings; since preliminary data exploration revealed that the relationship between work experience and earnings is not linear, she applied a transformation to the predictor variable to rectify the relationship before proceeding with the multiple correlation analysis.

Multiple correlation models require all variables in the analysis to be, conceptually at least, measured at the interval-scale level, although categorical predictors may be used by creating a dichotomous variable for each category of a nominal predictor (dummy variables). In the example cited above, Taylor employs two dummy variables for the categorical predictor, veteran status: disabled veteran and other veteran (each scored 1 = yes, 0 = no). The use of these two dummy variables permits inclusion of the three-category predictor in the analysis (the third category, not a veteran, is of course redundant since those who answer negatively on both dummy variables give the researcher the same information as would inclusion of the third category; there are mathematical reasons as well why only $n = 1$ dummy variables may be included in the equation to represent a nominal variable with n categories). Multiple correlation models assume that the independent variables are linearly related to the dependent variable, and that the independent variables are not highly correlated with each other. These two assumptions must also be examined in the preliminary data exploration. Additional assumptions about the data are necessary if the analysis will include hypothesis testing or testing casual models.

Multivariate Analysis of Covariance is a type of dummy-variable regression model where some of the predictors are qualitative variables and some are quantitative variables. As in regression analysis, the relationship between the interval-scaled dependent variable and the interval-scaled predictor variables may be assessed; analysis of covariance permits that relationship to be compared across categories of the qualitative predictor variables. Alternatively, as in analysis of variance, the relationship between categorical predictors and a continuous dependent variable may be assessesd, with the added feature of controlling for the effects of a set of continuous variables (covariates). Seen as a blending of analysis of variance and regression analysis, analysis of covariance enables the investigator to ascertain if the assumed efforts of classification factors such as sex, religion or political party on some dependent variable should be ascribed to covariates such as earnings, age or years of schooling. This type of comparison is useful for assessing sex effects in social processes, as Robert Levine et al. (1982) do in "Individual Differences for Sex Differences in Achievement Attributions?"

To answer questions of whether the continuous predictor variables operate the same way across all categories of the covariate, F-tests for equal slopes may be applied. In addition to testing for no interaction overall, we may also test each predictor separately. Similarly, F-tests for equivalent intercepts will allow testing for the effects of the categorical predictors on the dependent variable, controlling for the continuous covariates.

As with all variations on the general linear model, multivariate analysis of covariance assumes a linear relationship between the dependent variable and the predictors, as well as the absence of multicollinearity among predictors. In order to apply F-tests to these models, the researcher must make the additional assumptions that the dependent variable is normally distributed within categories of independent variables, that observations are independent of each other, and that the variance in the dependent variable is equal across categories of the independent variables.

Another, and very much neglected, variation of the general linear model is *Multiple-Partial Correlation,* in which all variables are interval-scaled and the predictor variables are grouped into clusters on the basis of theoretical or practical concerns. Multiple-partial correlation analysis allows us to estimate the relationship between a dependent variable and a set of predictor variables controlling for another set of variables. Given the multidisciplinary nature of many debates in sex roles research, investigators may find the little used multiple-partial correlation analysis useful for addressing questions about the relative importance for a given outcome of psychological traits compared to social factors, or economic variables compared to structural variables. This is the type of question guiding the analysis by Robert Bibb and William Form (1977) in "The Effects of Industrial, Occupational, and Sex Stratification on Wages in Blue-Collar Markets." Bibb and Form compare the effects on women's and men's wages of factors predicted by human capital theory to factors predicted by structural-stratification theory. Although their analysis follows the logic of multiple-partial correlation, they examine squared multiple correlation coefficients and regression coefficients and neglect the multiple-partial correlation coefficients; these latter could serve as a neat, rigorous test of their research question.

The same data assumptions of multiple correlation apply to multiple-partial correlation as do the assumptions for F-tests described in the previous section. They apply as well to *Log Odds Analysis,* a form of multivariate regression analysis where the dependent variable is a dichotomy, redefined by the log-odds transformation. The predictor variables may be categorical variables, continuous variables most often is a measure of the presence or absence of some event such as divorce, employment or childbirth, and the analysis focuses on the proportion of cases experiencing the event. If the event is quite rare (or, alternatively, very common) and the observed proportion of cases experiencing the event is less than .25 or more than .75, ordinary least-squares procedures for estimating regression parameters may yield uninterpretable results. A log-odds transformation applied to the dependent variable, permits the use of ordinary least-squares estimation procedures. The transformation involves expressing the proportion, p, in terms of odds, $p/1=p$; a proportion of .4 is equivalent to odds of 2 to 3 against. The log of the odds has the virtue of no theoretical floor or ceiling, in contrast to the proportion whose range is 0 to 1. Log-odds analysis is appropriate for examining the effects of the predictor variables on the proportion of cases experiencing an event. Examples of log-odds analysis abound in sex-roles research; for two substantively and theoretically interesting examples see Joan Huber and Glenna Spitze (1980), "Considering Divorce: An Expansion of Becker's Theory of Marital Instability" and Linda J. Waite's (1980) "Working Wives and the Family Life Cycle."

For applications of some other variations of the general linear model, additional assumptions need to be made. Specifically, factor analysis, canonical correlation analysis and path analysis are all causal models that require further restrictions for their application.

Factor Analysis is another general linear model variation employed with continuously distributed variables, where underlying unities among a set of variables may be explored. These unmeasured, unobserved unities or factors often help explain the basic structure of a set of variables. The factors are hypothetical contructs, often given names by the researcher to reflect the observed variables with the highest factor loadings (factor loadings are indices of the amount of variance a factor contributes to the estimation of the observed variables, analogous to regression weights). Factor analysis is a type of causal model where one or more unobserved factors are hypothesized to cause several observed variables. These factors may then be used as predictors in further multivariate analyses, as Millicent Poole and B.C. Law (1982) do in "Who Stays? Who Leaves? An Examination of Sex Differences in Staying and Leaving." In their report, the authors employ factor analysis to explore the structure of thirty-three independent variables in an investigation of school leavers and stayers.

The use of factor analysis requires a few additional assumptions, as do all causal models based on the general linear model. We need to be able to make the logical assumption that the (unmeasured) factor hypothesized to cause the measured variables indeed precedes them, and the methodological assumption of high reliability and validity of all measurements. The results of factor analysis are sensitive to errors of measurement and must be interpreted with caution. When some variables employed in a factor analysis are poorly measured, the well-measured variables are more likely to have high factor loadings.

As noted above, researchers pick names for factors on the basis of the meaning of the measured variables with the highest factor loadings, and may be misled in their interpretation of the underlying structure of a set of variables because of poor measurement. Namboodiri et al. point out another pitfall in factor analysis that may result from measurement error; instead of the unobserved factor being a cause of all the observed variables, suppose one observed variable is the cause of all the others but is poorly measured. In this case, the unobserved variable inferred from factor analysis would be purely an artifact of measurement error (Namboodiri, Carter, and Blalock 1975, pp. 546–47). Because of the measurement difficulties in much social research, factor analysis tends to be of limited utility at present.

FIGURE 10.1. A Factor-Analysis Model

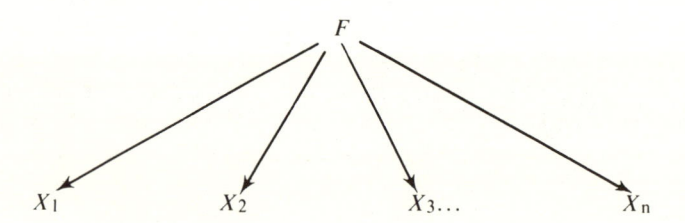

$F \to X_1, X_2, X_3 \ldots X_n$

Related to factor analysis is a second causal model, *Canonical Correlation*, a linear model with any number of dependent variables and any number of predictor variables. Canonical correlation may be viewed heuristically as the linking of two factor analyses: for the set of predictors, the (unmeasured and unobserved) first factor is calculated. For the set of dependent variables, the first factor is calculated. Then, the canonical correlation is the correlation between those two unobserved factors, and the square of the canonical correlation coefficient is interpreted as the variance shared by the two factors. Canonical correlation may be useful for studying the underlying relations between two sets of variables since, as in factor analysis, more than one source of common variance may be identified and interpreted. The difficulties arising from poorly measured variables described for factor analysis apply to canonical correlation analysis as well.

For a clear but fairly technical example of the use of canonical correlation analysis, see Arthur James (1982) "A Multivariate Comparative Analysis of Work-Related Symptoms of Distance and Campus Undergraduates." James's analysis estimates the effects of eight psychoneurotic and motivational factors on three measures of educational attainment for commuting students and dormitory-based students.

Path Analysis is a form of multiple regressison analysis employing standardized partial regression coefficients in a causal model. In addition to the data restraints common to all variations of the general linear model, path analysis requires the additional assumptions of causal models: There must be a basis for assuming an unequivocal time ordering of the variables in a path model, all variables must be reliably and validly measured, and the set of variables in the path analysis must be inclusive of all major influences on the dependent variables. Path analysis is useful for making explicit all the indirect as well as direct causes of a particular variable as they are implied by a set of structural equations. In path analysis, the correlation between an independent variable and a dependent variable is decomposed into direct causal effects,

FIGURE 10.2. A Canonical Correlation Model

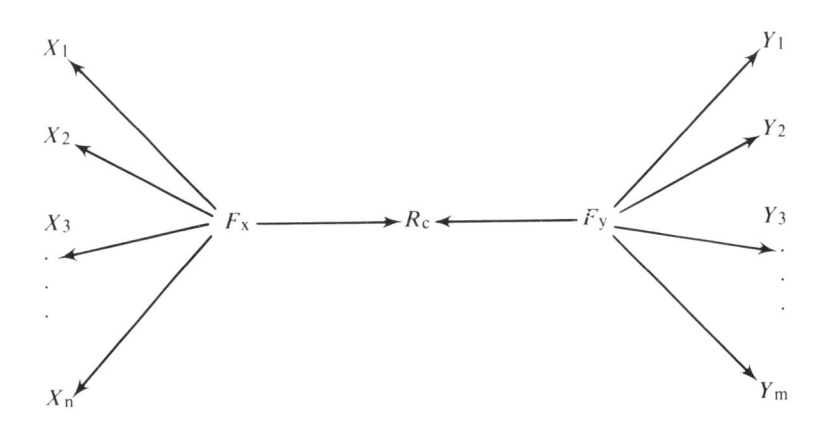

indirect causal effects and noncausal effects. Path analysis is best suited for areas of research where theory is well-developed, since, as with factor models and other causal models, there are many possible path models that will be consistent with a particular set of data. Path models often incorporate measures of the same variables at two or more time points, and therefore require careful inspection of the patterns of residuals. The section in this book on structural models presents a more detailed discussion of path analysis (cf. Boruch, Chapter 13).

FIGURE 10.3   A Path-Analysis Model

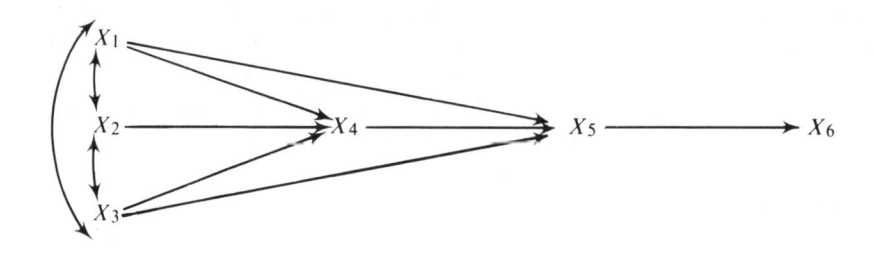

$$X_1, X_2, X_3 \rightarrow X_4 \rightarrow X_5 \rightarrow X_6$$

All the techniques discussed so far are variations of a single model. A departure from the general linear model is multivariate contingency-table analysis, familiar to most researchers but somewhat unwieldy in application after two or three control variables are included in the analysis. Contingency table analysis requires none of the restrictive assumptions of the general linear model, but may require very large samples as the number of cells in the table becomes large. Log-linear analysis is a form of multivariate contingency-table analysis, analogous to multiple correlation, where all variables are categorical.

In the case of a dichotomous dependent variable and categorical predictor variables, log-linear analysis is preferable to log-odds analysis if the researcher is interested in investigating relationships among the categorical predictors. Since log-linear analysis is applied to multivariate contingency tables, fairly large sample sizes may be necessary. This technique proceeds by comparing the observed data to successively more complex models (main effects only, main effects and first-order interactions, etc.) and discarding models that are inconsistent with the data on the basis of goodness-of-fit statistical tests. Log-linear analysis is relatively new, so appropriate examples are not common. However, this method for the analysis of multiway contingency tables seems well suited for the analysis of social processes from survey research since some restrictive assumptions of regression-based techniques are absent. One recent example of log-linear analysis in sex roles research is Wesley Jamison and Margaret Signorella (1980), "Sex-Typing and Spatial Ability: The Association Between Masculinity and Success on Piaget's Water-Level Task," in which the authors examine social factors as explanations of the well-replicated finding of sex differences on Piaget's horizontality task.

Log-linear analysis of a 2 × 2 × 3 × 2 contingency table reveals that sex-role orientation predicts task performance independent of gender.

This brief overview of techniques for analyzing large numbers of variables is meant as an introduction to an array of possibilities beyond multiple regression and analysis of variance. To aid the researcher who desires more details, a short, annotated list of fuller presentations of these techniques that I and my students have found to be readable is given.

- Feinberg, Stephen E. *The Analysis of Cross-Classified Categorical Data.* Cambridge: MIT Press, 1977.
  Feinberg provides a readable and compact introduction to log-linear models, and their applications.
- Green, Paul E. *Analyzing Multivariate Data.* Honesdale, Ill.: Dryden Press, 1978.
  Green's text assumes one course in statistics and no knowledge of matrix algebra. The major multivariate statistical methods are presented in the context of the general linear model. Most of the applications are chosen from business management substantive areas.
- Heise, David R. (ed.). *Sociological Methodology 1976.* San Francisco: Josey-Bass, 1975.
  Included in this annual series of papers dealing with problems of research methods and statistics are the papers from a 1973 seminar on causal models with nominal and ordinal data. Several approaches to incorporating ordinal data into causal models are presented. Examples are mainly from sociology and social psychology.
- Kerlinger, Fred N. and Elazar J. Pedhazur. *Multiple Regression in Behavioral Research.* New York: Holt, Rinehart & Winston, 1973.
  Kerlinger and Pedhazur's presentation assumes one course in basic statistics. Multiple regression and its major variations are presented, with a richness of detailed examples from educational psychology and sociology. This is a very readable regression to solve data analysis problems.
- Namboodiri, N. Krishnan, Lewis F. Carter, and Hubert M. Blalock, Jr., *Applied Multivariate Analysis and Experimental Design.* New York: McGraw-Hill, 1975.
  This text presents multiple regression analysis and its variations for readers who have had one basic statistics course. The unique feature of this book is the emphasis on the relationship between research design, statistical analysis and the conceptualization of the research problem. It includes an excellent chapter on measurement problems in the context of multivariate data analysis.
- Reynolds, H.T. *Analysis of Nominal Data.* Sage University Paper series on Quantitative Applications in the Social Sciences, 07–007. Beverly Hills and London: Sage Publications, 1977.

Reynolds covers most methods of cross-tabulation analysis, including multivariate methods such as log-linear. A simple introduction to the topic. One data set is analyzed throughout for excellent opportunities to compare methods.

CONNECTING THEORY TO DATA ANALYSIS: SOME ILLUSTRATIONS AND SUGGESTIONS

A common difficulty in the statistical analysis of social processes is the inadequate translation of the dynamic form of the social process into an appropriate data analysis plan. In its extreme form, inadequate attention to substantive theory leads to trivial findings or to masses of inappropriately analyzed data—the classical sociological nightmare of everything being correlated with everything else at the .15 level. We all recognize the abuse of statistical computation guided by half-formed ideas. But even with carefully conceptualized research problems, investigators often fall short of what is possible by not confronting complexities of dynamic theories with equally complex data analysis. Two examples from recently published essays in sex-roles research will serve to illustrate this problem. Both essays are based on clearly conceptualized research questions and are rewarding to read. I present them as illustrations of how, occasionally, data are under-analyzed with respect to the research questions posed and how a flexible approach to multivariate data analysis may improve on insights gained from competent but perhaps incomplete data analysis strategies.

In their essay, "Sexual Inequality and the Reproduction of Consciousness: An Analysis of Sex Role Stereotyping Among Children," Scott Cummings and Delbert Taebel (1980) develop a conceptual framework carefully grounded in theory to test "whether children, over time, develop values and attitudes which endorse or legitimate existing patterns of sexual segmentation in the work force." The authors present a series of 4×4 tables with accompanying chi-square and gamma statistics to test the relationship between grade level (3, 6, 9, 12) and sexism (ordinal dependent variable collapsed to four levels from a 13-point scale). The tables are broken out separately for two categories each of sex, race, socioeconomic status (SES), and mother's employment status.

The clear presentation of theory and data makes a beautifully constructed essay, but the authors themselves note in their conclusion that the dynamic form of their hypothesis is ignored in the data analysis: The hypothesis describes a cumulative-effects process on the individual level and cannot be addressed adequately by cross-sectional data aggregated by grade level. Further, the hypothesis implies a convergence toward a (empirically identifiable) fairly stable point ("existing patterns of sexual segmentation") as the dynamic form of the social process. The authors make no attempt to locate the stable point or to measure the subjects' distance from it. They merely show

TABLE 10.1. Degree of Sex Role Stereotyping by Grade Level, Controlling for Minority Status (Percent)

		Grade level			
Race	Sexism scale	3	6	9	12
Whites[a]		(n=48)	(n=38)	(n=47)	(n=59)
	4 (high)	22.9	15.8	12.8	8.5
	3	52.1	60.5	36.2	33.9
	2	22.9	18.4	34.0	27.1
	1 (low)	2.1	5.3	17.0	30.5
Non-Whites[b]		(n=63)	(n=45)	(n=9)	(n=9)
	4 (high)	27.0	28.9	22.2	11.1
	3	44.4	42.4	66.7	44.4
	2	25.4	28.9	.0	22.2
1 (low)	3	.2	.0	11.1	22.2

[a] χ^2=28.42, df=9, significance = .0008, gamma = -.39.
[b] χ^2=15.18, df=9, significance = .0862, gamma = -.06.
Source: Cummings and Taebel (1980, p. 639).

that sexism is weaker in the higher grade levels. This result lends no support to predictions from the theoretical framework, and the authors conclude by suggesting that social psychological processes are irrelevant for the reproduction of social inequality.

My quarrel with this essay is of opportunities foregone: Something is going on in the data. With a more creative approach to statistical analysis within the limitations of cross-sectional data, we may be able to discover what it is. Some suggestions: (1) Attempt to refine rather than collapse the dependent variable. Why collapse the original 13-point sexism scale to four levels? If there is measurement error in the original scale, it will inevitably be exacerbated in the collapsed scale. This is a very common situation in social research. Obviously, a 4 × 4 table is easier to read than a 13 × table, but most of us are willing to cope with the added complexity in order to avoid magnifying measurement errors in our dependent variable.

An exploratory analysis of the 13-point ordinal scale might indicate that it may, with some adjustment, reasonably substitute for a conceptually interval-scaled variable in an analysis based on the general linear model. Try it and compare results to the tabular analysis. (2) Utilize existing data from other sources to supplement the data at hand in order to reshape the data analysis to fit the research question. Why ignore in the data analysis the convergence process implied by the hypothesis? Make the implied process explicit in the data analysis strategy. Throughout the essay, comparisons are implied between student sexism scores and the "existing patterns of sexual segmentation in the work force," but no comparisons are carried out. Construct this comparison score, from census data perhaps, either as a point (total sexism score of the existing patterns of sexual segmentation in the work force) or a vector (13 values, representing the sexual segmentation in each of the occupations investigated) in order to make comparisons. The convergence hypothesis could then be tested by constructing a new dependent variable consisting of distance scores (comparison score-student score). (3) In place of a series of bivariate tables, or as a supplement to them, examine the simultaneous influence of all five independent variables on sexism. All five characteristics coexist simultaneously in the children themselves, and theoretically interact to influence the formation of individual consciousness. Why ignore multivariate statistical techniques? If the sample is sufficiently large, carry out a log-linear analysis of a six-way contingency table; or enter all five independent variables into a Multiple Classification Analysis (MCA, a form of multiple regression using all dummy variables for categorical predictors) of sexism. Examine interaction effects, especially of sex of subject with grade level, in order to compare boys' and girls' differential patterns of change at each grade level. For this problem, some loss of information will result from ignoring the ordinality of grade level; no totally satisfactory method for the multivariate analysis of ordinal variables exists at present. But look back at the theory: Grade level is employed as an imperfect indicator of age. Would it be possible at this point to go back to school records or a vital statistics registry to extract the ages of the children? Or, try an additional data analysis strategy and compare results: Enter the four dichotomies of sex, race, SES and mother's employment as dummy-variable predictors, and grade level as an interval-scaled covariate, in an analysis of covariance framework with the sexism scale as dependent. Significant interaction terms from the MCA could be entered as predictors as well. As with MCA, this data analysis procedure will permit direct comparisons of effects of levels of each independent variable on the dependent variable. Entering grade level as an interval-scaled covariate avoids the loss of information of MCA, but risks unreliable results because of the restricted range of values of grade level in the data. Then, compare MCA results with the analysis of covariance results to see what the trade-offs are.

In all fairness to Cummings and Taebel, they may have explored all these strategies and rejected them. In any event, their interest is not in exploring the process of change in sexist attitudes but in testing a prediction derived from neo-Marxist social psychological theory of the reproduction of social relations via individual consciousness. They chose each variable on the basis of a well-developed theoretical framework. This is a secondary analysis of data collected for other purposes; had the authors conceptualized the statistical analysis in advance of data collection, they would have been able to collect data at each grade level from the same panel of students, or at least at a second time point for each grade cohort. Although there is no strictly statistical method for separating out the effects of age, cohort and time period, with data from four cohorts at two time periods comparisons can be made and inferences drawn by appealing to theory or additional information from outside the data.

An excellent exposition of problems and methods in cohort analysis is Norval Glenn's brief monograph (1977) on the topic. For a clear illustration of a creative approach to the multivariate analysis of data with problems similar to those discussed here, see Denise Kandel et al. (1978), "Analytical Strategies for Studying Transitions Into Developmental Stages." The authors present two strategies for analysis of panel data and discuss drawbacks and advantages for each. One strategy involves separate analyses of cohorts at risk for transition to the next stage in a developmental process, and the second strategy employs a pooled sample of all cohorts. Their essay is exemplary in its sensitivity to conceptualizing data analysis to fit the hypothesized dynamic forms of a social process—in this case a developmental process of hierarchical stages. For a creative use of MCA to investigate possible explanations for the sex differences in U.S. morbidity, see Walter Gove and Michael Hughes (1979), "Possible Causes of the Apparent Sex Differences in Physical Health: An Empirical Investigation."

Inadequate attention in the data analysis to the dynamic form of the hypothesized social process can take more subtle forms than suggested by the extended illustration presented above. When theory guides data exploration, and the results of data exploration feed back to theory we expect the statistical analysis to parallel the theoretical discussion. Sometimes the statistical analysis falls short because the theorist does not follow through on the implications of preliminary data analysis. This appears to be the case in Rachelle Canter's "Achievement-Related Expectations and Aspirations in College Women," an excellent preliminary work (1979). Canter develops a multivariate path model of the development of aspirations in women from her exploration of cross-sectional data.

For the purposes of data exploration, this technique (via correlations and factor analysis) is often suitable and desirable. However, because all the variables in the model except ability (Scholastic Achievement Test scores) and achievement (grade-point averages) are psychological perceptions, their intercorrelation will tend to be greatly exaggerated as a function of being measured simultaneously. As Cook and Alexander (1980) demonstrate, data from longitudinal designs tend to favor ascriptive factors and structural constraints over social psychological explanations, since psychological variables are likely to be less strongly intercorrelated if the variables are measured at different times. The converse, relatively strongly intercorrelated psychological variables, is what we notice in Canter's cross-sectional data, especially since the psychological variables are closely interrelated conceptually. The result is that Canter concludes from her factor analysis that "there is considerable consistency in what women expect from themselves and their social environment," which may be too strong a conclusion. For exploratory analysis purposes, this problem of artifactually inflated correlations of

FIGURE 10.4. Path Model of Relationships Among Aspirations, Expectations, Past Achievement, and Ability

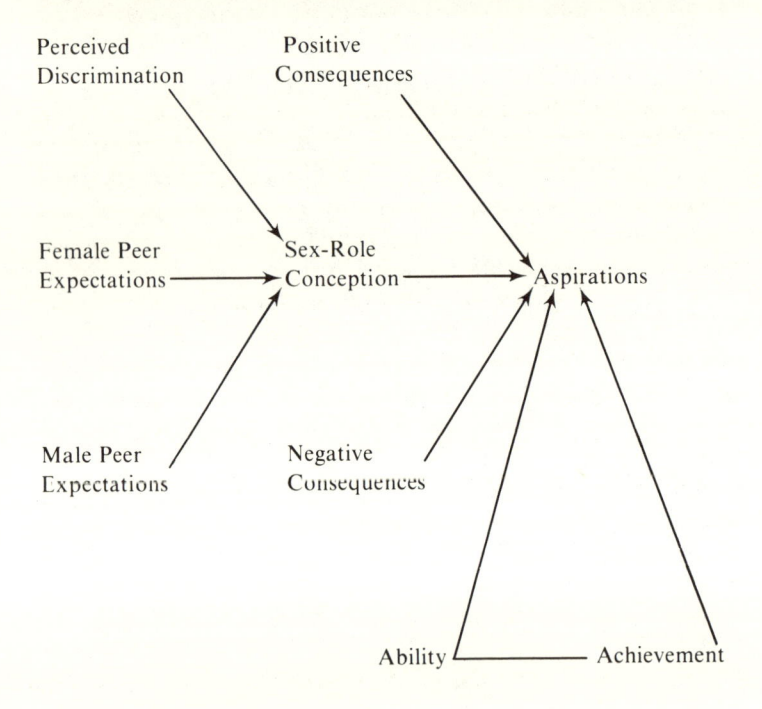

Source: Canter (1979, p. 463).

psychological variables may be mitigated by collecting the data for different psychological variables over a period of weeks. For a test of her developmental theory however, panel data is indicated, with the timing of data collection waves conforming to theoretical conceptualizations.

Canter's path model predicting aspirations was developed via the method of disappearing partial correlations (analogous to elaboration procedures in contingency table analysis) but indirect and direct effects in the path model are not explored by Canter with the available data. Although it is not persuasive to test a model with the same data used to develop it, the indirect effects discussed in the narrative are contradicted by the model as presented. In addition, the data exploration suggested that aspirations and expectations, the two outcome variables, are reciprocally related. Instead of incorporating reciprocal causation into her theoretical model, Canter drops the expectations variable from the model. Causal models permitting reciprocal causation between variables may be estimated by recognizing explicitly that the disturbance terms of those variables may be correlated; then one can proceed with two-stage least-squares estimation procedures. A creative example of this procedure in the context of age cohort analysis is presented in Ross

TABLE 10.2. Correlations of Aspirations with Expectations, Achievement, and Ability (N = 200)

	Aspirations
Sex role conception	.29[b]
Negative consequences of success	-.14[a]
Positive consequences of success	.40[b]
Expectations for success	.70[b]
Perceived discrimination	.16[a]
Female peer expectations	.16[a]
Male peer expectations	.12
Grade point average (achievement)	.25[b]
Scholastic Aptitude Test (ability)	.14[a]

[a] $p < .05$.
[b] $p < .01$.
Source: Canter (1979, p. 461).

Stolzenberg and Linda Waite's "Age, Fertility Expectations and Plans for Employment" (1977).

I chose Cummings and Taebel's and Canter's essays as pedagogical illustrations because, in both cases, the authors develop cogent and sophisticated theoretical arguments and present them in clear prose. It is entirely possible that the investigators tried most of the strategies I suggest and rejected them. Full exposition of data analysis strategies seldom appears in a published article; it may be that social researchers, like magicians, never publicly reveal all their secrets. What is more likely, I suspect, is that editors impose severe space limitations on authors and tend to suggest cutting out explorations of the data. In addition, many authors themselves are under pressure to publish their work in little dribbles to maximize the number of publications.

One result of the social conditions of social research publishing, I hypothesize, is that little help is available in print to the novice data analyst aside from textbooks that offer perhaps more than she needs to know about analyzing messy data, and polished journal articles that offer less. My aim in this essay has been to offer some help between these two extremes and to encourage sex-role researchers to connect the creativity and complexity of their theories with creative, complex data analyses.

REFERENCES

Acker, J. Issues in the sociological study of women's work. In A.H. Stromberg and S. Harkness (eds.), *Women Working*. Palo Alto: Mayfield, 1978.

Bean, F.D., and G. Swicewood. Intergenerational occupational mobility and fertility: A reassessment. *Amer. Sociological Review* 44(4), (August 1979):608–19.

Bibb, R., and W.H. Form. The effects of industrial, occupational, and sex stratification on wages in blue-collar markets. *Social Forces* 55(4), (1977):974–96.

Canter, R.J. Achievement-related expectations and aspirations in college women. *Sex Roles* 5(4), (1979):453–70.

Cook, M.A., and K.L. Alexander. Design and substance in educational research: Adolescent attainments, a case in point. *Sociology of Education* 53 (October 1980):187–202.

Cummings, S., and D. Taebel. Sexual inequality and the reproduction of consciousness: An analysis of sex-role stereotyping among children. *Sex Roles* 6(4), (1980):631–44.

Glenn, N.D. Cohort analysis. *Sage University Paper Series on Quantitative Applications in the Social Sciences, 07–005.* Beverly Hills and London: Sage, 1977.

Gove, W.R., and M. Hughes. Possible causes of the apparent sex differences in physical health: An empirical investigation. *Amer. Sociological Review* 44 (February 1979):126–46.

Huber, J., and G. Spitze. Considering divorce: An expansion of Becker's theory of marital instability. *Amer. Journal of Sociology* 86(1), (1980):75–89.

James, A. A multivariate comparative analysis of work-related symptoms of distance and campus undergraduates. *Research in Higher Education* 16(4), (1982):303–22.

Jamison, W., and M.L. Signorella. Sex typing and spatial ability: The association between masculinity and success and Piaget's water-level task. *Sex Roles* 6(3), (1980):345–53.

Kandel, D.B., R.Z. Margulies, and M. Davies. Analytical strategies for studying transitions into developmental stages. *Sociology of Education* 51 (July 1978): 162–76.

Leinhardt, S., and S.S. Wasserman. Exploratory data analysis: An introduction to selected methods. In *Sociological Methodology,* 1979.

Levine, R., M.-J. Gillman, and H. Reis. Individual differences for sex differences in achievement attributions? *Sex Roles* 8(4), (1982):455–66.

Namboodiri, N.K., L.F. Carter, and H.M. Blalock, Jr. *Applied Multivariate Analysis and Experimental Designs.* New York: McGraw-Hill, 1975.

Poole, M.E., and B.C. Law. Who stays? Who leaves? An examination of sex differences in staying and leaving. *Journal of Youth and Adolescence* 11(1), (1982):49–63.

Schuessler, K. *Analyzing Social Data.* Boston: Houghton Mifflin, 1971.

Stolzenberg, R.M., and L.J. Waite. Age, fertility expectations and plans for employment. *Amer. Sociological Review* 42(October 1977):769–83.

Taylor, P.A. Income inequality in the federal civilian government. *Amer. Sociological Review* 44(3), (1979):468–79.

Waite, L.J. Working wives and the family life cycle. *Amer. Journal of Sociology* 86(2), (1980):272–94.

11

Methods for Integrative Reviews

Gregg B. Jackson

Reviews of research are a fundamental activity in the behavioral sciences; they usually precede any major new research study and also are done as independent scholarly works. The focuses and purposes of such reviews vary substantially. Some investigators are primarily interested in sizing up new substantive and/or methodological developments in a given field. Some are primarily interested in verifying existing theories or developing new ones. Some are interested in synthesizing knowledge from different lines or fields of research, and still others are primarily interested in inferring generalizations about substantive issues from a set of studies directly bearing on those issues.

This study is addressed only to reviews with the last purpose. They are referred to as "integrative reviews." Parts of the chapter are probably applicable to other reviews, but no attempt has been made to discuss all types.

Given the importance and widespread conduct of integrative reviews, one might expect a fairly well-developed literature on methods, techniques, and procedures for conducting such reviews, but this is only now becoming the case. An earlier examination by this author of a convenience sample of 1960–75 books on general methodology in sociological, psychological, and educational research revealed very little explanation of matters other than the use of card catalogs, indexes to periodicals, and note taking. Of 39 books, only

---

The research reported herein was supported by Grant No. DIS 76-20398 from the National Science Foundation to the Social Research Group of the George Washington University. It is reprinted here by permission from the *Review of Educational Research* 50(3) (Fall 1980) pp. 438–460. Copyright American Educational Research Association, Washington, D.C.

four discussed how to define or sample the universe of sources to be reviewed, three discussed criteria by which to judge the adequacy of each study, and only two discussed how to synthesize validly the results of different studies. None of the discussions exceeded two pages in length.

Similarly, a preliminary examination of journal article titles in *Sociological Abstracts* (from January 1973 through October 1975), *Psychological Abstracts* (from January 1973 through December 1975), and *Current Index to Journals in Education* (from January 1973 through June 1975) revealed a dearth of work on integrative review methods. Entries under the following subject headings were examined: literature reviews, methods, methodology, research methods, and research reviews. Only five of the titles from approximately 2,050 entries appeared directly relevant. Upon examination, one of the sources proved to be inappropriate and another could not be located. The remaining three are discussed briefly later in this section.

Doing a good integrative review is never easy. It might seem that if all or almost all of the studies on the topic yielded similar results, the work would be easy, but this is incorrect because a careful reviewer is still obliged to determine whether all the studies have biases in the same direction that cause similar but invalid results. In the more prevalent case where the studies on the topic have different and apparently contradictory results, the work is obviously difficult. A good review of such research should explore the reasons for the differences in the results and determine what the body of research, taken as a whole, reveals and does not reveal about the topic.

Feldman (1971) wrote that there is "little formal or systematic analysis of either the methodology or the importance of... reviewing and integrating... the 'literature'" (p. 86). He suggests that "half-hearted commitment in this area might account in part for the relatively unimpressive degree of cumulative knowledge in many fields of the behavioral sciences" (p. 86). Feldman mentioned the problem of not being able to know the parameters of the universe of relevant studies. He suggested the utility of examining the distributions of results in more than one manner and indicated that inconsistent results can sometimes be explained by differences in subjects, treatments, settings, and the quality of the research methods. He warned that reviews should avoid hypercriticalness as well as hypocriticalness and indicated that a good review of research "shows how much is known in an area, [and] also shows how little is known" (p. 100).

Light and Smith (1971) discussed the present lack of systematic efforts to accumulate information from a set of disparate studies. They used a four-category typology to characterize most integrative reviews. The first category comprises those reviews that merely *list* any factor that has shown an effect on a given dependent variable in at least one study. A second category comprises reviews that *exclude* all studies except those supporting one given point of view. The third category is for those reviews that in one way or another *average* the relevant statistics across a complete set of studies. The fourth category is comprised of *vote taking*. This entails counting the positive significant results, the nonsignificant results, and the negative significant results; if a plurality of studies have one of these findings, then that finding is declared the truth. Light and Smith pointed out the weaknesses and resulting consequences of these procedures and proposed as a superior alternative a paradigm for secondary analysis of data from various studies having a common focus. The paradigm suggests that the data be analyzed within strata that take into account different characteristics of subjects, treatments, contextual variables, and effects of interaction among these. Ironically, Light and Smith failed to point out that such a paradigm could also be useful for integrating results of different studies when secondary data analysis is not feasible. (Time constraints, promises about the confidentiality of data, lost data sets, and other factors can sometimes preclude secondary data analysis.)

During the last few years, at least four investigators have initiated lines of work on improved methods for integrating results across studies. All began their work independently and without knowledge of the others' work, but luckily most of their efforts have been complementary rather than duplicative. In his 1976 AERA presidential address, Gene Glass (1976a) stated the need for "a rigorous alternative to the causal narrative discussions of research studies which typify our attempts to make sense of the rapidly expanding research literature," and proposed an approach that he calls meta-analysis; that approach is discussed later in this article. Rosenthal (1978) recently published a paper on aggregating results of independent studies by combining their probability values; his approach assumes that the studies are essentially replicates of each other, an assumption that is not necessary for Glass's approach. Schmidt, Hunter, and their colleagues (1973, 1976, 1977, 1979, 1982) have analyzed variations in the observed criterion validity of some personnel tests over repeated validation studies and demonstrated that the variation is substantially due to statistical artifacts rather than to situation-specific validity as had formerly been thought; their analysis is applicable whenever there are several independent studies using the same or similar measures, particularly when the studies have relatively small sample sizes. This writer (1978) has recently conducted an empirical investigation of the methodological approaches used in published review articles and queried journal editors and federal research agencies on the standards they used to judge integrative reviews. Some of the results of that work are discussed in this article.

This study primarily focused on the methods recently used for integrative reviews of empirical research in educational research, psychology, and sociology. The study had four objectives:

- to develop a conceptualization of the various methodological tasks of integrative reviews and of the alternative approaches to each task;
- to estimate the frequency with which recent reviews published in high-quality social science journals used each of the alternative approaches;
- to evaluate critically the strengths and weaknesses of the alternative approaches; and
- to suggest some ways in which more powerful and valid integrative reviews might be done.

DATA COLLECTION

Estimates of the frequency of approaches used in recent reviews were based on the coding of 36 review articles from prestigious social science periodicals. The articles were selected with stratified random sampling. Three articles were sampled from each of the 1975 and 1976 volumes of *Psychological Bulletin, Annual Review of Psychology, Review of Educational Research,* and *Annual Review of Sociology;* three articles were sampled from each of the 1974 and 1975 volumes of *Review of Research in Education;* one article was sampled from each of the 1975 and 1976 volumes of *American Sociological Review, Sociological Quarterly,* and *Social Problems.* Not all the sampled reviews were primarily directed towards inferring generalizations about substantive issues from a set of studies directly bearing on those issues, but all used at least part of the review for this purpose.

It appears useful to conceptualize the methodology of integrative reviews as involving six basic tasks: (1) selecting the questions or hypotheses for the review; (2) sampling the research studies that are to be reviewed; (3) representing the characteristics of the studies and their findings; (4) analyzing the findings; (5) interpreting the results; and (6) reporting the review.

These tasks are analogous to those performed during primary research (research that involves collecting original data on individual subjects or cases). Indeed, this conceptualization was based on the presumption that reviewers and primary researchers share a common goal and encounter similar difficulties. The common goal is to make accurate generalizations about phenomena from limited information.

RESULTS AND DISCUSSION

Task 1: Selecting the Questions or Hypotheses

This task was reconceptualized after coding the 36 randomly sampled review articles. Consequently, data were not coded for several important aspects of it.

Sometimes reviewers start with one or more very broad questions about a body of research, such as asking what the available research indicates about the relationship of X to other factors. Sometimes the initial questions may be more narrow, such as asking what increases Y. Occasionally the questions are quite specific, such as asking whether X_1 or X_2 increases Y.

The first two kinds of questions require a search for tentative answers and then verification of those tentative answers. The last kind of question is adequate for beginning the verification or hypothesis-testing stage.

Skill in asking good questions is probably as important to the progress of science as skill in finding tentative answers or verifying those answers. Zetterberg's work (1965, pp. 68–100) on propositional statements outlines alternative forms of relationships among variables. Questions for reviews can reflect any of these forms.

There are two distinct levels at which questions can be asked in a review. One level concerns only the phenomenon itself. For example, does X causally influence Y, or does X causally influence Y when Z_1 prevails but not when Z_2 prevails? The second level considers what variations in the methods of studies $S_1, S_2, \ldots S_n$ might account for variations in the results. If the findings of the studies appear consistent, the second level of question is superfluous. But if the findings of the studies display apparent inconsistencies, this level is essential for a productive investigation. Without it one may conclude that available research on the question is inconclusive when that is not true.

There are at least four important sources that ought to be consulted when developing questions, searching for tentative answers, or formulating hypotheses for a review. The time at which these sources ought to be consulted may vary with many circumstances, but it would seem that almost all reviewers can benefit from consulting them.

One source is available theory that bears on the topic. Just as theory can be useful in formulating questions or hypotheses for investigation in primary research, it can be helpful in formulating questions or hypotheses for a review. Theory can suggest potentially important relationships for investigation. It also can provide a framework for a series of questions.

The discerning examination of prior research on a topic is well-known to be useful for preparing and interpreting subsequent research on the topic. Similarly, the discerning examination of prior reviews on a topic can be useful when conducting subsequent reviews on that topic.

Seventy-five percent of the 36 randomly sampled integrative review articles cited previous reviews on the topic or on similar topics. But only 2 of these 27 provided any critique of the previous reviews.

The uncritical acceptance and use of previous reviews is as undesirable as the uncritical acceptance and use of any other research. One of the widely recognized responsibilities of a researcher is to examine critically all evidence used in his or her research. Important decisions about the focus, methods, and interpretations of a review are probably sometimes heavily influenced (consciously or unconsciously) by examinations of previous reviews on the topic or similar topics. There is nothing incorrect or undesirable about this if the reviewer uses scholarly judgment in evaluating the strengths and weaknesses of the previous work.

A third important source to consult when developing the questions or hypotheses for a review is the primary research that is expected to be reviewed. It is inadvisable to finalize the questions or hypotheses before examining the research studies that are expected to be used in the review. The examination may indicate that the initial questions or hypotheses are broader or narrower than is desirable. It may reveal that few studies directly bear on the selected questions or hypotheses, but that much more or better research is available on others of equal importance; or it may suggest that additional questions must be asked in order to interpret the answers to the initially selected ones.

One's intuition, insight, and ingenuity is a fourth source that ought to be consulted before finalizing the questions or hypotheses for a review. The most common challenge of integrative reviews of modern social science is finding order in apparent chaos. Intuition, insight, and ingenuity can help by suggesting new questions or hypotheses. These resources have so often proved important in virtually all fields of scientific endeavor that they shouldn't be overlooked when doing reviews. It should be remembered, however, that intuition and insight are grossly inadequate means of verifying tentative answers.

Task 2: Sampling

The results of any integrative review will be affected by the population of primiary studies upon which the review is focused and by the manner in which the actually reviewed studies are selected from that population.

Only one of the 36 randomly selected review articles reported the indexes (such as *Psychological Abstracts* of *Dissertation Abstracts*) or information retrieval systems used to locate primary or secondary studies for possible inclusion in the review. Only 3 of the 36 review articles reported the bibliographies of previous reviews that were searched to locate appropriate sources for the review.

It seems reasonable to assume that these results mainly reflect the failure of reviewers to report how they searched for sources, rather than a failure to use the indicated means for the search. It is almost inconceivable that most reviewers do not use indexes or bibliographies. The failure of almost all integrative review articles to give information indicating the thoroughness of the search for appropriate primary sources does, however, suggest that neither the reviewers nor their editors attach a great deal of importance to such thoroughness.

It is desirable that a reviewer locate as many of the existing studies on the topic as possible. There is no way of ascertaining whether a set of *located* studies is representative of the full set of *existing* studies on the topic. Consequently, the best protection against an unrepresentative set is to locate as many of the existing studies as possible. Cost-benefit considerations will, however, often suggest a search that is somewhat short of being thorough. In such cases, it is particularly important for the investigator to report the search strategy so that others can judge its adequacy. Reports of this information also allow subsequent reviewers to expand upon previous searches without needless and expensive duplication.

Data were collected on the extent to which the reviewer analyzed or discussed the full set of *located* studies on the topic. One of the 36 randomly sampled reviews analyzed or discussed the full set of located studies; 6 of the reviews clearly did not; and for the 29 other reviews, the information given in the published article was insufficient for making a judgment on this matter.

Data were not collected on how reviewers selected studies for analysis or discussions from the located studies. The coders' impressions from reading the reviews are that subsets were usually purposive samples of "methodologically adequate studies" or of "representative" studies. For instance, Glass (1976a) analyzed only those studies that had a control group. Sechrest (1976) indicated "No pretense of breadth or depth of coverage is made here. The materials cited were chosen because they fit a topic or illustrate a point to be made" (p. 9). Demerath and Roof (1976) indicated "It is manifestly impossible to summarize the entire recent literature. Instead, we have highlighted empirical studies that mark significant conceptual and/or methodological advances" (pp. 19–20).

If one wishes to analyze representative studies, there seems to be good reason for selecting the studies at random from the set(s) to be represented. Such selection does not assure a representative sample, but neither does any other approach, and random samples have the advantage of allowing an estimate of the probability of drawing a significantly unrepresentative sample.

Many reviewers wish to eliminate from their analyses those studies with results that have been seriously biased by methodological inadequacies. This seems reasonable and desirable, but it faces several difficulties. First, almost all research studies have at least a few methodological inadequacies. Second, methodological inadequacies do not always cause biased findings (as is discussed in more detail later in this paper). Third, it sometimes is difficult to determine reliably when methodological inadequacies have caused biased findings and when they haven't.

Some reviewers are inclined to use the simple strategy of eliminating all the studies with methodological flaws. They often end up with only one or two studies. When there is good reason to think all the eliminated studies have substantially biased results this strategy seems justified, but that seldom is the case.

Generally it is desirable to include in the analyses all studies for which there is not good evidence of biased findings. Replication is widely considered one of the most powerful tools for validating findings. If there is a consistent pattern in the findings of numerous studies on a topic, that pattern is more likely to be valid than a pattern exhibited by one or two allegedly unflawed studies.

When including studies with methodological inadequacies, it is important to analyze whether the different inadequacies are correlated with the studies' findings. When such correlations occur, they must be taken into account when making inferences about the phenomena being investigated. This is discussed further in respect to Task 4.

Task 3: Representing Characteristics of the Primary Studies

The representation of the characteristics of the primary studies is, in effect, the data collection of integrative reviews. The manner in which this is done can substantially affect the results and interpretation of the review.

Eight of the 36 reviews did not report the findings of most of the reviewed studies and did not indicate how many or what percentage of the studies had each type of finding or result. Only 18 of the 36 represented any of the findings of the primary or secondary research with an indication of the direction and magnitude of the result, and few did this for each analyzed finding. Only four of the reviews made any clear distinctions among significant positive findings, nonsignificant positive findings, nonsignificant negative findings, and significant negative findings.

It was fairly common for the reviewer to report the findings of individual studies in a manner such that it was impossible to judge how the reviewer had represented most of the findings when analyzing them. The impression of this writer is that such ambiguities were present in about 80 percent of the review articles. For instance, it was common to find reports that "Johnson found a relation between X and Y, but Alexander and Henderson did not." It was often impossible to know whether reported relations were statistically significant or included those that were "substantially" different from zero but not statistically significant. It also was common for findings of primary studies to be reported as statistically significant with no explicit indication of their direction.

Every reviewer has to represent the findings of the primary studies in some manner. Of the alternatives, magnitude measures with a directional sign are clearly the preferred way of representing the findings of the primary studies. To analyze these it is necessary to reduce them to a common metric, a chore that is not always easy but one on which some developmental work is currently being done (Glass et al. 1977a; Glass 1977c). The next best alternative is representing the findings as significant positive, nonsignificant positive, zero, nonsignificant negative, and significant negative. This alternative may be best if magnitude measures, or the data needed to calculate them, are not reported in most of the primary studies, but it is quite inferior to the first approach. This is discussed further in the next subsection. The worst of the alternatives is representing findings as a significant difference in one given direction or not so. This alternative should usually be avoided, for it produces ambiguous data unless most of the primary studies being reviewed used one-tailed tests of their hypotheses. For instance, if 9 out of 23 findings are significiantly positive, is this good evidence of a positive relation for the studied phenomena? It largely depends on how many of the remaining 14 studies had significantly negative findings.

Only one of the 36 randomly sampled review articles indicated that the reviewer, when encountering reports of primary and secondary studies that did not have all the information needed for the analyses, sought to get the information from other sources. It is just about inconceivable that 35 of the 36 reviewers did not encounter problems with missing information. What cannot be determined from this study is whether the failure of review articles to report efforts to obtain such information reflects an omission in the reports or a failure to seek the information. This writer suspects that it is some of each, but predominantly the latter.

In primary research today it is quite common for the investigators to make rather extensive efforts to minimize missing data and to report those efforts briefly. It would appear that similar efforts and reporting procedures are equally desirable for reviewers.

Task 4: Analyzing the Primary Studies

Analysis is the process by which the reviewer makes inferences from the primary studies. It includes judgments about the implications of identified methodological strengths or weaknesses in the primary studies, estimates of population parameters of the studied phenomena, and assessments of how varying characteristics of subjects, content, and treatments or suspected causal variables may affect the phenomena.

The analytic task of a review is seldom simple. Usually the findings of the examined studies vary moderately. Sometimes they vary so much as to appear contradictory.

Even in the rare case when the findings of the different studies are quite similar, a careful reviewer has some work. He or she should examine whether all of the findings are invalid. Congruent but invalid findings can occur if one or more methodological flaws are common to all the studies or if all the findings have about the same net bias (caused, however, by different methodological flaws in different studies). The latter is not particularly likely, but it is possible.

When the findings of the reviewed studies vary moderately or substantially, there can be at least three causes. The variations may be due to sampling error, differences in the methodological adequacy of the studies, or differences in the phenomena that were studied.

Sampling theory indicates that when there is a set of studies from a given population, the findings will vary some. About one-half of the study findings will be greater than the population parameter and about one-half will be less than the population parameter. In addition, in a large set of studies, if each study's findings are tested for statistical significance at the .05 level with the null hypothesis being the true population parameter, as many as 2.5 percent will have findings statistically significantly greater than the population parameter, and as many as 2.5 percent will have findings statistically significantly less than the population parameter. This sampling error has to be taken into account when judging whether or not variations in the findings should be considered congruent.

In the random sample of 36 examined reviews there were *at least* 18 that did not provide adequate information for judging whether or not the reviewer had interpreted variations in the findings of the primary studies in light of expected sampling error. In addition, there were several reviews where the authors clearly failed to take sampling errors into account when drawing inferences from a set of primary studies. For instance, Barnes and Clawson (1975) reported "The efficacy of advanced organizers has not been established. Of the 32 studies reviewed, 12 reported that advanced organizers facilitate learning and 20 reported that they did not" (p. 651). An examination of their evidence, however, indicates that the 12 studies yielded statistically significant positive findings and that the other 20 may have yielded nonsignificant (+) findings, zero difference, nonsignificant (−) findings, and perhaps significant (−) findings. Barnes and Clawson did not report how many of the 20 studies yielded each type of finding. If the population value was zero, and all 32 studies tested their hypotheses at the .05 level, only about one of the studies would be expected to have statistically significant (+) findings, rather than the 12 that actually did. Unless several of the 20 studies had statistically significant (−) findings, Barnes and Clawson's data strongly suggest that advanced organizers have at least a small positive effect on learning. If there are considerably more than the expected number of both significant (+) and significant (−) findings, it is possible that the population has a bimodal distribution or that the examined studies are of two or more populations, despite appearances to the contrary.

Twenty-six of the 36 reviewers described what were considered to be the major methodological difficulties or shortcomings of the primary research that was reviewed. Some of the other 10 reviewers may have examined these difficulties or shortcomings but failed to report on them.

If more than a small portion of the reviewed studies have serious methodological weakness, these limitations can sometimes lead to invalid inferences unless their effects are considered before drawing inferences about the topic. No data were collected on how identified weaknesses in the methods of the primary studies were taken into account when making inferences from those studies. The impression of this writer is that the most common approach was to indicate that inferences about the topic were unreliable if many weaknesses were found. The second most common approach appeared to be to discard the methodologically "inadequate" studies and base the inferences on the remaining ones. A third approach was to identify weaknesses in the research that supported one point of view, thus discrediting the evidence for that point of view, without applying the same standards of methodological adequacy to research that supported another point of view.

All three strategies raise the question of what constitutes a serious threat to the validity of a given study and what does not, but there is no simple answer. It should be noted, however, that the actual threat to the internal and external validity of a study is not determined exclusively by the design of the study. Campbell and Stanley's (1973) important and widely read monograph on experimental and quasi-experimental designs shows which threats are controlled by various different designs; but the monograph does not indicate which threats are likely to be trivial in a given study or which threats can be reasonably controlled by other means. For instance, instrument decay may be a serious threat to internal validity when using a rater's judgment of people's emotional health, but is unlikely to be a serious threat when measuring children's heights using the kind of device that is common in physicians' offices. Similarly, obtrusive measures of a variable pose a more serious threat of testing effects than do unobtrusive measures. Also, studies where the data are collected over a brief period of time are less likely to have their validity threatened by history and maturation than are studies where the data collection extends over a longer period of time.

It is the impression of this writer that some reviewers will label as methodologically inadequate any studies not having experimental or strong quasi-experimental designs. Sometimes this is appropriate, but the above discussion ought to indicate that it is not always appropriate.

A third reason for varying findings among a set of studies on a given topic is that the phenomena investigated in the studies varied. The variables may have been measured by instruments that appeared to tap the same constructs but did not. Supposedly similar levels of variables may have differed because the instruments used had dissimilar metrics despite tapping the same constructs. In addition, contextual variables that were unmeasured in some or all of the studies may have varied among the studies. Under any of these circumstances it is possible for all findings in an apparently incongruent set to be valid.

When the findings of the reviewed studies vary, statistical analyses can be used to explore which differing aspects of the studies may have contributed to differences in the findings. For instance, in a set of 20 studies, there may be: (1)

15 that had adequate controls for instrument decay and 5 that did not; (2) 11 that used measurements that may have had obtrusive effects and 9 that did not; (3) 7 that used only male college freshmen as the participants, 5 that used both male and female college freshmen, and 8 that used a random sample of adults aged 20–25 in a middle-sized industrial town; and (4) 6 that used a recall measure of the criterion and 14 that used a multiple-choice measure of the criterion. The findings of each study need to be expressed in terms of a common magnitude measure (how this can be done is discussed later); statistical procedures can be used to explore the extent to which the differences above *may* have affected variations in the findings. Given the small number of studies in this example, univariate tests would need to be used. If the results were not statistically significant when tested at a modest probability level, such as .10, we would be able to conclude that there is little reason to think that any of these characteristics seriously affected the findings. If one or more of the statistical tests yielded significant results, however, then we would conclude that some of the characteristics *may* have affected the results.

None of the 36 randomly sampled reviews did such an analysis in a multivariate manner, where two or more of the varying characteristics of the primary and secondary studies were simultaneously tested for relationships with the varying results. Two of the 36 reviews did univariate analyses, examining the relationship of a single characteristic of the studies to the varying results. Another 5 of the 36 reviews made such analyses in a systematic discursive manner, whereby they discussed how one or more characteristics of the primary and secondary studies were related to differences in the findings across the full set of analyzed studies. A total of only 7 out of the 36 articles reported analyses by any of the above three means.

The impression of this writer is that most of the reviews did suggest some explanation for the observed differences in the findings, and many offered some evidence for the explanation, but the evidence was usually less systematic than that coded as "systematic discursive." Reviews were not coded as using systematic discursive analyses unless they discussed how a characteristic of the study related to differences in the findings across *all or most studies* in the analyzed set. Most reviewers failed to be so thorough. Instead, they would do something like point out that the study having the highest Y also had a higher X than the study that had the lowest Y, while not mentioning the relation between X and Y in the other studies on the topic.

It is not at all clear why systematic analyses of the correlates of varying findings are not done more often in integrative reviews. Clearly, it is not because reviews fail to encounter discrepant findings; 32 of the 36 sampled reviews examined primary studies with at least some discrepancies in the findings. Perhaps it is because the reviewers find so many differences among studies that they despair of being able to find systematic relations, or perhaps it is because the reviewers simply have not thought to do such analyses.

Whatever the reasons, the effect of this omission is obvious and serious. Without such analyses reviewers will sometimes incorrectly infer that the findings of a reviewed set of studies are contradictory and that the available evidence is inconclusive. It seems almost certain that some of the confusion that surrounds many topics in the social sciences is a result of reviewers' frequent failure to search systematically for explanations of the varying results. Multicolinearity or weak correlations will sometimes preclude explanations of the variations, but the search ought to be conducted despite such possibilities.

Glass's Meta-analysis

Glass's meta-analytic approach involves transforming the findings of individual studies to some common metric, coding various characteristics of the studies, and then using conventional statistical procedures to determine whether there is an overall effect, subsample effects, and relations among characteristics of the studies and the findings. The original data for each unit of analysis in a study are *not* used. Rather, the unit of analysis is the study, and summary data from each study are analyzed. For instance, if there is a set of experimental studies that investigate the impact of X on Y, for *each* study one might code the average age and social-economic status of subjects, the duration of treatment (X), the setting in which the treatment was applied, an estimate of the reactivity or "fakeability" of the outcome measure used, an estimate of the internal validity of the research design, and the date when the study was conducted. Then these variables would be used in a univariate or multivariate manner to predict a standardized measure of the findings. Glass (1977c, p. 39) suggests that when most of the studies are experiments with a control group, the standardized measure of the findings should be a standard score difference measure calculated by the mean difference of the experimental and control groups divided by the within-group standard deviation of the control group. He suggests that if most of the studies are correlational and use different measures of association, the standardized measure should be a product-moment correlation; he provides formulas for estimating product-moment correlations from various other measures of association such as the point-biserial correlation, Spearman's rank-order correlation, and Mann-Whitney U, as well as t and F (Glass et al. 1977a, pp. 4–10).

The meta-analytic approach has a number of strengths. First, it is a systematic, clearly articulated, and replicable approach to integrating findings from a set of studies. Second, it can be used with information from both the best and the less-than-best studies on a topic, but with controls for possible biases caused by various flaws in the available studies. Third, it can provide estimates of the population parameters. Fourth, when using multivariate statistical procedures, it provides a method for simultaneously investigating the relationships among studies' methods, population of subjects, scope conditions, duration of treatments, and findings. No approach used to date for integrative reviews has been capable of doing this. There are, however, some limitations and problems in the application of this approach. It should be noted that *most* of these difficulties are common to all analytic approaches to integrative reviews. Nevertheless they are important to keep in mind when doing or interpreting meta-analyses.

One limitation of the meta-analytic approach is that it can assess only relatively direct evidence on a given topic. Sometimes a topic of importance has not been directly investigated but there are studies with indirect evidence that can be reviewed and woven together. For instance, if the topic is "Will substance X reduce chronic depression in adults?" there may not have been any studies on that question, but there may have been studies of the effects of X on depression in baboons and studies of the similarity of effects of other chemicals on depression in baboons and humans. The meta-analytic approach can be used for evaluating the results within each set of studies, but it cannot weave together the evidence across sets of studies on related topics.

A second limitation of the meta-analytic approach is that it cannot be used to infer which characteristics of studies on a given topic *caused* the differing results. Statistical analyses can provide good evidence of causal relations only when the data are from experiments or strong quasi-experiments, or when there is a clear temporal ordering of the independent variables—which is not the case when analyzing characteristics of completed studies. The characteristics of reviewed primary studies are not systematically manipulated in an experiment or quasi-experiment, even when all the studies used experimental designs to investigate the given topic.

A third problem when doing meta-analysis is the lack of common metrics for the measures used and reported in the various primary studies on the topic. There are at least three aspects of this problem. First, different constructs are sometimes studied under a single topic. For instance, the outcomes of various studies on the effects of psychotherapy include emotional health, happiness, social relations, and others. Second, for any given construct there are alternative measures, the metrics of which may not be equivalent. For instance, what is described as upper-middle SES on one measure mãy be described as middle SES on a second measure. Third, the statistics used to measure a relationship between two or more variables can vary in different studies. Studies may use r_p, t, rho, tan, or others.

Glass has suggested the first aspect of the problem is often not serious and can be ignored (1977d). He argues that all the various outcomes mentioned above in the example of psychotherapy are aspects of mental health and can be lumped together for a general investigation of the effects of psychotherapy. When the effects are thought to perhaps vary among different outcome constructs, Glass suggests including data that indicate major distinctions among the constructs and using them as a predictor in multiple regression analyses or a stratifying factor for nested analyses. Though Glass directs his suggestion to variations in the construct of the criterion, it is equally appropriate for variations in the construct of predictors.

The second aspect of the problem is one that past reviewers have often complained about. When different studies use different measures of the same construct, and when the measures have not been validated, there is a serious question about the equivalence of the values generated by the different measures. For some characteristics such as age and sex, there is seldom any problem, but for others such as self-image and social support, there often will be a problem for which there is no simple solution. It should be noted that it is incorrect to rationalize that variations existing in the metric of some variable will only serve to reduce the strength of the relationship between that variable and some second variable and therefore can be ignored if strong relationships are found. This will be true if the variations in the metric are not correlated with the second variable, but generally there is no assurance that this will be the case.

Glass and his students have already completed some work that reduces the third aspect of the problem. They have assembled equivalency functions for some statistics and developed others (White 1976; Glass et al. 1977a). Some of these functions are mathematical identities, but others are approximations. To date that work has not indicated the conditions under which the approximations become poor ones. This is a fertile subject for future research.

It should be noted that Glass's proposal of analyzing standardized effect measures obscures the absolute magnitude of the effects. It is possible for the average standardized effect for one subset of studies to be twice that of another subset of studies whereas the absolute magnitude of the difference is trivial for all practical purposes.

A fourth problem faced in meta-analysis is achieving valid and reliable coding of the characteristics of the primary studies to be analyzed. When the set of reviewed studies is relatively small, the coding is likely to be done by a single investigator, but coding, say, 40 studies may require as many as 60–80 hours, and this work may be stretched over a 4- to 6-week period, thus raising serious threats to coding stability. When large numbers of studies are being reviewed, a number of coders may be used, which raises the additional problem of intercoder reliability. Memory failures, boredom, and migraine headaches can undermine sustained coding reliability. When the coding is done over a lengthy period of time, intercoder reliability should be assessed more than once; reliability over time should also be assessed, and periodic retraining may be needed.

A fifth problem faced in meta-analysis is how to control for the effects of poor research design among the reviewed studies. Glass provocatively argued that it is wasteful to discard poorly designed studies from the analysis because "a study with a half-dozen design or analysis flaws may be valid...[and] it is an empirical question whether relatively poorly designed studies give results significantly at variance with those of the best designed studies" (p. 4). Glass suggests testing whether methodological characteristics such as the reactivity of the outcome measure and the internal validity of the design are related to the distribution of findings. He does not specify how this should be done other than by examining the covariation between the design characteristics and the findings. This analysis, however, is not as straightforward as it may appear.

The results of the analysis may be misleading if there is not at least a modest number of studies with good overall design. Since there usually is no reason to think that the relationship between the quality of design and the findings is linear or monotonic, there is no basis for extrapolating from the relation that holds for studies of poor and mediocre design to the studies with good design. In integrative reviews of some topics, there may be very few, if any, primary studies with good control of the threats to internal and external validity, and thus in these cases the possible effects of less-than-good design cannot be assessed.

If there is a modest number of well-designed primary studies, but a much larger number of studies with poor or mediocre design, regression slopes computed for the full sample of cases can still provide misleading results. This is because regression lines are fitted so as to minimize the squared deviations of the bivariate or multivariate points, and relatively little weight would be given to the small number of points from the well-designed studies.

In short, the meta-analytic approach is an important contribution to social science methodology. It is not a panacea, but it will often prove to be quite valuable when applied and interpreted with care.

In general, it appears that current integrative reviews often fail to proceed beyond the stage of grounded hypothesis development. The reviewers carefully examine the available primary research, discover some apparent pattern or lack of pattern, and then report it. Seldom do the reviewers systematically and rigorously determine the extent to which the primary research coincides with the perceived pattern. Rigorous hypotheses testing is as desirable in reviews as it is in primary research, and, as was discussed above, there are better methods for doing it than were recently applied in most reviews.

Task 5: Interpreting the Results

Seven of the 36 randomly selected reviews induced and reported new theory, confirmed old theory, or disproved old theory; 6 of the 36 induced and stated recommendations for policy or practice, and 4 of those 6 discussed conditions that might affect the impact of the policies or practices; 28 of the 36 suggested desirable focuses or methods for future primary or secondary studies on the topic; and only 3 of the 36 suggested desirable focuses or methods for future *reviews* on the topic or related topics.

There are other types of conclusions that the review articles may have stated that were not coded, but it is surprising that only one-third made conclusions about theory, policy, or practice. It may be that most integrative reviews are oriented toward making suggestions for improving the primary research, or it may be that most start with the aim of making suggestions for theory, policy, or practice, but subsequently decide to withhold inferences because they judge the available evidence to be inconclusive. The latter reason seems unlikely since 32 of the 36 studied reviews reported one or more inferences about the topic.

This writer has no strong suspicions as to why most review articles do not make suggestions for future reviews. Perhaps it is because reviewers do not think carefully about the methods of doing a review; perhaps it is because after completing the often herculean task of doing a review, the reviewers would not want to wish the task on anyone else, or perhaps it is for some other reason. Regardless, it is quite apparent that the resulting omission is unnecessary and harmful to the progress of science. As with primary research, it is virtually impossible to do a major review carefully without encountering some ideas for improved methods and some additional questions that need to be answered. These ideas and questions may be a valuable contribution to other investigators and ought to be reported, even if they can be used only after the accumulation of further primary research.

Task 6: Reporting the Review

A widely held precept in all the sciences is that reports of research ought to include enough information about the study that the reader can critically examine the evidence. This precept probably also should apply to integrative reviews, since such reviews are a form of research. As a minimum, it is widely held that the report ought to describe the sampling, measurement, analyses, and findings. Where unusual procedures have been used, it is expected that they will be described in some detail.

The previously discussed results indicate that many of the 36 review articles failed to report important methodological aspects of the review, particularly with respect to sampling and representing characteristics of the primary studies. Only 1 of the 36 articles reported the indexes and information retrieval systems used to search for primary studies on the topic. Only 3 of the 36 reported the bibliographies used as a means of locating studies. Only 7 indicated whether or not they analyzed the full set of located studies on the topic, instead of some subset. Only one-half of the 36 reported the direction and magnitude of the findings of *any* of the reviewed primary studies, and few did this for *each* finding. In addition, very few review articles systematically reported characteristics of the primary research that may have affected the findings.

One-half of the 36 reviews often reported findings of the primary studies by stating a generalization followed by the citation of some studies that support the generalization. Such reporting can be very misleading. Unless used in conjunction with reporting the findings of each study, this practice also precludes the reader from critically examining the inferences of the reviewer without consulting the original reports of each study. For instance, Dusek (1975) reported "there is considerable evidence that during classroom interactions teachers treat groups of students differently (e.g., Davidson 1972; Good and Brophy 1970; Schwebel and Cherlin 1972)" (p. 662). Hoffman (1972) reported "Several investigators report that while dependency in boys is discouraged by parents, teachers, peers, and the mass media, it is more acceptable in girls (Kagan and Moss 1962; Kagan 1964; Sears, Rau and Alpert 1965)" (p. 144). Both of these statements give an implication of consensus among the available research evidence, but neither of the statements would be *incorrect* even if the majority of the located evidence contradicted their points. Jacoby (1976) made a similar type of statement, reporting "Not surprisingly studies which utilized price as the only independent variable (261, 262, 316, 452) generally found a significant main effect" (p. 336). Though "generally" in this statement provides an explicit warning that the evidence was not entirely consistent, it still does not indicate what percentage of the studies supported the finding, nor does it indicate the magnitude of the findings. Some reviewers stated juxtaposed generalizations such as "Several studies found that X causes Y (Ace 1967; Bace 1953; Cace 1969; Dace 1970), but a few did not (Eace 1968; Face 1970)." This type of presentation is less ambiguous than the above examples, but it still obscures the magnitude and statistical significance of the findings.

Taken together, these results indicate that integrative review articles commonly fail to report their studies in the detail that is fairly common for primary research articles.

CONCLUSION

It appears that prior to 1976, relatively little thought was given to the methods for doing integrative reviews. Such reviews are critical to science and social policymaking and yet most are done far less rigorously than is currently possible. It seems likely that some of the confusion that surrounds many topics in the social sciences is partly a result of nonrigorous reviews of research on the topic.

Serious consideration of the following suggestions should substantially improve the validity and usefulness of integrative reviews. The suggestions are enumerated under the six tasks discussed in earlier parts of this article.

Task 1: Selecting the Topic(s)

1. The topic(s) of a review should be specific and stated as a question or hypothesis for investigation. "Sex stereotyping," "social stratification," "intelligence," and "psychosis" are not topics but rather subjects under which there are a large number of possible topics.

2. When the topic involves both factual and value issues, those issues ought to be clearly distinguished.

3. If the evidence available on a selected topic is mostly indirect, it may be desirable to revise the topic so that it is more congruent with the available evidence.

4. An effort should be made to ascertain whether a tentatively selected topic has recently been, or is currently being, reviewed.

5. Previously completed reviews of the topic or similar topics ought to be consulted to assess what is already known on the topic, to refine questions or hypotheses for the forthcoming review, to anticipate problems that may be encountered when doing the review, to gain familiarity with alternative ways of doing the review, and to acquire ideas for interpreting the results of the forthcoming review.

6. When searching for previously completed reviews of the topic or similar topics, one usually should search at least four kinds of sources: published reports of primary research, books, doctoral dissertations, and published review articles.

7. When searching for previous reviews of the topic or similar topics, it is often desirable to consult the literature in more than one discipline. Many topics that have been researched in one discipline have also been researched in other disciplines.

8. Previous reviews of the topic or similar topics should be examined critically in respect to their methods, results, and interpretations.

Task 2: Sampling

9. The search for primary research on a topic ought to be thorough within clearly stated boundaries. These boundaries are ideally defined in terms of the topic scope, but practical limitations of time and cost-effectiveness will usually require that they be defined in terms of the reference sources, descriptors, and years of publication that are initially searched. An unthorough search yields a convenience sample of unknown bias, and such samples are as undesirable for cumulative reviews as they are for primary research.

10. Searches for primary research can cover at least eight types of sources: books, published articles, doctoral dissertations, government reports, unpublished reports to major funding organizations, papers presented at professional meetings, works in progress, and works that have never been publicly reported.

11. Searches for primary research of a given topic can be done by at least six methods: using computerized information retrieval systems; using printed indexes to research literature; examining bibliographies of located sources ("snowballing"); consulting experts on the topic, including proponents of alternative points of view; skimming journals most likely to publish research related to the topic; and perusing books on library shelves near those books located by other means. The first three methods are usually the most efficient, but experienced reviewers usually find the latter three methods to be valuable supplements.

12. Some of the most useful indexes to social science research studies are the following: ABI/INFORM (C); Abstracts in Anthropology (P); Books in Print (P); Child Development Abstracts and Bibliography (P); Cumulative Book Index (P); Current Contents—Social & Behavioral Sciences (P); Current Index to Journals in Education—ERIC (P & C); Dissertation Abstracts International—Comprehensive Dissertation Abstracts (P & C); Education Index (P); Government Reports Announcements & Index (P); Index Medicus (P & C); Index of Economic Articles (P); International Bibliography of Economics (P); International Bibliography of Political Science (P); International Political Science Abstracts (P); Journal of Economic Literature (P); Library of Congress Catalog (P & C); Management Contents (P & C); National Clearinghouse for Mental Health Information (C); National Institute for Mental Health Grants and Contracts Information System (C); National Technical Information Service (C); Psychological Abstracts (P & C); Research in Education—ERIC (P & C); Smithsonian Science Information Exchange (C); Social Science Citation Index—SOCIAL SCISEARCH (P & C); Sociological Abstracts (P & C); Subject Guide to Forthcoming Books (P). The letters in parentheses indicated whether the index is printed (P) and/or computerized (C).

13. The difficulty in effectively using computerized and printed indexes should not be underestimated. The appropriate subject descriptors for any topic not only vary from one index to another, but they also vary within any index over a period of years (because common terminology varies over the years). In addition each index's coverage of sources on a given topic is limited, but in different ways for different indexes, and in different ways within an index over the years. Information retrieval experts who are experienced in using the chosen indexes can substantially facilitate a search. Such experts are sometimes available at university libraries or computer centers.

14. All located sources on the topic ought to be cited in the bibliography. This can save future reviewers of the topic a great deal of effort, and allow scholars knowledgeable about the topic to judge the thoroughness of the literature search.

15. Either the full set of located studies, or some sort of random sample of the full set of located studies ought to be analyzed in the review. Purposive

samples and convenience samples have the same weaknesses for integrative reviews as they do for primary research, but a purposive sample may sometimes be a useful supplement to a random sample, especially one selected as exemplary in some respect.

Task 3: Representing Characteristics of the Primary Studies

16. The findings of each primary study should be represented by a standard score difference measure or a common measure of association, if possible. Such representation provides the most flexibility and power for statistical analysis. A reviewer should never represent findings as statistically significant in one direction or not so, unless most of the primary studies used one-tailed tests of their hypotheses.

17. When reports of the primary studies do not have all the information needed for the review, the information usually ought to be sought from detailed final reports of funded research or from the authors.

18. When more than 20 or 30 research reports are to be coded, the reliability of coding over time should be checked. If two or more coders are being used, intercoder reliability also ought to be assessed periodically. Retraining should be provided as needed. The primary studies should be coded in random order, and if there is more than one coder, assigned randomly to coders. This helps to randomize some of the systematic coding biases that may exist.

19. If the reliability of the data that are to be analyzed is low (say below 0.65) interpretation of the results ought to be made with full recognition that characteristics of the studied phenomena could have been masked by the coding error variance. Low reliability will not affect point estimates if the errors tend to cancel each other out (over coders or over time). But low reliability will cause substantial underestimates of the associations among two or more variables.

Task 4: Analyzing the Primary Studies

20. Substantial advances in methods for analyzing and synthesizing the findings of primary studies have been made during the last few years. It is the opinion of this writer that every responsible reviewer must be fully familiar with at least the methods developed by Gene Glass and his colleagues and those developed by Jack Hunter and Frank Schmidt. The Glassian methods are now collected and expanded in a book (Glass, McGaw, and Smith 1981). Hunter and Schmidt have developed methods to estimate the amount of variance in a set of findings that is likely to be due to random sampling error and other sources of spurious variance. Their contributions are described in a recent monograph (Hunter, Schmidt, and Jackson 1982).

21. When there is a serious question about the sets of primary studies, the units of analysis, the variables, the weights, or the methods that are appropriate for the analysis, it is often desirable to do the analyses using each of the alternatives, and to compare the results. When the results are similar, the questions need not be resolved; when the results are quite different, the question does need to be resolved, or conclusions should be withheld.

22. An integrative review should not test just a single hypothesis, but rather, to the extent possible, the full set of plausible competing hypotheses. When some of the plausible hypotheses are not tested, they should at least be briefly mentioned in the report of the review. Such an approach is the basis of firm inference, whether used in a primary study or a cumulative review (Platt 1964).

Task 5: Interpreting the Results

23. The magnitude as well as the significance of the results of the review's analyses ought to be taken into account when interpreting the results.

24. The results of review analyses ought to be compared with the results of previous reviews on the topic or related topics. When there are substantial differences, explanations for them ought to be sought.

25. The reviewer should help the readers make inferences about theory, policy, practice, future primary research, and future reviews on the topic, when a review provides a basis for such inferences. Good cumulative reviews require substantial resources and consequently ought to be made useful to as wide an audience as is possible.

Task 6: Reporting the Review

26. The methods used in the review ought to be described in enough detail so that it would be capable of being replicated by another investigator. When publication space limits prohibit this, the most important methodological features (including sampling, representation of characteristics of the primary studies and their findings, and analysis) ought to be most thoroughly described, and reference should be made to a full report that can serve as an adequate guide for replication.

27. The topics of the review should be clearly and explicitly stated. Sometimes a topic can be usefully clarified by stating what is not included in the topic, but might be thought to be included by the readers.

28. The descriptors and the years of literature covered with each index that was used, should be reported.

29. The report should clearly indicate if the analyzed sets of studies do not include all the located studies, and if so, how they were selected from the full set of located studies.

30. When fewer than about 40 primary studies are being reviewed, the data on the major characteristics of the studies and their findings ought to be reported in concise tables. The findings ought to be reported in the form in which they were analyzed in the review and perhaps in their original form.

31. The major descriptive and inferential statistics from all the analyses of the review ought to be reported, not just those that had substantial or statistically significant results, or those the reviewer finds particularly interesting. A large number of results usually can be presented quite compactly in a matrix or table.

REFERENCES

Barnes, B.R., and E.V. Clawson. Do advance organizers facilitate learning? Recommendations for further research based on an analysis of 32 studies. *Review of Educational Research* 45 (1975):63759.

Bracht, G.H., and G.V. Glass. The external validity of experiments. *American Educational Research Journal* 5 (1968):437–69.

Campbell, D.T., and J.C. Stanley. *Experimental and quasi-experimental designs for research.* Chicago: Rand McNally, 1963.

Coleman, J.S. Recent trends in school integration. *Educational Researcher* 4(7), (1975):3–12.

Demerath III, N.J., and W.C. Roof. Religion—recent strands in research. *Annual Review of Sociology* 2 (1976):19–33.

Dusek, J.B. Do teachers bias children's learning? *Review of Educational Research* 45(4), (1975):661–84.

Feldman, K.A. Using the work of others; some observation on reviewing and integrating. *Sociology of Education* 44 (1971):86–102.

Glass, G.V. *Primary, secondary, and meta-analysis of research.* Presidential address to the Annual Meeting of the American Educational Research Association, San Francisco, April 1976(a).

Glass, G.V. Primary, secondary, and meta-analysis of research. *Educational Researcher* 5(1976):3–8 (b).

Glass, G.V., D. Coulter, S. Hartley, S. Hearold, S. Kahl, J. Kalk, and L. Sherretz. *Teacher 'indirectness' and pupil achievement: An integration of findings.* Unpublished manuscript, Universitiy of Colorado, 1977 (a).

Glass, G.V. Personal communication, October 1977 (b).

Glass, G.V. Integrating findings: The meta-analysis of research. *Review of Research in Education* vol. 5. 1977 (c).

Glass, G.V. Personal communication, November 1977 (d).

Glass, G.V., B. McGaw, and M.L. Smith. *Meta-Analysis in Social Research.* Beverly Hills: Sage, 1981.

Hoffman, L.W. Early childhood experiences and women's achievement motives. *Journal of Social Issues* 28(2), (1972):129–55.

Hunter, J.E., F.L. Schmidt, and G.B. Jackson. *Meta-Analysis: Accumulating Research Findings Across Studies.* Beverly Hills: Sage, 1982.

Jackson, G.B. *Methods for reviewing and integrating research in the social sciences.* Final report to the National Science Foundation 1978. (NTIS No. PB28374-7/AS).

Jacoby, J. Consumer psychology: An octennium. *Annual Review of Psychology* 27 (1976):331–58.

Light, R.J., and P.V. Smith. Accumulating evidence: Procedures for resolving contradictions among different research studies. *Harvard Educational Review* 41 (1971):429–71.

Light, R.J. Capitalizing on variation: How conflicting research findings can be helpful for policy. *Educational Researcher* 8(9), (1979):7–14.

Platt, J.R. Strong inference. *Science* 146 (1964):347–53.

Rosenthal, R. Combining results of independent studies. *Psychological Bulletin* 85 (1978):185–93.

Rosenthal, R. and D.B. Rubin. Interpersonal expectancy effects: The first 345 studies. *The Behavioral and Brain Sciences* 3 (1978):377–415.

Schmidt, F.L., J.G. Berner, and J.E. Hunter. Racial differences in validity of employment tests: Reality or illusion? *Journal of Applied Psychology* 58 (1973):5–9.

Schmidt, F.L., J.E. Hunter, and V.W. Urry. Statistical power in criterion-related validation studies. *Journal of Applied Psychology* 61 (1976):473–85.

Schmidt, F.L., and J.E. Hunter. Development of a general solution to the problem of validity generalization. *Journal of Applied Psychology* 62 (1977):529–40.

Schmidt, F.L., J.E. Hunter, K. Pearlman, and G.S. Shane. Further tests of the Schmidt-Hunter Bayesian validity generalization procedure. *Personnel Psychology* 32 (1979):257–76.

Schultz, C.B., and R.H. Sherman. Social class, development, and differences in reinforcer effectiveness. *Review of Educational Research* 46 (1976):25–59.

Sechrest, L. Personality. *Annual Review of Psychology* 27 (1976):127.

Smith, M.L., and G.V. Glass. Meta-analysis of psychotherapy outcome studies. *American Psychologist* 32 (1977):752–60.

White, K.R. The relationships between socioeconomic status and academic achievement. (Doctoral dissertation, University of Colorado, 1976). *Dissertation Abstracts International* 38, 1977, 5067A-5068-A. (University Microfilms No. 77-3250.)

Zetterberg, H.L. *On theory and verification in sociology* (3rd ed.). New York: Bedminster Press, 1965.

12

The Impact of Societal Biases on Research Methods

Patricia B. Campbell

BIAS AND "OBJECTIVE RESEARCH"

Bias is a particular tendency or inclination which prevents reasonable, knowledgeable, thoughtful consideration of a question (Harmon 1973). Since bias prevents reasonable consideration of a question, one who is affected by bias will have difficulty dealing "objectively" with questions related to that bias. With objectivity the basis of the scientific method and empirical research, it would appear that, conceptually, the presence of bias renders objective research impossible.

Yet this is not an issue that has received great attention in the research community. Perhaps this lack of attention occurs because the researcher, the follower of the scientific method, is presumed to be "objective," unmoved by bias. Bias is frequently seen as something that can affect the subjects of social science, but not the author. This is unfortunate because, as Thomas and Sillen (1972) have concluded, researchers are not immune to the "disease and superstition of American racism." Too, as Gideonse (1977) has suggested, if a society is sexist, then so perhaps is its science and its scientists. The myth of the objective researcher is one which most of us believe; yet it is a myth.

Writers in the philosophy of science have long commented on the difficulty of attaining scientific objectivity. As Nagel (1961) wrote, "It is not easy in most areas of inquiry to prevent our likes, aversions, hopes, and fears from coloring our conclusions" (p. 488). Russell's (1959) comment is even stronger: "As soon as any strong passion intervenes to warp the experts' judgment, he [sic] becomes unreliable, whatever scientific equipment he [sic] may possess" (p. 276).

There are some data to support the opinions of philosophers about the difficulties of obtaining objectivity. Sherwood and Nataupsky (1968) found that scientists' conclusions as to the relative importance of heredity and environment in determining race differences in intelligence could be predicted reasonably well from biographical characteristics of the investigator such as the researcher's age when the research was published, family background, and education.

Once people have made a decision or accepted a judgment, it is difficult to get them to change. For example, in a study of student behavior, half of the subjects in a class were told that a new instructor was a "warm person" while the other half were told that the instructor was "cold." Even though all the subjects saw the same instructor in the same setting, the ones who expected the intructor to be cold described the person as "cold," while the ones expecting the instructor to be warm rated the person as "warm." These results continued even when the subjects were told that the initial information they were given was arbitrary (LaBrecque 1980).

Neither research nor researchers are value-free or even value-neutral. Researchers frequently believe that values and assumptions enter the research process only when subjective measures are employed and that science (and scientists) should be value-neutral (Sherif 1979). But as Gideonse (1977) has explained, social science cannot be separated from the confounding effects of human values, time and the phenomena of human consciousness. More specifically:

- Everything in social science research is susceptible to one's value premises.
- The social scientist is always conceptually inside the system or phenomena being studied.
- Every social scientist must adopt some vantage point for analysis, be it their own values or those of society (Gideonse 1977, p. 7).

Much of the basis of the objectivity of research is founded on the assumptions of: (1) an objective researcher; (2) the openness of researchers and the general public; and (3) the value-free nature of science. Yet, these assumptions have questionable validity. A purely objective social science is, as Nagel (1961) informs us, a vain hope. Knowledge is socially distributed; what one takes for reality is determined by his/her place in the social structure (Long Laws 1978) and that perception of reality has influenced research methods including topic selection, design and data analysis, sampling, measurement, and the generation of conclusions.

BIAS AND TOPIC SELECTION

"The things a social scientist selects for study are determined by his [sic] concept of what are socially important values. The student of human affairs deals only with material to which he [*sic*] attributes 'cultural significance'" (Nagel 1961, p. 485). Traditionally the "cultural significance" of women (and minority men), other than in a pathological sense, has been minimal, as has the amount of research being done on them. Topic selection has been related to this "cultural significance" as well as to a number of other factors including funding and publishing opportunities.

In today's world, few institutions and even fewer individuals are willing or able to assume the financial burdens of doing research. Most researchers must look to private and public funding sources for support and thus match their research interests to the interests and priorities of the funding agency. In general, research on women, on equity, and other issues is less likely to receive funding from either the private or public sector than is work in many other areas (Klein and Goodman 1980; Saario 1980).

Another large influence on topic selection is the opportunity for publishing. Most researchers want or need to publish their work. Through publishing, research is disseminated, feedback is generated, and decisions are made about hiring, firing, and promotion. "Publish or perish" is still very much a reality in the academic and research and development worlds. The unpublished researcher is soon the unemployed researcher. Thus the research focus of journals is an important influence on topic selection. In general, research journals publish little research specifically related to women.

In an analysis of the articles published in five leading education journals from 1973 to 1978, Lockheed and Stein (1980) found that 303 or 13.5 percent of the 2,239 articles dealt with women, girls, and education. The percentage of articles on women and education ranged from 5.0 percent of the articles that appeared in *Journal of Educational Measurement* to 17.4 percent of the brief reports appearing in *Child Development*.

An analysis of the *American Educational Research Journal* (AERJ) produced similar findings. In 1978, two of the 44 articles published focused on women in education. In 1979, two of the 33 articles published by AERJ were on women in education.

When work related to women is published, it is frequently in the area of sex differences. However because of the tendency for journals to publish positive findings, it is studies which find sex differences rather than those finding "sex similarities" or "sex-unrelated characteristics" which are published and become "part of the literature" (Jacklin 1979).

Research topics dealing with women are frequently devalued. Steinem found during her tenure as a Wilson fellow:

> My own work on theories of gender-based power was academically suspect as single-factor analysis while my neighbor's work on one man's military acts during one decade was thoughtful, scholarly and basic. (Steinem 1980, p. 98)

This devaluing must, of necessity, influence the research that is done. As Shakeshaft concluded from her 1979 study of the content of dissertations in educational administration, we have asked "Why can't Johnny read?" not "Why can't Janey add?" or "Are women feminizing our schools?" not "Are men polarizing our schools and causing them to become violent places?"

As a result of these biases on research topic selection, "At a period when the public is demanding information and explanations about social inequity, the academic professions are unable to provide them, in large part because the relevant questions are not on their research agenda" (Long Laws 1978, p. 10).

Minority females are particularly left out of research agendas. Lightfoot (1978) and Pollard (1976) concluded, after surveying the literature, that minority females have not been the focus of the research agenda of social science research, and in fact, are presented in the literature minimally if at all.

The absence of information on minority females is not surprising. Babladelis (1976) concluded that, "a significant portion of what is considered important to study is determined by male investigators," and that male investigators, particularly majority males, rarely study females, particularly minority females. Babladelis is not alone in her conclusions. Researchers from education (Shakeshaft 1979; McDonald 1977), sociology (Tresemer 1975) and psychology (Acker and Van Houton 1974; Kearney 1979) have all commented on how the preponderance of male researchers has limited the selection of research topics.

The bulk of work in the social sciences has focused on phenomena and areas in which men dominate: territoriality, aggression, politics and economics (Shakeshaft, 1979). Work on patterns of research, in early childhood education, has found that the majority of male researchers (who are themselves the majority of researchers) tend to study control of persons and institutions, philosophy and methodology; while women tend to study the family, the role of women and the development of young children (McDonald 1977).

Stereotypes about appropriate behavior for people also affect selection. For example, investigating subjects' desires to remain teachers rather than to move from teaching to administration is seen as a study of deviant behavior rather than a study of different types of aspiration (Shakeshaft 1979). Similarly, other than work by people like Oakley (1975), unpaid housework and child rearing are not considered "work" and studies on the labor force or on working do not deal with the millions of full-time homemakers. Topics of interest to women (e.g., victimization by rape and abuse) have often been ignored or have received less attention than other topics such as aggression (Frieze, Koeske, and McHugh 1981). Bias can affect topic selection when researchers give the topic a different name based on the sex of respondents. For example, a study of male competitive game playing would be seen as "achievement behavior" while a comparable study of females is described as "female game playing behavior" (reported in Frieze, Koeske, and McHugh 1981).

While not reflecting the dominant male model may be considered deviant, so may acting outside prescribed sex roles. As the Committee on the Status of Women in Sociology (1980) has commented, there is an emphasis in research, on the problems of female-headed households and single-parent families, but there is an absence of studies of problems associated with two-parent families, because, just as situations outside prescribed sex roles are defined as problematic, situations in which people conform to prescribed sex roles are assumed to be nonproblematic. In the same vein the problems of "working" mothers and the problems of children in child care are studied, not the problems of "nonworking" mothers nor of children who are at home full time. The problems of "nonworking" fathers are examined but never, at least in relation to the family, are the problems of "working" fathers. Mother-child interactions are studied extensively, father-child interactions rarely.

Bias in topic selection has contributed to gaps in the knowledge base. It has also allowed us to close our minds to testing alternative hypotheses or explanations for behaviors that fall outside our expectations.

BIAS AND DESIGN

Bias can affect the design of research in a number of ways, such as familiarity with the appropriate literature; selection of independent variables; control of sources of invalidity and data analysis. Bias can affect our knowledge of appropriate literature in a number of ways. First, as indicated earlier, one of the results of bias in topic selection is the existence of gaps in research areas, where information pertinent to a research topic just does not exist. The devaluing of research on women may also mean that the research that is done is published out of the mainstream, in sources that may be difficult to find and are not routinely read by the majority of researchers. Even if work is available, too often the biases mentioned in the section on topic selection, discourage researchers from seeing how work on, for example, sex-roles or racial bias in testing could affect their work on achievement motivation or self-concept.

Lack of researcher awareness of relevant literature can cause the selection of independent variables to become a source of bias. For example, socioeconomic status is often used as an independent variable with a mixed sex example. This occurs even though common methods of categorizing people according to socioeconomic status use the status of the husband or father as determinants of a woman's status (Acker 1973; Edelsky 1979).

A third source of bias can be found in the controlling of potential sources of invalidity. Obviously if one is not aware of, or sensitive to possible threats to validity, it is impossible to control for them. For example, much research has failed to take into account the different socialization of females and males. Although most studies attempt to control for situational factors by making the external situation the same for females and males, what is overtly the same may be psychologically very different for females and males (Frieze, Koeske, and McHugh 1981).

Finally, the techniques used in the analysis of the data can themselves be a source of bias. Data which do not fit the expected pattern can be thrown out as was the case in Yerkes's research on sex roles in chimps, often used as evidence of the genetic basis of sex roles. Yerkes threw out the data for two females "because they were highly dominant" (Herschberger 1948).

Biased analysis techniques are also seen in analyses of sex differences in intellectual performance. Using separate regressions for each sex, sex differences are concluded when significant beta weights are found for one sex but not the other. This is not correct. "In order to establish a sex-related difference, one must show that the relation of two variables has a *significantly different* relation for boys than it does for girls. This can only be established if both sexes are included in the same regression equation" (Jacklin 1979, p. 6). This is also true in correlational analysis. Only when significant differences between correlations of females and males are found, can a sex-related difference be concluded.

A major effect of bias on design has been in the lack of use of existing information about women and men in the design to increase the validity of the study. For example, Caplan (1975) found that the presence of an adult investigator caused boys to become more antisocial, while the absence of an adult was more conducive to finding no sex differences in antisocial behavior. A study of antisocial behavior designed without knowledge of this information and without the necessary controls could then lead to an inaccurate conclusion about sex differences and a reinforcing of stereotypes about boys' antisocial behavior. Based on her work, Caplan (1975) concluded that the elements of the experiment may play a greater role in producing or abolishing sex differences in behavior than do real sex differences.

Her conclusions have been supported by several other researchers. For example, Serbin and O'Conner found that children were more apt to play with stereotypically sex appropriate toys when there were others in the room than when they were alone (Greenberg 1978). Thus studies of children's play behavior designed with others in the room may be apt to find "sex appropriate" behavior.

In their extensive review of the literature, Maccoby and Jacklin (1974) reviewed a number of studies whose results could affect studies of sex differences. They found that college men performed better when observed by peers while college women's performance did not change. They also found that boys persisted longer in a task with a boy watching than when an adult was watching—while the age and sex of an observer had little effect on girls.

Different situations were found to affect boys' activity levels and speed of work, while not affecting girls' activity levels. Not knowing or controlling for information like this, particularly in studies of sex differences, means that the independent variable being studied may be the *interaction* of the situation with the sex of the subject rather than subject's sex.

Controlling for confounding variables may not be enough, because some of the variables are themselves biased. The most obvious of these, as mentioned earlier, is socioeconomic status. Nichols described the ways that socioeconomic status can be biased and the way that the bias can affect research in one area, language, in the following passage:

> Unfortunately, common methods of categorizing people according to SES use the husband's or father's status as the determinant of the women's status even though the woman may have more education than the man in question. In addition, "stenographer" and "mechanic" may be classified as same status occupations. The result is that women are often misclassified because of a bias in the methodology and are found to use different language than men. What those language differences may actually reflect, in some cases, is the fact that women are being compared to men of presumably the same, though in reality, lower-class status and also to men whose jobs are likely to be less language oriented (Nichols reported in Edelskey 1979, p. 7).

The major result of bias in design is the generation of inaccurate information and incorrect conclusions based on that information. Particularly in areas involving sex roles and differences, bias in design may have influenced research toward researcher expectations and away from examinations of complex realities—a dangerous direction for both research and resarchers.

BIAS AND SAMPLING

The composition and selection of samples and the generalizations made from those samples can all be affected by bias. In the past several years, a number of researchers from different fields have commented that, traditionally, males have been the population studied in social science research. Babladelis wrote, in 1976, that "a significant portion of our knowledge is based on the study of male behavior only." Her conclusion, which related to research in psychology, has been supported by other psychologists (Kearney 1979; Long Laws 1978) and has been generalized in other social science areas such as education (Shakeshaft 1979), anthropology (Carey 1979), and sociology (Committee on Women in Sociology 1980).

The concerns of these researchers have their basis in fact. Of the 226 studies published by the *Journal of Personality and Social Psychology* in

1968, 31 percent studied males, 15 percent studied females, 44 percent had mixed sex samples, and 10 percent did not indicate the sex of the sample (Carlson 1971). A 1970–71 replication of the study found 27 percent male samples, 7 percent female samples, 53 percent mixed sex samples, and 14 percent sample sex not indicated (Schwabacker 1972). A further replication, in 1974, found 12 percent male samples, 28 percent female samples, 43 percent mixed sex samples, and 15 percent sex unspecified (Reardon and Prescott 1977).

At least for this journal, a number of single sex samples were used. Previously, these samples were disproportionately male; however, the most recent data have found the single sex samples to be predominantly female.

There are a number of widely known research studies that have used single sex samples (e.g., McClelland's work on achievement motivation). There is some indication that McClelland and his co-workers were aware that sex differences probably existed in achievement motivation; however, they neither pursued these possible differences nor expanded their samples to include females. Neither did they adequately specify that their theories or conclusions applied only to men (Atkinson 1958).

Another example can be found in the area of management and careers. Until recently, research on management and careers typically examined white, middle-class male subjects. Surveys on educational levels might cover females and males; however, when occupations and other work-related variables were examined, the subjects were primarily male. For example, in her analysis of "The Relation of Education and Status of Work to Economic Differences Between Blacks and Whites," Gottfredson (1977) used a sample composed of 20,000 white men, 1,500 black men, and no black or white women. Similarly, in 1978, Blau and Duncan published a massive study of occupational structure based on a survey of 20,000 men (race unspecified).

More recently, a major study of occupational changes at midlife, currently being completed, has used a sample of 370 midlife males, but generalizes its results beyond the sample to "individuals" (Osherson 1981). As Jelnick (1978) concluded, patterns and norms brought to light by this type of research are not necessarily applicable to a wider population.

Although such results are not necessarily applicable to wider samples, authors frequently try to generalize them to the population as a whole. An analysis of single sex studies found that in 1970–71, 92 percent of the studies with male subjects and 61 percent of the studies with female subjects, published in the *Journal of Personality and Social Psychology,* were generalized to both women and men (Schwabacker 1972). By 1974, 97 percent of the studies with female samples, and 92 percent of the studies with male samples, were generalized to both sexes (Reardon and Prescott 1977). Other work in 1972 found 92 percent of the studies with male subjects were overgeneralized, while 62 percent of the studies with female subjects were (Dan and Beekman 1972).

Some work has been done on why researchers study only one sex. Prescott and Foster (1974) found that the reasons 67 researchers gave for working with single sex samples fell into three major categories: (1) scientific; (2) practical; and (3) extra scientific. "Scientific" reasons given were, for example: "sex differences were known to exist in the phenomena and the investigator did not wish to explore them," and "the theory being studied was restricted to one sex." The sex of the subject pool and the need to keep the number of subjects to a reasonable size were given as the "practical" reasons for using single sex samples, while the "extra scientific" reasons were that the use of one sex reduced the variability of the data and that the experimental conditions favored the use of one sex over the other.

The use of single sex samples seems to be related to the topic being studied. McKenna and Kessler (1974) found that while men were more apt than women to be studied, whether women or men served as subjects depended, to some extent, on the topic. If a research topic was in an interpersonal area, researchers were more apt to include women than they were if the topic were, for example, on aggression or on careers. Eagly found, as well, that research on aggression has typically studied males, while research on social influence has relied on females (Frieze, Koeske, and McHugh 1981). Also, women have been more apt to be included in samples of research on topics stereotypically considered to be feminine, such as parent-child interaction (in reality, mother-child interaction) (Condry and Condry 1976) and on questions dealing with children, child rearing and work around the house (Steinmetz 1974).

However, studies about the family and its economic and social status have relied almost totally on male samples. The male "head of the household" has been the basic unit for much data collection on the family. If, for example, the husband was a bricklayer, then the family was construed as blue collar, regardless of whether the wife was a teacher, a waitress, or unemployed. The U.S. Census, source of much of the data for studies on families, has encouraged the use of male only samples. In 1850, the census dealt only with "male persons over fifteen." By 1970, the census had changed considerably but "for ease of tabulation" the male was still considered head (and representative) of the household (Steinmetz 1974).* This step, for ease of tabulation, helped to continue to encourage studies on families with male samples.

Sampling procedures can also contribute to the selection and use of skewed samples. For example, the Gallup poll has a very well-developed sampling procedure to gather information on its sample of 1,500 "representative" subjects; however, male subjects are interviewed beginning at 6:00 P.M.,

---

*The 1980 U.S. Census had respondents indicate themselves, which household member was "head of household." It may be, however, that years of assuming that the head of household was male, and that female head of household indicated male absence, will mitigate the impact of this change.

while female subjects are interviewed beginning at 4:00 P.M. (Gallup 1980). Most of the female interviews are conducted from 4:00 to 6:00 P.M., thus eliminating the responses of most professional "working women" who would not be home before 6:00 P.M.

Except in stereotypically feminine areas dealing with care of children and of home, men and boys have traditionally been the population studied. And except in the case of research specifically on minorities and on pathological areas such as cultural deprivation, delinquency and the effects of discrimination, the men and boys that have been studied have been white.

Another effect of bias on sampling is the inaccurate attribution of characteristics to one sex based solely on the study of the other sex. Witelson (1977) found male dyslexics less lateralized than males who are not dyslexic. Only boy dyslexics were studied, yet the study has been used to explain sex-related differences (McGee 1979).

Nowhere is the effect of bias on sampling more evident than in the popular and growing field of the life cycles or stages. Beginning with Erikson's (1959) work on the "Eight Stages of Man" to Levinson's *Seasons of a Man's Life* (1978), the study of life cycles has focused on male subjects. When women are examined, it is in terms of how they fit or don't fit the male model. Without empirical verification, women are said to go through the same cycles as men (Stewart 1977) or are said to go through cycles that are antithetical to mens' (Sheehy 1977).

Based on a survey of the literature on life cycles, Sangiuliano (1978) concluded that "Mostly we (researchers) persist in seeing her (woman) in the reflected light of men" (p. 44). Her conclusion seems to hold in a number of other social science areas as well.

BIAS AND MEASUREMENT

Since tests and measures are the basis of data collection for research, bias in measurement has a large effect on research. One of the largest areas of testing for research and evaluation purposes is in achievement and aptitude. It appears that sex bias in the content of these tests can affect performance. Milton (1957) found that females did better on test problems dealing with stereotypically feminine activities than they did on problems with a more stereotypically masculine orientation. This finding was substantiated by other studies which found that girls tended to do better on questions dealing with human relations and that boys tended to do better on questions dealing with science and economics (Coffman 1961; Donlon 1971). Tests have a tendency to include more items dealing with "masculine" areas than "feminine" areas.

The number of females and males appearing in a test item may also have an influence. A 1977 analysis of four achievement tests found a tendency for adolescent girls to be more apt to get an item correct, if more girls than boys, or if equal numbers of boys and girls were mentioned (Donlon, Ekstrom, and Lockheed 1977).

Donlon (1971) has also suggested that changing the content of items on the math section of the Scholastic Aptitude Test (SAT) to include more subject matter of greater familiarity to females, had the potential to reduce the sex difference in test scores by about twenty points.

The influence of item content on performance seems primarily to affect adolescents and adults. To date, research on younger children has been mixed; findings range from effects similar to those found in older students (Montemayor 1974) to no effect (Plake, Hoover, and Loyd 1978) to a reverse effect, with black girls doing better on traditionally masculine content and black boys doing better on traditionally feminine content (King and Blount 1975).

Test format has also been shown to affect the performance of females and males. Murphy (1977) found that switching from essay or fill in the blank questions to more objective items such as multiple choice, produced higher scores for males. This was found to be true in a wide range of subjects, including those stereotypically considered masculine, such as math, and those stereotypically considered feminine, such as reading comprehension.

"Sex differences" can be created or eliminated through the selection of items to be included in a test (Dwyer 1976). A test can be slanted toward either sex or balanced to assure sex equity through the format (multiple choice, fill in the blank, essay) or the proportion of stereotypically masculine, feminine, or neutral contents of items selected to make up the test (Campbell and Scott 1980).

While a number of tests may be unconsciously "balanced" or "unbalanced" by sex, intelligence testing is one of the few areas in which some tests have been deliberately designed so that females and males will score approximately equally. These "balanced" IQ tests may then be used in research on sex differences in intelligence. The results of this research would not provide accurate data on sex differences in intelligence. Results would be biased by one of the original intentions of the test—to equalize female and male scores. Studies using unconsciously, unbalanced tests have greater problems. For example, sex differences found in mathematics may be real differences or may just be indicators that the test was slanted by item content or type to favor one sex or the other.

The effects of bias in measurement go beyond aptitude and achievement tests to other areas as well. In the past, vocational interest inventories severely limited test takers' job choices by sex. Interest inventories had separate questions and even separate tests for females and males. Even when the same person took both forms of a vocational interest inventory, the feminine form indicated the person's interests were in low paying, low status job areas, while the masculine form indicated the person's interests were in high paying, high status job areas. Routinely, females were given job options such as nurse, executive secretary and stewardess, while males with similar interests were given job options such as physician, business executive and airline pilot (AMEG 1973). Title IX of the Education Amendments of 1972 prohibited the use of vocational tests which suggested one set of occupations for males and another for females. The implementation of this law has changed the situation and now, as Tittle and Denker (1977) conclude, "many of the characteristics of vocational interest inventories that caused charges of sex bias in interpretive materials and gender linked items are being eliminated."

Bias can also have an impact on personality tests. For example, social value scales base their scoring on a knowledge of common social values. The correct answer is the common social value, while an incorrect answer is assumed to be based on ignorance of common social values. Answers that are not based on ignorance but rather on opposition to common social values, or to differences in situations are still considered incorrect and are not differentiated from answers based on ignorance (Jorgensen 1973).

Almost any measure can be influenced by bias and, as a result of that influence, cause inaccurate results to be generated. These results can be influenced by such obvious factors as the language of a question such as, "Should Jews be forced to leave the country?" (Bettelheim and Janowitz 1964); or to more subtle factors such as using the Scholastic Aptitude Test to track changes in sex differences in mathematics, but not accounting for the potential effect of a test content change to the SAT, as in removing item types that favored females (Dwyer 1976).

Campbell and Scott (1980, p. 9) concluded that "in a society that professes educational equity as a goal, equitable nonstereotyped test content is a simple matter of justice." It is also a matter of good research.

BIAS AND CONCLUSIONS

After the design has been developed and implemented, the data collected and analyzed, the researchers' final task is to generate the section of the research article that is most often read and quoted—the conclusion. It is to this section most harried practitioners most often turn to find the short- and long-term meaning of a study. It is also from this section that textbook authors, journalists and politicians find their "research" quotes. The researchers' expectations, colored by stereotypes, can—and frequently do—have more effect on the generation of conclusions than do the data.

Stereotypes can be found in the explanation of data as well. The data are reported, but the explanations of results are based on stereotypes rather than other, equally plausible but nonstereotyped explanations. For example, based on their study of infant behavior when confronted with a barrier keeping them from a desired object, Goldberg and Lewis (1965) concluded that boys attack and girls give up. This is a reasonable explanation of the data showing that girls tend to cry and boys tend to try to push or climb the barrier and is also an explanation that reinforces our stereotypes. An equally plausible nonstereotyped explanation that the more verbal girls were crying not because they gave up, but to attract the attention of those who could remove the barrier was not, however, reported. Thus the reader was left with the impression that one sex sought to solve problems while the other did not, instead of the alternative that both sexes sought to solve problems, but used different styles (reported in Parlee 1975).

Researchers do fit stereotyped conclusions to the reality of the data, but this is not always the case as Nobles (1973) asserts, "oftentimes researchers have demonstrated only one insignificant finding and regardless of their own results, concluded their studies with assertions which were contrary to their own evidence."

CONCLUDING REMARKS

While this paper has attempted to be a comprehensive look at bias in research, it has several limitations. The first is that it has been limited to an examination of the effects of sexism on research methods. It has been shown that the effects of racism can be just as negative on research and indeed, racism and sexism often combine to affect research methods (Campbell 1982). Also, the paper has been based on the acceptance of a traditional, statistically oriented model of research. Little has been said about the role that bias has played in the development of this model itself and the ways that the use of "scientific method" of research has limited the generation of knowledge.

Bias does indeed affect researchers and the research that they do. As the preceding has indicated, because of the sexism in our society—and in researchers who are part of that society—research findings can be limited and inaccurate. However efforts can and are being made to rectify some of the negative effects. More work is being done by people like Gilligan (1980) to involve multiethnic samples of women and men in the development and testing of theories. Social science organizations like the American Psychological Association (Frieze, Koeske, and McHugh 1981) and the American Sociological Association (Committee on the Status of Women in Sociology 1980) have developed guidelines on nonsexist research and are working, as are other groups such as the American Educational Research Association, to insure that the research of tomorrow is more accurate than that of yesterday and today.

REFERENCES

Acker, J. Women and social stratification: A case of intellectual sexism. *American Journal of Sociology* 72 (4), (1973):936–45.

Acker, J., and D.R. Van Houten. Differential recruitment and control: The sex structure of organizations. *Administrative Sciences Quarterly* 6 (1974):152–69.

AMEG Commission Report on Sex Bias in Interest Measurement. *Measurement and evaluation in guidance* 6(3), (1973):171–74.

Atkinson, J.W. (ed.). *Motives in fantasy, action and society.* Princeton, N.J.: Van Nostrand, 1958.

Babladelis, G. Editorial. *Psychology of Women Quarterly* 1(1), (1976):3–10.

Bettleheim, B., and M. Janowitz. *Social change and prejudice.* New York: Free Press, 1964.

Blau, P.M., and O.D. Duncan. *The American occupational structure.* New York: Free Press, 1978.

Campbell, P.B. Race and sex bias in research methods. In H. Metzel (ed.) *The encyclopedia of educational research,* New York: Macmillan, 1982.

Campbell, P.B., and E. Scott. Non-biased tests Can Change the Score. *Interracial Books for Children Bulletin* 11(6), (1980):7–9.

Caplan, N., and S.D. Nelson. On being useful: The nature and consequences of psychological research on social problems. *American Psychologist* 28(3), (1973):119–211.

Caplan, P.J. Sex differences in anti-social behavior: Does research methodology produce or abolish them? *Human Development* 18(6), (1975):444–60.

Carey, C.B. The anthropology of women: An advocacy position. ERIC Document, ED 156543, 1979.

Carlson, R. Where is the person in personality research? *Psychological Bulletin* 75 (1971):203–19.

Coffman, W.E. Sex differences in response to items in an achievement test. *Eighteenth Yearbook, National Council on Measurement in Education,* 1961, 117–24.

Committee on the Status of Women in Sociology. Sexist biases in sociological research: Problems and issues. *ASA Footnotes* 1 (1980):8–9.

Condry, J., and S. Condry. Sex differences: A study of the eye of the beholder. *Child Development* 45 (1976):812–19.

Dan, A.J., and S. Beekman. Male vs. female representation in psychological research. *American Psychologist* 27(11), (1972):1078.

Donlon, T.F. Content factors in sex differences on test questions. A paper presented to the annual meeting of the American Educational Research Association, Boston, 1971.

Donlon, T.F., R.B. Ekstrom, and M.E. Lockheed. Performance consequences of sex bias in the content of major achievement batteries: Final report. ERIC Document ED151415, 1977.

Dwyer, C.A. Test content and sex differences in reading. *Reading Teacher* 29 (1976):753–57.

Edelsky, C. Genderlects: A brief review of the literature. ERIC Document ED165187, 1979.

Erikson, E. Growth and crises of the healthy personality. *Psychological Issues* 1(50), (1959):1–171.

Frieze, I., R.D. Koeske, and M. McHugh. *Guidelines for non-sexist research.* Washington, D.C. APA Division 35 Task Force, Washington, D.C., 1981.

Gallup, G. *The Gallup poll: Public opinion, 1979.* Princeton, N.J.: Scholarly Research, 1980.

Gideonse, H.D. Sex roles, inquiry and social policy. A paper presented to the American Educational Research Association, New York, 1977.

Gilligan, C. Woman's place in man's life cycle. *Harvard Educational Review* 49 (1980):431–46.

Goldberg, S. and M. Lewis. Play behavior in the year-old infant: Early sex differences. *Child Development* 40 (1969):21–31.

Gottfredson, L.S. The relation of education and status of work to economic differences between blacks and whites. ERIC Document, ED150059, 1977.

Greenberg, S. *Right from the start.* Boston: Houghton Mifflin, 1978.

Harmon, L.W. Sexual bias in interest measurement. *Measurement & Evaluation in Guidance* 5(4), (1973):496–501.

Herschberger, R. *Adam's rib.* New York: Pellegrini and Cudahy, 1948 (Reprint edition: Harper & Row, 1970).

Jacklin, C.N. Methodological issues in the study of sex-related differences. A paper presented at the Annual Meeting of the American Psychological Association, New York, 1979.

Jelnick, M. Career management and women. ERIC Document ED150272, 1978.

Jorgensen, C.C. IQ tests and their educational supporters. *Journal of Social Issues* 29(1), (1973):33–40.

Kearney, H.R. Feminist challenges to the social structure and sex roles. *Psychology of Women Quarterly* 4(1), (1979):16–31.

King, P., and H.P. Blount. The influence of sex-typed math test problems on performance of sixth grade students. A paper presented to the National Council on Educational Measurement, Washington, 1975.

Klein, S.S., and M.A. Goodman. *Federal funding to promote sex equity in education: 1980.* Washington, D.C.: Women's Educational Equity Act, U.S. Department of Education, 1980.

LaBrecque, M. On making sounder judgments. *Psychology Today* (June 1980):33–42.

Levinson, D.J. *The seasons of a man's life.* New York: Knopf, 1978.

Lightfoot, S.L. Socialization and education of young black girls in schools. In *Conference on the Educational and Occupational Needs of Black Women,* vol. 2. Washington, D.C.: NIE, 1978, 3–32.

Lockheed, M.E., and S.L. Stein. The status of women's research in educational publications. *Educational Researcher* 9(2), (1980):11/0915.

Long Laws, J. Feminism and patriarchy: Competing ways of doing social science. ERIC Document, ED166081, 1978.

Maccoby, E., and C.M. Jacklin. *The psychology of sex differences.* Stanford: Stanford University Press, 1974.

McDonald, G. Two windows on research. ERIC Document, ED133053, 1977.

McGee, M.G. Human spatial abilities: Psychometric studies and environmental genetic, hormonal and neurological influences. *Psychological Bulletin* 86 (1979):889-918.

McKenna, W., and S.J. Kessler. Differential treatment of males and females as a source of bias in social psychology. A paper presented to the annual meeting of the American Psychological Association, New Orleans, 1974.

Milton, G.A. The effects of sex role identification upon problem solving skills. *Journal of Abnormal and Social Psychology* 55 (1957):208-12.

Montemayor, R. Children's performance in a game and their attraction to it as a function of sex typed labels. *Child Development* 45 (1974):152-56.

Murphy, R.C. Sex differences in examination performance. A paper presented to the International Conferencce on Sex Role Stereotyping, Cardiff, Wales, 1977.

Nagel, E. *The structure of science:* New York and Burlingame: Harcourt, Brace and World, 1961.

Nobles, W.W. Psychological research and the black self concept: A critical review. *The Journal of Social Issues* 29(1), (1973):11-31.

Oakley, A. *The sociology of housework.* New York: Pantheon, 1975.

Osherson, S.D. *Adaption to occupational changes at midlife: A predictive longitudinal study.* NIE Project G-77-0049, 1981.

Parlee, M.B. Psychology. *SIGNS: A Journal of Women in Culture and Society* 1(1), (1975):119-38.

Plake, B.S., H.D. Hoover, and B.H. Loyd. An investigation of differential item performance by sex on the Iowa tests of basic skills. A paper presented to the National Council on Measurement in Education, Toronto, 1978.

Pollard, D. Special needs of black women in educational research and development. In Doris Leckie (ed.), *NIE/AERA planning conference to increase the participation of women and minorities in educational research and development.* Washington, D.C.: NIE, 1976, 31-58.

Prescott, S., and K. Foster. Why researchers don't study women: The responses of 67 researchers. A paper presented to the annual meeting of the American Psychological Association, New Orleans, 1974.

Reardon, P., and S. Prescott. Sex as reported in a recent sample of psychological research. *Psychology of Women Quarterly* 2(2), (1977):57-61.

Russell, B. *The scientific outlook.* New York: Norton, 1959.

Saario, T.T. The Ford Foundation. In L. Hunter and J. Marzone (eds.), *Funding for women's educational equity.* San Francisco: Women's Educational Equity Communicators Network, 1980.

Sangiuliano, I. *In her time.* New York: Morrow, 1978.

Schwabacker, S. Male vs. female representation in psychological research: An examination of the *Journal of Personality and Social Psychology,* 1970, 1971. *Journal Supplement Abstracts,* 1972.

Shakeshaft, C. Dissertation research on women in academic administration: A synthesis of findings and paradigm for future research. Ph.D. Diss., Texas A&M University, 1979.

Sheehy, G. *Passages.* New York: Bantam, 1977.

Sherif, C.W. .Bias in psychology. In J.A. Sherman and E.T. Beck (eds.), *The prism of sex: Essays in the sociology of knowledge.* Madison: The University of Wisconsin Press, 1979.

Sherwood, J.J., and M. Nataupsky. Predicting the conclusions of Negro-White intelligence research from biological characteristics of the investigator. *Journal of Personality and Social Psychology,* (1968):53–58.

Steinmetz, S.K. The sexual context of social research. *The American Sociologist* 9(3), (1974):111–16.

Steinem, G. Feminist notes. *MS* 9(3), (1980):98–103.

Stewart, W.A. A psychosocial study of the formation of early adult life structure in women. DPJ 77-08289. Ann Arbor, MI.: Dissertation Abstracts, 1977.

Thomas, A., and S. Sillen. *Racism and psychiatry.* New York: Brunner/Mazel, 1972.

Tittle, C.K., and E.R. Denker. Re-entry women. *Review of Educational Research* 47(4), (1977):531–84.

Tresemer, D. Assumptions made about gender roles. In Marsha Millman and Rosebeth Kanter (eds.), *Another Voice.* New York: Anchor Books, 1975, 308–39.

Van Tassel, E. The science of sexism. *Politics and Education,* (Fall 1979):28–30.

Witelson, S.F. Neural and cognitive correlates of developmental dyslexia: Age and sex differences. In C. Shagass, S. Gershon, and A.J. Friedholl (eds.), *Psychopathology and brain dysfunction,* New York. Raven Press, 1977.

13

Causal Models: Their Import and Their Triviality

Robert F. Boruch

INTRODUCTION

The thirteenth century's great Arab philosopher, Ibn Khaldun, maintained that the more an individual's "reflective power is capable of comprehending a regular chain of causes and effects, the more fully is the human quality of the individual developed. Some...are capable of two or three links...others push on" (Issawi 1950, p. 166). This paper discusses work that Khaldun might find kindred to his own, notably methods that are designed to make scientific speculation about cause and effect more orderly, coherent, and verifiable. The methods, like Khaldun's announcements, can be formidable.[1]

The focus here is on structural equations, a class of causal models used to analyze numerical information generated usually from quasi-experiments and surveys. The treatment is introductory but there are numerous references to more advanced work in education, economics, sociology, and psychology. Definitions of the models and their purpose are discussed briefly. There is considerable stress on the logic underlying the models and the inferences that they permit. There is also a discussion of the relations between structural

---

A contract with the National Institute of Education supported development of this paper. Background research on related topics has been supported by NIE-79-G-0128. I am indebted to Jeana Wirtenberg for broaching the idea for this paper and to Richard Berk and John Bynner for their comments. The abstracts of sex-equity projects compiled by Klein (1980) are the basis for illustrating practice here.

models and other more familiar approaches to data analysis. Applied and basic research are considered here, but the former is emphasized.

DEFINITION, PURPOSE, AND ANALOGS

A structural model is a statistical equation representing a causal linkage among variables. By "statistical" as used here, we mean the equation contains an error term—a random element representing a packet of ignorance—on one side of the equal sign. Because most social phenomena are complex, a number of compatible models are usually constructed to represent the observations. It is critical that prior theory or field experiments be used to specify the causal links and the equations.

The approach does not demonstrate that A causes B. It does help determine whether supposed causal linkages are consonant with the data. To the extent that theory is strong, the fit between model and observations will be good. To the extent that tests of consonance between data and theory are possible, and many formal statistical tests of hypotheses that exist are pertinent, the approach permits new inferences to be made about social processes or about the effects of intervention on the processes. Here, as in most science, we can reasonably expect that the increments to understanding will be small despite the new methods.

The idea of understanding whether a mathematical model is compatible with data is old. The use of structural or related models then does not differ in spirit from the task of assaying fit in ordinary least-squares regression. The approach exploits more information, however: that is partly where its merit lies. One is forced to be explicit in laying out each causal equation, thus fostering orderly thinking and opening the process to independent criticism. It invites sequential testing and fitting so that one gradually develops a verifiable characterization of reality rather than an unverifiable one. Finally and perhaps most important, the advanced work encourages explicit recognition of errors in measurement and misspecification of models, an emphasis not always evident in conventional statistics texts. In this respect, it is a more realistic approach.

The major disadvantages are related to the advantages. It may give considerably more mathematical legitimacy to data than the data deserve, as any elaborate analytic technology may do. It may obscure flaws, in that the difficulty of the mathematics is sufficient to prevent able criticism from the substantive expert who is mathematically inept or simply not familiar with the methods. The obtuseness of social scientific reporting exacerbates the problem. It may distract attention from alternative and better sources of evidence, e.g., good randomized field tests, time series, or ethnographic approaches in some cases. Finally, the more powerful techniques are generally useful only for large samples, especially when the social phenomena under examination is complex.

The process of developing a literal story line from observable evidence in clinical work is not dissimilar from what the causal modeler does. Where the clinician might use words to describe the size of a program's effects ("the group seems to be much improved by..."), the structural modeler uses numbers ("The group has improved by an eighth of a standard deviation."). The number has the merit of being more specific, provided that it has some meaning. Where the clinician may prefer to be vague or may be ignorant of what should be explicit, the modeler must make everything explicit. Where the clinician can exploit information and theory that is inchoate or cannot be articulated well in words much less in symbols, the modeler is at a considerable disadvantage.

This analogy is crude as all such analogs are. Briefly put, the idea is that structural models fall somewhere between the usual extensivity of statistics and the intensivity of qualitative knowing.

THE STATISTICAL MACHINERY AND THE ROLE OF THEORY

The analysis process involves specifying all causal linkages in a process, then translating those statements into statistical models. The variables, their sequence and placement in causal chains, their causal-effect and noncausal relations are supposed to be based on decent theory and evidence. The resulting system of equations is set up to assure that parameters can be estimated and, where possible, the system is modified to permit tests of hypotheses about the causal linkages.

A Simple Example

Consider, for example, a simple problem in which the process underlying mathematics achievement is posited to be a direct function of math anxiety and an indirect function of spatial ability. It is further thought that ability also influences anxiety. The process is made visually explicit in Chart 13.1, using a path diagram. The error terms introduced there add a bit of reality since the relation is bound to vary across individuals. From the diagram, one may derive two models to show how the variables depend on one another. From the models, we may then derive expected variances and covariances of observations, information that is necessary to estimate parameters in the models.[2] This particular model can be tested in the sense that if the model is true, the equation shown in stage 4 must be true. Duncan (1975), among others, provides a fine introduction to this class of models—small systems that involve few perfectly measured variables.

CHART 13.1

Simple Illustration

1. In words, spatial ability (X) is a major influence on math anxiety (or confidence, Z) and this in turn influences math achievement directly (Y). Random error affects our observations of both anxiety and ability and must be taken into account.

2. In path diagram form;

$$\begin{array}{cc} X \to Z \to Y & \qquad U, V \text{ are random independent errors} \\ \uparrow \quad \uparrow & \\ U \quad V & \end{array}$$

3. The models implied by the diagram are:

$$Z = \rho_{zx}X + U$$
$$Y = \rho_{yz}Z + V$$

4. For the models to be true, the following relation must hold:

$$\rho_{xy} = \rho_{xz}\rho_{zy}$$

A formal test of the null hypothesis that this relation holds helps us to understand whether the models are actually consonant with the data.

5. One ought to recognize that other theories lead to exactly the same test, notably:

$$\begin{array}{cc} Y \to Z \to X & \qquad Z \begin{array}{c} \nearrow Y \leftarrow U \\ \searrow X \leftarrow V \end{array} \\ \uparrow \quad \uparrow & \\ U \quad V & \end{array}$$

If these can be ruled out on theoretical grounds, the test of the null hypothesis is a test of only the model given earlier. These might be ruled out, for instance, if one reckoned that though math achievement Y could affect anxiety directly, anxiety could not affect spatial ability (X), for the left-hand diagram. And one might know that anxiety simply cannot be a joint influence on both spatial ability and math achievement.

Subsequent stages of the analysis are important but often ignored. Competing models, different sequences of variables, and so on, may be equally plausible and may fit the data equally well. It is the analyst's responsibility to identify them, develop a system of equations to represent each theory, and if possible assay the relative goodness of fit of each. This task, critical to any scientific enterprise, is analogous to the search for alternative explanations about the causes of an event that are discussed by Campbell and other methodologists, scientists, and philosophers.

The test of H_0: $\rho_{xy} = \rho_{xz}\rho_{zy}$ helps one understand, for example, whether the model is compatible with the data. As the chart suggests, however, two other models are, in effect, tested with the same statistical test. Failing to reject the null hypothesis implies that at least one of the models can tentatively be accepted. Which one we can accept cannot be designated without theory since without the latter all may be equally plausible.

Other sets of models, each testable with a single equality, can be generated and the equalities are distinct from one set to another. Duncan (1975) presents two other sets analogous to the one presented here, along with the more general message that determining "causal ordering of variables is beyond the capacity of any statistical method" (p. 50).

A Slightly More Complicated Example that Gets More Complicated

The simple illustration involves the outlandish assumption (theory aside) that the observed variables, x, y, and z, are perfect indicators of ability, anxiety, and achievement.[3] Expanding the theory to recognize measurement error seems sensible. Such expansion generally requires more information so that parameters in the model can be estimated. It also requires that we include measurement models to represent fallible measures in the system, and that we distinguish between those measurement models and the underlying structural relation.

For instance, one may posit that there are durable structural relations among the variables, lay out path diagrams and models of the kind given in Chart 13.2. Adapted from Carmines and McIver (1981), the chart exploits conventional notation and matrix algebra.[4] The model differs slightly from the earlier one in that here traits are latent; i.e., not observable directly and spatial ability is said to operate both directly and indirectly (through math anxiety).

One may then posit that what we observe from achievement test scores and the like does not constitute truth. Rather, the observations of achievement, y, are a weighted sum of true score and random error. The weight, analogous to a regression coefficient, or factor loading in orthodox factor analysis, can be regarded as an index of true score variability. The next chart (13.3), lays out these measurement models for both the latent traits of mathematics achievement and math anxiety.

Both structural relations and measurement models may be combined into a compact equation, represented in matrix form in the next chart (13.4). The equation is a vehicle for displaying parameters that need to be estimated, i.e., parameters that indicate the strength of causal linkages, if indeed the model is appropriate. The actual estimation process for complex models is handled by available computer programs.[5]

CHART 13.2

Structural Relations

1. In words, the structural relations among math achievement, η_2, with math anxiety, η_1, and spatial ability (ξ_1) such that ability has a direct influence on achievement and anxiety, and achievement is also influenced directly by anxiety. Random errors, ζ_1 and ζ_2, affect η_1 and η_2.

2. In path diagram form:

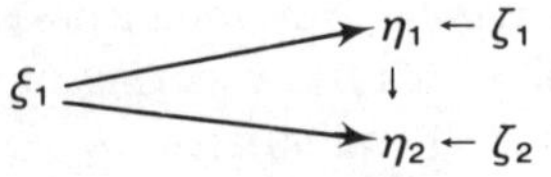

$$\xi_1 \begin{matrix} \nearrow \eta_1 \leftarrow \zeta_1 \\ \downarrow \\ \searrow \eta_2 \leftarrow \zeta_2 \end{matrix}$$

3. The models implied by the diagram are:

$$\eta_1 = \gamma_{11}\xi_1 + \zeta_1$$
$$\eta_2 = \beta_{21}\eta_1 + \gamma_{21}\xi_1 + \zeta_2$$

or more compactly:

$$B\eta = \Gamma\xi + \zeta$$

where

$$B = \begin{bmatrix} 1 & 0 \\ -\beta_{21} & 1 \end{bmatrix}, \quad \eta = \begin{bmatrix} \eta_1 \\ \eta_2 \end{bmatrix}, \quad \Gamma = \begin{bmatrix} \gamma_{11} \\ \gamma_{21} \end{bmatrix} \quad \xi = [\xi_1] \quad \zeta = \begin{bmatrix} \zeta_1 \\ \zeta_2 \end{bmatrix}$$

CHART 13.3

Measurement Models

1. In words, observations, y, are regarded as composed of a latent true score, η, and an error of measurement, ε.

2. In path diagram form, if we have three measures of the trait, η_1, math anxiety:

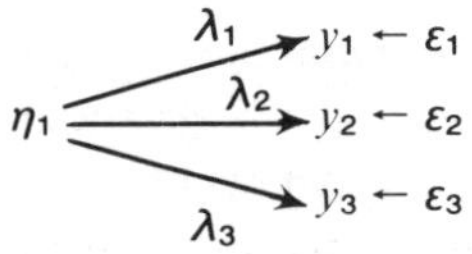

$$\eta_1 \begin{matrix} \xrightarrow{\lambda_1} y_1 \leftarrow \varepsilon_1 \\ \xrightarrow{\lambda_2} y_2 \leftarrow \varepsilon_2 \\ \xrightarrow{\lambda_3} y_3 \leftarrow \varepsilon_3 \end{matrix}$$

3. The models then are:

$$y_1 = \lambda_1\eta + \varepsilon_1,$$
$$y_2 = \lambda_2\eta + \varepsilon_2,$$
$$y_3 = \lambda_3\eta + \varepsilon_3$$

or $\quad y = \Lambda_y\eta + \varepsilon$ in matrix terms.

4. Observations, X, of the characteristic ξ may also be influenced by error δ:

$$X = \Lambda_x\xi + \delta$$

CHART 13.4

Combining the Models

1. In words, the latent traits math anxiety and achievement are influenced directly by latent spatial ability. Achievement is also affected by anxiety directly, and both are affected by random variation (ζ). Further, the traits are measured imperfectly, and any observed score is regarded as a function of true score plus error – multiple measures of each trait are obtained.

2. The path diagram is:

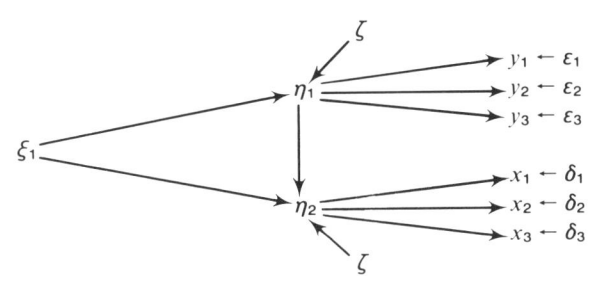

```
                    ζ
                    ↓
                   η₁ ────→ y₁ ← ε₁
                   ╱  ╲───→ y₂ ← ε₂
                  ╱    ╲──→ y₃ ← ε₃
                 ╱
              ξ₁
                 ╲
                  ╲    ╱──→ x₁ ← δ₁
                   ╲  ╱───→ x₂ ← δ₂
                   η₂ ────→ x₃ ← δ₃
                    ↑
                    ζ
```

3. The equations for the system can be represented in matrix notation as a function of the expected variance-covariance matrix ζ:

$$\zeta = \begin{matrix} \Lambda_y(B^{-1}\Gamma\phi\Gamma^1 B^{1-1} + B^{-1}\Psi B^{1-1})\Lambda_y^1\Theta_\varepsilon & \Lambda_y B^{-1}\Gamma\Phi\Lambda_x^1 \\ \\ \Lambda_x\Phi\Gamma^1 B^{1-1}\Lambda_y^1 & \Lambda_x\Phi\Lambda_x^1 + \Theta_\delta \end{matrix}$$

where Φ is the expected variance-covariance matrix for ξ
Ψ is the expected variance-covariance matrix for ζ
Θ_ε is the expected variance-covariance matrix for ε
Θ_δ is the expected variance-covariance matrix for δ

The Role of Theory

Of course, all this is much easier said than done. It is typical of most scholarly papers on causal models that the critical process of developing the statistical models from literary theory and the available evidence is not made clear. It is also typical that the appeal to theory is scientifically pious and glib. We can expect to be seduced sometimes by the appeal despite the feeble state of theory in the social sciences.

A fascinating exception to the usual treatment is given by Rossi, Berk, and Lenihan (1980) in a report on randomized field tests of income subsidy for men and women paroled from prison. There, the authors take pains to explain how causal models were built to help understand the surprising outcome of the experiment. The outcome, that providing income subsidies has no remarkable effect on recidivism, decreases work effort rather than increases it, and is not encouraging to those who view humanity, including parolees, as hardworking and thoughtful. Rossi, Berk, and Lenihan (1980) and Nancy Jurik (1980) exploited the models in building a post facto explanation that may be wrong, but *is* explicit and persuasive.

To begin, they recognize that though there are many theories of deterring crime, those theories are not especially pertinent to individuals who, like parolees, have not been deterred. Because there is so little sociological theory applicable to this group, the authors were forced to exploit theory from another discipline—economics. However, economic theory appears to be little better than others in laying out specific causal expectations, so the process of building crude theory to understand parolee recidivism had to be tailored and ad hoc. (Ad hoc has a bad name but remember its splendid exploitation by Watson and Crick in the search for DNA's structure.)

So for instance, the parolees' subculture of dependence, the stereotypical ways of spending their time and their determinants are not clearly covered by the sort of population and process that economic theory addresses. One can, as Rossi and his colleagues did, lift variables regarded as important in economic theory, e.g., allocation of time to work and leisure, job skills, etc. One can be, as they were, sensitive to the common sense idea that different outcome variables imply different causal models, e.g., ex-offenders' recidivism for property crimes implies a mechanism different from one for arrests for disorderly conduct, since police arrest practices for each may differ. Because most criminal theory is developed on the basis of data on men rather than women, and because causal influences on recidivism can differ across gender (as work opportunity, training, time allocation, and so on differ), the authors, through Jurik, try to determine if the statistical models that stand for men also apply to women. Apart from the choice of variables, the direction of their expected influence on recidivism and *some* relations among the variables though, the full set of relations has to be thought out heuristically. That is, theory is insufficient, as it usually is in complex social systems, and what little independent evidence and common sense we can bring to bear must also be exploited as Rossi, Berk, and Lenihan did (1980).

The Statistical Models and Scales of Measurement

The models are typically linear. The dependent and independent variables they include are usually regarded as random, with random disturbances and perhaps random measurement error. This focus on linear models and random variables permits one to exploit a good deal of the statistical machinery already developed for estimation and testing. The methods of estimation of parameters in the models vary a bit depending on nature and complexity of the system—one and two stage least squares and maximum likelihood being common.

Most methods for handling structural models are appropriate for variables that are measured on equal interval scales (Bentler and Woodward 1979). The newer methods permit one to exploit models using ordinal and categorical data. Muthen (1977), for instance, has developed a categorical analog to methods of estimation developed during the late 1960s and 1970s by Jöreskog. His approach presumes that the categorical variables are merely crude surrogates for continuous variables. The presumption is reasonable in some instances, e.g., school versus no school is a surrogate for what can be regarded as a continuous latent trait—schooling. Handling an observed variable with several categories of response (e.g., high, medium, low) in the context of model systems is difficult and methods for estimating parameters have only recently been developed (see Amemiya 1978, for instance).

Standards for Fit

The degree of fit between model and data is established usually by using the model and parameters one has estimated for it to reestimate original observations or predict new ones. So, for example, one may use a correlation matrix as a basis for estimating parameters in a structural model, then exploit the model to get the predicted correlation matrix. The differences between actual values of the correlations and predicted values, i.e., residuals, is one indicator of goodness of fit. Predicting values of correlations or covariances in a new sample, as in cross validation, is less common but builds considerably more confidence. Predicting new values of individual observations in a new sample is still less common, but probably ought to be regarded as a sine qua non. The main point is that if one cannot predict or postdict observations or functions of them decently, then one is not justified in announcements that the model fits the data.

As a practical matter, the fitting process is usually sequential and supported at times by formal tests of the hypothesis that the model accords with data. Structural models developed using maximum likelihood theory, such as Jöreskog's, can be appraised using a chi-square test when the sample is large and raw observations can be assumed from a sample of a normal population.

The general theory together with illustrations of such tests is given in Jöreskog (1979) based partly on seminal work by Lawley and Maxwell (1973). Formal tests are of limited value, partly because in large samples even models that fit well will be rejected (i.e., Type I errors). At least as important are the properties of the solution, e.g.: Does it make sense? Do estimates of parameters fall within permissible bounds? Is the solution unique in the sense that up to a rotation only one such solution exists? Technical criteria that address such questions have been invented and are still being debated, e.g., Rubin and Thayer (1982).

CLASSES OF APPLICATIONS

Causal analysis based on structural models has been applied in a variety of settings, appropriate and otherwise. In the following, broad classes of application that seem sensible are considered briefly. The classes are pertinent to research on sex-related differences and development and on social phenomena that are expected to affect each.

Measurement Theory

One important, relatively safe class of applications of structural models is dedicated to understanding the fallibility of social measurement and the implications that poor quality measurement has for inferences about social processes. That imperfections in measurement can have dramatic effects on conventional analytic techniques is clear. For instance, unreliability and misspecification in conventional regression is generally more important in producing biased estimates of parameters than nonnormality (e.g., Bohrnstedt and Carter 1971). In principle, one could produce conclusions opposite to those which should be drawn because of this (e.g., Campbell and Boruch 1975, in compensatory education). Failure to attend to the matter has been identified by Jacklin (1981, also this volume) as a crucial methodological issue in research in sex-related differences, among others.

Classical theory of errors in measurement, so-called true score theory, is strong partly because of its long history, partly because it deals with microprocesses. This theory about what causes error and how severe it is can be extended nicely using structural models. For instance, they permit more realistic assumptions about error structures. That is, reporting errors may be random or systematic, or both; they may differ in magnitude depending on occasion, cohort, gender, and so on; and they may be independent of the true state of affairs or correlated with true state and so on. Tests of these alternative structures are possible in principle—and practice turns out to be not far from principle here.

Consider for example, that we must often be satisfied with children's reports on parental occupation, income, and education, rather than parental reports, in field surveys of sex roles, attitudes, etc. and influences on the latter.[6] Nonetheless, children's reports are, for many thoughtful scientists, not at all trustworthy. The practical implication is that the influence of parental socioeconomic status cannot be judged in a causal analysis based on such reports. Not content to simply accept causal analyses or to reject them on account of the measurement error, Mare and Mason (1981) assayed quality of reporting using both conventional regression and structural models to understand the data. In examining white boys' reports about their parents, for sixth, ninth and twelfth graders, they find remarkable increases with higher grades in simple reliability of response with increasing grade, better reporting of father's occupation than other traits, and no remarkable differences in reporting parents' educational attainment. More important, they determined that structure of errors in reporting is stable across grade regardless of change in magnitude. They exploited structural models that permitted them to verify that indeed the models fit the data well by statistical standards and to exploit data across grade levels and reporting type simultaneously, rather than with a sequence of regression models.

Mary Corcoran's (1981) interest lay in understanding how young adults' misreporting can affect one's conclusions about the role of gender in social and educational status attainment. Poor quality reporting, for instance, of parental socioeconomic status can inflate or deflate the importance of gender educed where importance is registered by regression coefficients in conventional regression analyses. There has been little study of the influence of error despite its implications. She approached the problem by identifying alternative structural models that could plausibly be expected to underlie misreporting; she tested the fit of models to available data from Michigan's Panel Study of Income Dynamics. The alternative models involve assuming, for instance, that errors in response are random and independent, correlated with themselves or with the true state or condition to which questions are addressed. For instance, a son or daughter may guess imperfectly about one parent's occupational status based partly on the second parent's status; husbands may overstate the consistency between their own and their wife's status. Corcoran's sequential tests of ten models provide strong evidence that the error structure can be specified well, that there are indeed remarkable differences in quality between men's and women's reports of parental SES, and that sons' retrospective reports of their mothers' schooling were considerably less reliable than were daughters' retrospective reports. Finally, she shows that making inferences based on regression of adults' education on parental attributes change slightly, but notably in magnitude, when the error structure is taken into account.

The approach has been used to better understand the latent traits that underlie observed measures of alienation, hostility, and the like. One can construct a system of models, for example, to represent multitrait, multimethod matrices, and so help to establish that methods of measuring given traits perform as advertised, distinguishing between traits and providing measures that are consistent across measures. See Boruch and Wolins (1969) and Jöreskog's (1979) adaptation of their approach. Similarly, observed scores on four correlated tests of what is purported to be the same ability can be regarded as an effect of true ability, random variation, and characteristics specific to the test. Jöreskog (1973, 1977, 1979) lays out applications designed to understand the relation between true score and error variance in sets of tests that are equivalent, for determining whether a single factor underlies sets of tests, and the structure of observations from repeated trials. *Most such applications have ignored potential sex-related differences, but it is possible to test the fit of the models across groups of males and females.*

Internal Analysis and Randomized Field Experiments

The technology for randomized field tests has developed apart from the technology for structural models. So, for example, developers of such models justify their efforts partly on grounds that such models are useful when one cannot do experiments (e.g., Goldberger 1973; Rogosa 1979).

Still, there are mathematical links between the two approaches; it seems sensible to expect that their coupling can be useful. This seems especially true when field experiments are mounted to estimate the effects of new programs or variations. For the theory underlying such programs is often weak and rarely strong. Illustrations are few, though, partly on account of the separation of the technologies, and partly because mounting randomized field tests is very demanding.

For example, the Seattle and Denver Income Maintenance Experiments (SIME/DIME) are randomized field tests designed to estimate the effects of new income subsidy programs on the work activity of eligible recipients. The effects of the subsidy on labor supply were addressed, using both conventional analysis of variance (ANOV) models and more elaborate structural models, by Robbins and West (1981). The basic ANOV provides interpretable evidence of a work disincentive effect for some groups, i.e., subsidy lowers hours worked, exploiting the benefit of randomization to make the cause and effect relation clear. The structural models exploit this known causal relation and its directionality. But they incorporate independent information and theory to help understand how the results fit into a larger framework of economic theory and to facilitate comparisons between the field test results and the results of earlier work based on observational (nonrandomized) studies. The structural models employ continuous, theoretically important variables such as net wage rate and net change in disposable income to represent latent variables, rather than dummy variables that represent receipt of treatment, i.e., the income subsidy, in ordinary ANOV.

The TARP research (Rossi, Berk, and Lenihan 1980) is based on randomized experiments designed to understand the effects of postprison subsidies on work activity and recidivism of male and female parolees. Here, as in SIME/DIME, two parallel analyses were undertaken. The first, based on simple and appropriate analysis of variance of randomized groups suggest strongly that, as administered in Texas and Georgia, the subsidy's effect on property crimes was negligible and there was a work disincentive. The second analysis exploited crude theory to build structural models to understand the basic finding. So constructed, this analysis provides a different conclusion:

That the number of property crimes was "typically reduced" when one analyzes data from either men and women combined or women alone. The discrepancy between results of each analysis is still being debated. Some observers regard *only* the randomized results as sufficiently credible to use in policy decisions, since the structural models are based on theory that has not been well explored.

Nonrandomized Experiments and Observational Surveys

One merit that structural approaches have in principle is that they permit one to recognize reality better than older methods, and encourage establishing which of two or more competing views of reality are consonant with the data.

Recognizing reality here means, among other things, admitting that errors in measurement of various kinds exist, incorporating the admission into analysis, and in doing so, *not* being misled by the artifacts those errors frequently produce in conventional regression, covariance, and so on. Reality here also means that despite the effort required to set up such models, they may not fit the data well. The number of competing plausible models in such research is typically large, making the business of testing alternatives demanding, with no guarantee that any remarkably good models will be identified. To complicate matters, no prior theory is often used to guide data collection; consequently, data may be insufficient for estimation of parameters.

Some fine examples of application in this context have emerged from reanalyses of Head Start preschool programs. The form is generalizable, within limits, to other settings in which covariance analysis has typically been used to estimate program effects based on nonrandomized treatment and control groups. Magidson's (1977) layout, among the first to appear in print, involves admitting that the covariates used to adjust out preexisting differences between groups are fallible, and setting up measurement models to represent the fallible observations and structural models to represent underlying relations. His statistical tests suggest that the models do indeed fit the data well. His estimates of program effect lead to conclusions *opposite* to those reached in earlier analyses, i.e., that Head Start had a positive rather than negative effect on participants. Simplified treatments of the Magidson work are given by Rindskopf (1981). Alternative models that also fit the data well but yield different conclusions have been examined by Bentler and Woodward (1978).[7]

More general treatments of the mathematics and statistical methods for structural modeling in this context are given in Bentler and Bennett (1980), Bentler and Woodward (1979), Magidson and Sorbom (1980) and Sorbom (1978). The special case of longitudinal surveys is treated in Nesselroade and Baltes (1979) by Jöreskog, Rogosa, and others.

STEREOTYPICAL DIFFICULTIES AND MISTAKES

A variety of problems in statistical analysis are chronic. Some are tied to the use of new methods for causal analysis and four of these are considered in the following remarks. Others are more fundamental and affect conventional approaches, such as regression, as well as newer ones. A few of these are also considered.

The mistakes covered here are often overlooked by journal editors. So they may not harm the inept analyst professionally. Despite this, they can make analysis meaningless at best and misleading at worst. The list that follows focuses on statistical issues. See Jacklin (1981) and Wolins (1982) for alternative but related lists.

Competing Models

It seems fair to expect the researcher who exploits causal modeling to:

- recognize the existence of plausible competing models and to identify some of them clearly even if they are untested
- test the model used against plausible competing ones where possible, i.e., where information is sufficient
- report on the models fitted and rejected before settling on the model exploited most, for rejections are important

This is hard work of course. Its product is unlikely to be explicable in journal length articles, so unpublished reports need to be created, cited in the article and made available to interested readers.

"Arbitrary" Assumptions

It seems fair to expect investigators to identify the assumptions they regard as arbitrary, but necessary for estimation.

For instance, correlations among measurement errors or between latent factors and errors are often not based on clear theory or prior data. They are often exploited "merely" to make the model fit the data better. Readers need to know which these are, for they may be critical despite their arbitrariness. If they are not, this should be made plain.

Theory

Theory in some areas of research, especially new ones, is often weak. The theory actually exploited then to build models may be egocentric, fragmented, not particularly coherent, and will contain elements whose importance is not understood or is not known. As a consequence, a clear explanation of how the theory was evolved by the causal analyst would be helpful to most readers. See, for instance, the Rossi, Berk, and Lenihan (1980) work discussed earlier.

It is doubtful that such explanations can be incorporated neatly into journal length articles. It seems fair, however, for such explanations to be given along with other technical information in reports that are reproduced in limited quantity and cited in published articles.

Path Diagrams and the Models

It is not uncommon for structural modelers in psychology and sociology to draw path diagrams and to lay out the models they represent. The sequence is helpful, to the extent that any visual representation of a mathematical model is. Still, the practice is not uniform. As a consequence, the interested reader often cannot establish a clear link between literal and mathematical description or between mathematical description and the theoretical process at issue.

At the other extreme are investigators who map out a diagram with a large number of causal and correlational connections, but provide no assistance in developing or understanding their models. Often the testable and untestable relations are not identified.

Multiplicity of Models

The phrase "test the causal model" is a bit misleading in that: (1) rejecting a null hypothesis can leave one with an awesome array of competing models; and (2) tentatively accepting a null hypothesis may imply little because other plausible models may fit the data equally well. For a complex example involving structural analysis of longitudinal data on delinquency and its origins, see Bynner, O'Malley, and Bachman (1981), especially Table 1 on predicting theft and vandalism. Part of the problem here is usually an embarrassment of riches—there are several plausible theories.

Consider, for instance, research that involves only three variables A, B, and C, all of which may be causally related. Twelve simple recursive models can be set up: six of the form $A \rightarrow B \rightarrow C$, three of the form $A > C$, and three of the form $C > A$. Some of these are testable in the sense that the correlations among them have to have a certain pattern if the model is true. But such a pattern may be generated by two different models; failing to reject is tantamount to saying that at least two other theories can be correct.

Matters become much more complex with four variables: say peer attitudes *(A)*; parent attitudes *(B)*; school experience *(C)*; and attitudes about sex roles *(D)*. Over 80 simple models can be constructed from various ways in which these can be combined. The really bold researcher who chooses five variables will have to recognize that there are over 500 distinct causal models that can be generated. The number of models is low, incidentally, in that models that include random errors in measurement and the way these influence observations have been ignored.

However, the difficulty is exaggerated here in one respect. Not all models represent plausible schema and the number of models can be reduced greatly at times through theory, common sense, or external evidence. One *has* to ignore the competition, temporarily at least, to get anywhere.

Multiplicity of Tests

Causal models are often used in exploratory research—testing a variety of hypotheses on the same data set. Each statistical test may be made at the .05 significance level. The significance level for the totality of independent tests differs, however, being $1-(.95)^N$ where N is the number of tests. The fact that tests are related in most research, being based on the same data complicates matters, and no simple formula is possible.

One robust approach to this problem appears to be holding out a subsample or generating a new sample for confirmatory tests. The idea of using a cross-validation sample for this purpose is an old one. See Lord and Novick (1968) on validation samples and Bentler and Bennett (1980) on multiple tests in the context of factor analysis.

Imposing Constraints on the Models

Some models simply cannot be tested with available data unless special constraints are imposed on the model system or additional data is collected. One may have to assume, for instance, that there is no error of measurement or that certain types of errors are homogeneous in variance to generate models whose parameters are estimable, and which can be tested for compatibility with the data.

Identifying reasonable constraints is not easy. Indeed, some constraints are likely to be difficult to justify, despite their utililty in fitting the model, until we understand more about the measurement process (as in assuming errors of measurement). Jöreskog's (1979, p. 47) view is that some constraints will be "natural" but provides no advice on how to identify and exploit naturalness in an orderly way. His observation that in some cases restraints "can be chosen in an almost arbitrary manner" may be palatable to some theorists, but does not build confidence in others who have to educe something sensible from the results of analysis.

Power

Statistical power here means the probability of finding statistically "significant" differences among groups (categorized by gender or cohort, say) when indeed the differences exist in the population. This probability, of properly declaring significance when indeed the alternative hypotheses is correct, is often ignored. Failing to detect small differences is often attributable to the fact that the sample size is too small. Less obviously but perhaps more important, reliability in measurement and relevance of endogenous outcome variables, i.e., outcomes, are weak, and even more important, the integrity and reliability of measurement of exogenous and intervening variables may be poor. Both have dramatic effects on power (Boruch and Gomez 1979). For instance, where a laboratory experiment's design power might be .90, (i.e., the difference will be detected in 1 out of 10 cases), even moderate drops in quality of measuring outcome and of causes can produce decline in power to around .30. The consequence is an embarrassing number of nonsignificant results. The direct lesson is that in causal modeling as elsewhere, power analyses should be done and explained in any report of a causal analysis.

For the basic theory and advanced work on statistical power, see Cohen (1968) and Boruch and Gomez (1979) respectively and especially the references therein. For conscientious treatment in applied research, see Rossi, Berk, and Lenihan (1980) and Jurik (1980). A related matter is identified as a persistent methodological issue by Jacklin (1981). She believes few researchers report or even consider size of effect or of a difference despite its import. Of course, estimates of effect size are essential for power computations to avoid feeble experiments, quasi-experiments, and observational studies in equity and other gender-related investigations.

Regression to the Mean

Any sample selected on the basis of high or low scores on an earlier measure of achievement, for instance, will regress to the population mean. The result can be and often is ingenuous judgments about people who improved or who were actually hurt. The problem is as real in medical research (e.g., on labile hypertension) as it is in education (e.g., high math scores and what eventually happens to them). For illustrations, see Wolins (1982).

Additivity and Scales

Psychological measures yield data that have some properties which can mislead. Ceiling and floor effects are an obvious example of problems that can result in biased estimates of the effects of intervention in quasi-experiments and in biased estimates of the effect of naturally occurring events in longitudinal studies of human development. The problem and its damaging effect on inferences is discussed in Campbell and Boruch (1975).

Differences and Changes in Validity or Reliability

Changes in reliability of measurement over time can jeopardize inference in panel studies that are based on analyses that fail to recognize them. It is easy to show how estimates of the differences between groups, men and women for instance, can be artificially inflated or deflated relative to its true value when reliability differs between groups or when reliability increases or decreases differentially for each group. The result is that natural influences on the groups will appear to be more important or less important than they really are in conventional covariance and regression (Campbell and Boruch 1975), and in structural models that fail to recognize error in measurement. Jacklin (1981) maintains that ignoring such differences is chronic and illustrates her point with references to work on differences in the way boys and girls disclose their feelings to parents and their differential willingness to disclose information in other kinds of self-reports. Mary Corcoran (1981) among others, illustrates how the error might be accommodated. In her example, recognizing the error structure does not affect inferences much. Elsewhere it can.

Nonindependence

The data used in causal analyses are based on observations of various kinds of units. Children are observed within classrooms, classrooms within schools, children are asked to rate themselves relative to (an unspecified cluster of) peers, and so on. Most statistical methods rely on independent units of analysis, yet often those units are not independent (as for children within classroom) and the lack of independence is not recognized or cannot be compensated for in analysis. The aggregation problem is related but distinct: Models and estimates based on schools, for instance, may imply virtually nothing about models that are appropriate for children within classrooms. So for example, Coleman, Hoffer, and Kilgore (1982) exploit data on individual students in a large sample to support the conclusion that private schools, notably Catholic ones, have a greater effect on achievement than public schools. Peng, Owings, and Fetters (1982), using schools as the unit of analysis and related models, reach different conclusions, i.e., that private schools are not necessarily superior. Both sets of investigators used conventional regression approaches but the point holds for more elaborate structural approaches.

Little is known about the properties of test statistics when units are not independent for conventional tests. Even less is known about properties of large sample tests constructed for establishing goodness of fit in latent trait models.

DO THESE METHODS MAKE A DIFFERENCE?

Descriptions of causal analysis methods range from the elegant and tersely mathematical to ones composed in the interest of nontechnical but literate scholars. However, few descriptions contain any real evidence on why all this bustling and groping is important.

Jöreskog and Sorbom (1976), for instance, lead the reader conscienciously through the process of fitting models to panel data on verbal and quantitative achievement of boys and girls. But the substantive implications go unrecognized, the additions to what is already known and how important they are go unspecified. It is *not* quite fair to criticize these methodologists on substantive grounds, for their inventions are ingenious indeed; it *is* fair to expect guidance, and to begin to build opinion on the appropriateness and value of this new technology.

The Question and Its Elaboration

The question "Does it make a difference?" is crass; it may even be regarded as hostile. Still, it seems worth asking partly because actions we take are often robust against our ignorance.

Some policies, for example, are just not sensitive to evidence that is obtained incompetently. That is, the shape of policy is not influenced enough by the information to matter. Some measurement errors and error structure, for instance, are not sufficient to mask phenomena. And if the only objective is to identify the phenomena roughly, then advanced technology may be inappropriate. Some areas of social research lack coherent theory and exploiting the technology in such cases is likely to be impossible or difficult; the cost of the effort may not justify the product.

The question, crude as it is, is a small one in a larger net of questions, including: How do we evaluate any new technology and its impact? These larger questions cannot be answered here.

For simplicity's sake, suppose we frame rather more specific questions to understand whether application of the methods makes a difference:

- Can they help to identify what is wrong about an analytic method, and how important being wrong is?

- Can they help alter substantive theory, to illuminate beyond simple techniques, and how important is that illumination?
- Can they improve on conventional methods of analysis and how important is the improvement?
- Can they improve inferences for policy and management, and is the improvement important?

These are not unreasonable criteria for evaluating any methodological invention, despite their simplicity.

Identifying Flaws in Methods

Neither path analysis nor structural models more generally are necessary to show that a new or popular analytic method is wrong. But they are indeed helpful to judge from the evidence at hand.

Consider, for instance, the cross-lagged panel correlation approach to educing a predominant causal influence. The setup often involves measurement of two variables, X and Y at two points in time. The original idea was that one could determine from such data whether X is the predominant cause of Y or vice versa. In particular, if the correlation between X_1 and Y_2 is greater than the correlation between Y_1 and Y_2, one would infer that the predominant causal influence was X on Y.

Rogosa (1979) exploited simple path diagrams to make the situation mathematically clear and to uncover the assumptions underlying the approach. He exploited simple structural models to determine that the assumptions implicit in the approach are not likely to be tenable in real data (Chart 13.5).

To illustrate the point and its importance, Rogosa reviewed a variety of studies that rely on the method. So, for instance, published analyses of data on the relation between television and children's aggression invoked the approach and concluded that viewing TV violence does indeed cause children to be aggressive. He exploited path models to make explicit the assumptions underlying the original analysis, found that the assumptions did not hold. This then enables us to say that the original analysts' conclusions are unwarranted, based on the evidence at hand. To put it more bluntly, the scholar's judgment is probably no better than the journalist's in this instance. Rogosa also reanalyzed work on mother-child interaction in which the original analysts concluded, based on cross-lagged data, that the amount of mother's visual attention to the child influences the child's subsequent intellectual development. His conclusion, one that anyone now can make, is that no such conclusion is possible. He examined major growth studies which concluded that aural comprehension is a major causal influence on subsequent intellectual development. He found again that cross-lagged analysis

CHART 13.5

Cross-lagged Panel Correlation

1. Path diagram:

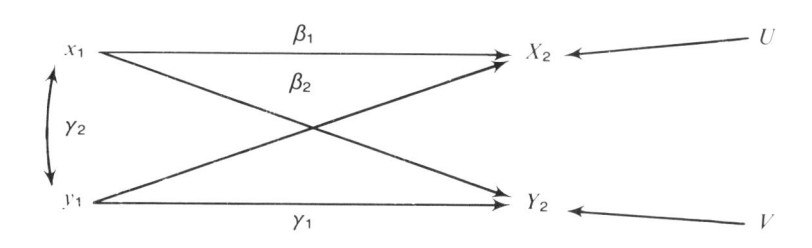

```
  X₁ ────────β₁──────────→ X₂ ←──────── U
   ↕        β₂
   │      ╲  ╱
   │       ╲╱
   │       ╱╲
   │      ╱  ╲
  Y₁ ────────γ₁──────────→ Y₂ ←──────── V
```

2. The models implied by the diagram are:

    $X_2 = \beta_1 X_1 + \gamma_2 Y_1 + U$
    $Y_2 = \beta_2 X_1 + \gamma_1 Y_1 + V$

3. The original interpretation of $\rho_{x_1 y_2}$ and $\rho_{x_2 y_1}$ posits that:

    if $\rho_{x_1 y_2} > \rho_{x_2 y_1}$, then X is the predominant cause
    $\rho_{x_2 y_1} > \rho_{x_1 y_2}$, then Y is the predominant cause

4. The relation between the correlations and path coefficients is (Rogosa, 1979):

$$\rho_{x_1 y_2} - \rho_{y_1 x_2}$$

$$= \left[1 - \rho_{x_1 y_1}^2\right] \left[\beta_2 \frac{\sigma_{x_1}}{\sigma_{y_2}} - \gamma_2 \frac{\sigma_{y_1}}{\sigma_{x_2}}\right]$$

$$+ \rho_{x_1 y_1} (\rho_{y_1 y_2} - \rho_{x_1 x_2})$$

5. The interpretation then is wrong, i.e., what one infers from the correlations will not accurately reflect reality, under common conditions, i.e.:

- stabilities differ, $\rho_{y_1 y_2} \neq \rho_{x_1 x_2}$
- variances of Y and X change from time 1 to time 2

used by the original investigators failed to recognize assumptions and are likely to have been violated. That is, the original analysis cannot sustain the conclusion.

A recent paper by Bynner, O'Malley, and Bachman (1981) is instructive in that it explores both conventional cross-lagged analysis and elaborate structural models to understand whether self-esteem among high school boys influences delinquency. The cross-lagged analysis suggests that it does (p. 417) and the latter approach suggests it does not (p. 429). The difference lies in the accommodation of plausible assumptions in the structural approach.

Substantive Theory

The inventors of structural approaches are persistent in their claims that their machinery will help to advance substantive theory. The intellective justifications for the claim are clear. Path diagrams can help one to visualize processes and provide an orderly accounting method. They serve both functions well.

In principle, the idea of laying out the models and testing elements of them is considerably more important. Despite this import in principle, professional practice often ignores the matter. The failure to test means we cannot attach much meaning to the claims. Still, it is possible to provide a few illustrations.

Stewart, Lykes, and LaFrance (1982), for instance, attempt to understand how family variables, such as the number of children a woman has and her age at marriage, and other variables, such as labor force participation, affect career achievement level. Examining simple correlations for a young cohort and an older cohort of women, they found substantial relations between number of children and career achievement ($r = -.28$ and $-.33$), and a very strong relation between labor force participation and achievement (.74 and .57). One might then be tempted to regard children as a direct influence on achievement. However, the authors make explicit what is for them a more plausible model; they estimate the parameters to show that the direct effect is small and indeed the only remarkable direct effect is of labor force participation itself on achievement. The effect is different for each cohort. Children do have a direct and notable effect on labor force activity and the parameters appear to be equal for each cohort. That is, the effect of children on how long one works is as strong for older women as for younger.

Two points are worth noting here. First, one's inferences about the role of childbearing changed as a consequence of exploiting the models. To the extent that the role itself is important for theory or practice, the use of the models is important. Second, the authors make no attempt to show that their models fit data any better than competing ones. In effect, they were unwilling or unable to advance their own theory or others beyond this.

Exploiting a structural approach can have an impact on the size of numbers, such as regression coefficients, that are supposed to reflect the importance of various causal influences in change studies. The impact depends on the specific setting, of course, and few general statements are possible. Applications to live data may be sufficient to provide order-of-magnitude effects, but their number are still too few for generalization.

For instance, Cuttance (1982) developed a model that is plausible and fits the data to clarify the error structure of educational panel data. He then compared a conventional regression of students' performance on parents' background and school variables to a regression that incorporated the structural analysis of errors in measurements of the independent variables. The estimates of regression coefficients that resulted from the structural approach range from eight times the magnitude of the conventional ones, in the case of mother's education, to a fifth of the magnitude, in the case of a variable concerning teacher's advising students. The practical implication is that the theoretical importance of mother's education in explaining school performance increases dramatically when measurement error is taken into account; the influence of teacher's advisory role declines substantially.

Alwin and Jackson (1980) reanalyzed a set of measures commonly used in economic and sociological research for socioeconomic stratification of men and women. The variables include: indices of the respondents' education; past and current occupational status; past and current job status; and father's occupational status and education. Their interest lay in understanding the fallibility of such data, notably the structure of error underlying response because such error can affect inferences. They assayed the fit of four distinct structural models to the data; the models ranged from assuming simple structural, i.e., completely random measurement error, to complex, i.e., assuming errors correlated with true score on a concept and errors correlated with true score on other concepts. Though they find the more elaborate models fit the data better than the simpler ones, all the fits are dismal. The models do yield estimates of reliability that vary considerably. For instance, reliability of responses about first job range from .6 to .8, a difference that is important substantively when reliability has to be taken into account in estimating the influence cohorts or epochs have on social change.

Improvement of Methods

The assumptions of least-squares regression, covariance and related analyses can be relaxed considerably using sophisticated structural models. For instance, one need not assume measurements are perfect, an assumption that is implicit in any explanatory use of conventional methods. One need not assume that random deviations from underlying relations are homogeneous, or independent of one another, or of major latent variables in the system of models. The result is more realistic at least in the abstract.

That the increased realism can be important seems clear. Magidson's (1977) reanalysis of Head Start evaluations, for instance, was based on a structural approach rather than conventional covariance analysis used by the original investigators. Recall that the original work yielded estimates of summer program effect that were negative, implying that the program hurt rather than helped white children. The negative effects were remarkable, and considering the size of the Head Start population, serious.

His reanalysis of the same data employed a true-score approach discussed earlier, and yielded estimates of program effect that are slightly positive rather than negative. The magnitude of differences between his results and those of conventional covariance analysis is substantial, to judge from correlations between the major response variables, achievement test scores symbolized by Y_1 and Y_2 below, and participation in Head Start adjusted under ordinary and true-score models.

	Covariance Model	True-Score Model
Y_1	−.04 (.06)	+.12 (.11)
Y_2	−.02 (.06)	+.14 (.11)

Because results are dramatic and analysis more realistic does not make the results correct, of course, nor does Magidson imply the latter.

Bentler and Woodward (1978) stand on Magidson's shoulders to make a remarkable contribution of their own. They try models that differ from Magidson's, but are no less plausible, and use a slightly different approach to obtain estimates of a Head Start effect that does not differ remarkably from zero. Magidson's (1978) rejoinder, among other things, reiterates a conclusion of the Bentler and Woodward critique, to wit, that the solutions are not final but are feasible and more realistic alternatives to conventional covariance approaches.

The more general point, made explicit by Box (1966) and others (see Campbell and Boruch 1975, and the references there) is that theory is often insufficient in such applications and as a consequence techniques for analysis of observational data, sophisticated or not, may be a blind alley. At worst, they may distract attention from development of managerial, political, and other kinds of solutions to the problem of generating less equivocal evidence (Boruch 1976). At their best, they help advance theory at this stage of the social sciences.

RELATIONS BETWEEN STRUCTURAL MODELS AND OTHER APPROACHES

As one might expect, structural modeling is related to a variety of other techniques that may be more familiar to readers. The following briefly describes its relation to ordinary regression and covariance analysis, quasi-experimental design and randomized experiments, and some other familiar topics.

General Distinctions

If we take as a basis for defining structural models the work of Goldberger (1973) and Jöreskog (1973) and others on whom they rely, structural models are distinct from other models and procedures exploited for data reduction in these respects. They stress:

- causal mechanisms, i.e., models that derive from theory
- a latent structure with or without random disturbance
- a measurement error structure
- a goodness of fit of the model rather than goodness of prediction of an individual response

The structural approach is not distinct from other approaches in that very general models are reducible to ordinary regression and other conventional models when constraints are laid on. It is not distinct in that it has its origins in the early path models of biometry and sociology, the structural relations of economics, the measurement models of psychology, and the framework of linear models and curve fitting of statistics (Jöreskog 1973).

Ordinary Least-Squares (OLS) Regression

The OLS regression methods typically presented in texts are most appropriate for use in prediction rather than explanation. Understanding the degree to which women's math achievement, for example, can be predicted from earlier play activity or from interaction with parents and peers, and so on, *is* important, regardless of whether one can explain the relation in any coherent way. Moreover, the machinery of OLS regression is designed to understand how good the prediction is, how to improve prediction, and where the weaknesses lie in our ability to predict. Inferences are constrained by confidence intervals that can be specified mathematically and verified empirically, and by the idea that all predictions are conditional on the observed independent variable.

However, the use of such models for educing cause and effect is another matter. The shortcomings of the approach in context is one reason for development of new technology. Goldberger (1973), for instance, presents a tidy explanation of three kinds of settings in which conventional regression does not yield estimates of the structural parameter in which the scientist must be interested if explanation rather than prediction is the aim. The cases include settings in which measures of (random) independent variables are fallible, where variables may be omitted from the model at issue, and where one expects independent and dependent variables to cause one another, i.e., reciprocal causation. In each of the cases, ordinary regression will not yield estimates of the structural parameter. We may go further as Duncan (1975, p. 35) does to recognize that the early regression analyst might have partitioned variance into components "uniquely" identified with particular independent variables. It is understood now that the partitioning does nothing of the sort except for a narrow class of data in which predictor variables are indeed independent (Duncan 1975, p. 65). Regardless of whether one uses stepwise regression, any causal model underlying such an approach is simultaneous, i.e., all the variables cause the dependent variable simultaneously. Of course, this is not usually the case.

The most general structural models direct attention to these problems and others. The statistical machinery will help to generate unbiased estimates of structural parameters under explicit conditions. For proofs, see Goldberger (1973). For elaboration of the relations between regression and structural models, see Lawley and Maxwell (1973) and Goldberger (1973).

Covariance Analysis

Cronbach et al. (1976) and others indicate that if the analyst knows either the fully complete covariate (one that predicts within-group outcome as fully as possible) or the complete discriminant (that fully represents initial group differences), then unbiased estimation of observational (nonrandomized) data using covariance analysis of observational data is possible.

In practice, the problem is that the analyst seldom knows whether imperfect prediction is due to errors of measurement or to poor specification of models or variables. Regression-discontinuity represents a limited subset of cases in which the complete discriminant is *known:* the covariates have been used to assign subjects to treatment groups and covariance and regression estimates will be unbiased (see Rubin 1973, 1976a; Kenny 1979; Overall and Woodward 1977).

If the data satisfy all of the other criteria for analysis of covariance (ANCOVA; e.g., the slopes of the regression line for each group should be the same), and the covariate set is complete except for random errors of measurement, then it is possible to do an ANCOVA with corrections for unreliability. Lord's (1960) technique, which is restricted to a single covariate and large samples, yields results similar to Porter's (1967) methods for estimating true covariates for any number of groups, given test-retest reliability. Stroud (1974) has derived a large sample test statistic for assessing differences between regression lines when the reliability of the covariate is known for the population. Still other approaches involve a combination of both blocking and covariance in which matching is conducted on regressed pretest scores (i.e., pretest regressed on posttest and estimates made of pretest scores); the regression might ignore unreliability altogether. There has been no attempt to compare results using these alternative methods or to lay out the relation among them. Expert statistical help may be necessary since there is disagreement about what kind of adjustment is appropriate in different situations (see, e.g., Kenny 1979; Linn and Werts 1977; Cronbach et al. 1976).

The model underlying all such approaches is a restrictive one. Less restrictive alternatives involve structural models. For the general analysis of nonequivalent control group designs, Magidson (1977) and Magidson and Sorbom (1980), for example, use less restrictive and more realistic models to estimate the effects of Head Start, obtaining results that differ from covariance analyses of the program during the 1960s. The results are still debatable, partly because data are not sufficient to sustain more complicated structural models that would accommodate other theories (Bentler and Woodward 1978).

Quasi-experimental design here refers to plans for collecting data on the effect of interventions in the absence of random assignment of the intervention to individuals or groups. The formal plans are such that they facilitate an inference that X produces an effect on Y by identifying and, where possible, accommodating plausible competing influences on Y. The remarkable work of this genre, by Campbell and Stanley (1966) and others, consolidates the spirit of a dozen statistical and philosophical approaches to evidentiary problems. The newest such approach, structural modeling, is pertinent in that many quasi-experimental designs can be framed in terms of the models. One may lose some benefit in doing so; for instance, the literal stress on competing causes that are identified but have not been measured. One may gain, however, in that where imperfectly measured or contaminated variables are at issue and where it is expected that competing mechanisms influence the estimated size of an intervention's effect, one can attach a numerical mean to the "plausibility" that is emphasized by the designers of quasi-experiments. The extent to which models fit the data is not the only numerical indicator, nor should the indicators be confined to the numerical. But it is useful.

The main benefit of using such models in this context is to make explicit the assumptions engendered by the designs and to recognize bias, independent of the intervention effects. The main drawback of structural models in this context is that not enough may be known about the phenomena under study to exploit models that demand one to specify structure or measurement mechanisms.

Randomized Experiments

A randomized experiment involves the random assignment of experimental units, individuals or institutions say, to one of two or more programs, program variations or components, in the interest of a fair estimate of relative program effects and a probability statement about one's confidence in the result. So, for example, one might randomly assign some members of a group of adolescents to a new youth employment program and some to conventional (control) condition. The objective is to estimate the benefits and costs of the program, relative to conventional conditions. If the experiment is run properly, the randomization guarantees long-run equivalence of the participants and nonparticipants in the new program, aside from program effect. The cost of the approach is that it demands considerably more managerial, institutional, and personal skills than many other designs with the same objective. Solutions to some of the problems they engender are given by Riecken et al. (1974).

Randomized experiments obviate the need for structural models in a single fundamental sense. They assure that the direction and magnitude of the causal link, between treatment and response is known. More specifically, the link is not modified by variables that might be omitted from a system of models based on nonrandomized data, such as self-selection into a program. Usually, available theory is not sufficient for specifying the self-selection process mathematically and so one can only speculate about its effect.

Structural models can, however, be used to illuminate the structure of randomized experiments. For example, the models that underlie mixed effects analysis of variance designs usually assume additivity of effects and homogeneous error. One can relax these requirements using a variety of structural models, notably one in which certain parameters have been fixed, to explore the consequences of relaxed assumptions for fit between model and data (see the appendix of the Boruch and Wolins (1969) paper).

Similarly, structural models can be used to generate and perhaps test hypotheses about how intervening variables, that are not controllable in the experiment, may influence the response variable or be influenced by natural variations in treatment intensity (Miller 1973). The examples of parallel structural modeling and analysis of variance by Rossi, Berk, and Lenihan (1980) and Robbins and West (1981) illustrate a related tactic.

Finally, where differential attrition, biased sampling, and the like may have an influence on estimates of program effect in a randomized design, structural models may be helpful in understanding the nature of biases and their magnitude. See, for instance, the papers in 1981 *Proceedings of the National Bureau of Economic Research.*

Factor Analysis

In a large class of situations, the main variables of interest are *not* directly observable. Instead, they are constructs and have meaning primarily when related to other constructs. In practice, the constructs are often measured in several ways. To reduce the measured variables to the constructs, the factor analyst builds models in which correlations or covariances among observed variables are described as functions of observable factors which influence them. The statistical models that are posited may be wrong and so the system warrants testing.

A main objective is to assay the structure of the data in a way that permits formal statements about consonance between data and model. Conceptually, this is no different from the approach taken in structural modeling, and Jöreskog (1973) lays out the mathematical relation neatly. Recent advances in estimating parameters have been made by Jöreskog (1973), based partly on work by Howe, Bock, Bargman, Lawley and Maxwell, and others. More technically advanced work has been produced by Jôreskog and Sorbom (1977), Jöreskog (1977), Muthen (1977), Magidson and Sorbom (1980), and others. Good introductions to factor analysis are given in Gorsuch (1974) and Mulaik (1972).

THE BOTTOM LINE

Structural models and their variations permit one to: (1) formally test and make probabilistic statements about how well a system of causal models, i.e., a theory represented mathematically, fits the data; (2) test competing systems of models on the basis of how consonant each is with data; and (3) deal with unobservable variables (constructs) and measurement error in an orderly way.

The technique requires: (1) explicit statements about causal influences and relations among variables; (2) large samples when the theory involves complex relations and numerous variables and when the relevant test statistics are based on large sample theory; and (3) careful explication and testing of competing models where possible.

The disadvantages of such methods are that they are: (1) complex, requiring considerable technical skill and experience; (2) their costs may not be justified by the product or, for that matter, by the original data; and (3) they can yield misleading results when theory is weak and attention to competing theories is inadequate.

Such methods are not a substitute for randomized field experiments when the object is to estimate the effects of intervention programs, program variations, or components—at least when theory is weak as it usually is in novel contexts. Nor are they a substitute for the better quasi-experimental designs, such as regression-discontinuity, in which part of the delivery of treatment can be controlled in certain ways. They are eminently suited to the situation in which theory or knowledge about process is strong and one would like to add incrementally to both theory and knowledge in a way that can be independently disconfirmed. They are a fine vehicle for orderly examination of small sets of causal arrangements in the interest of advancing our understanding about what might cause what. Adjoined to well-designed experiments or quasi-experiments, they enhance in a remarkable way one's ability to explain results beyond simple tests of hypotheses.

NOTES

1. I am unaware of any formal examination of the history of mathematical causal modeling, but Magidson (1979) and Rogosa (1979) exhibit an admirable awareness of developments over the past 30 years. It is a topic that deserves more attention from the historian.

2. Duncan (1975) covers the algebra of expected values of variances and covariances for observed variables in such systems. The mathematics of expected values is usually treated in greater detail in introductory texts on theory in statistics (e.g., Mood and Graybill 1963).

3. The paper stresses analysis of data that are fallible, generated by some unknown but potentially knowable process. Where measurement error is negligible and latent variables are not of interest, the statistical machinery for comparing models, causal or predictive, is considerable. See Specht and Warren (1976) for a nice review, using data on educational aspirations and marriage plans across sex as a vehicle for illustration, and Kenny (1979) for elaboration.

4. The matrix algebra that is sufficient to understand the framework of such problems is rudimentary. See, for example, Appendix B of Kmenta (1971) or Mulaik (1972).

5. Computer programs for handling structural models that involve no measurement error or latent traits are those ordinarily used in least-squares regression. They are available in most university computing centers. The new sophisticated programs developed by Jöreskog, Gruvaeus, Sorbom and others permit estimation and testing of models when multiple fallible measures of latent variables are used. The most recent programs of the kind, LISREL, is available at some university centers and directly from National Educational Resources in Chicago.

6. Studies that must use children's reports of economic status include those with substantial policy implications, such as Coleman, Hoffer, and Kilgore (1982) on private versus public schools, as well as research with basic rather than policy objectives such as Mason, Czajka, and Arber (1976) and Mare and Mason (1981) on changes in sex-role attitudes.

7. The existence of competing models is related to Simpson's paradox (Novick 1981), in nonrandomized studies. One can find that prison training increases recidivism when one analyzes and women together. But when one separates the two groups, one can find that training appears to *decrease* recidivism. The mathematics underlying the paradox has been elaborated by Novick, but it has not been linked to structural or path models in any texts that we are aware of.

REFERENCES

Alwin, D.F., and D.J. Jackson. Measurement models for response errors in surveys: Issues and applications. In K.F. Schussler (ed.), *Sociological methodology: 1980*. San Francisco: Jossey-Bass, 1980, pp. 68–119.

Amemiya, T. The estimation of a simultaneous equation generalized probit model. *Econometrica* 46 (1978): 1193–1205.

Bentler, P.M. Multivariate analysis with latent variables: Causal modeling. *Annual Review of Psychology* 31 (1980): 419–56.

Bentler, P.M., and D.G. Bennett. Significance tests and goodness of fit in analysis of covariance structures. *Psychological Bulletin* 88 (1980): 588–606.

Bentler, P.M., and J.A. Woodward. Nonexperimental evaluation research: Contributions of causal modeling. In L.E. Datta and R. Perloff (eds.), *Improving evaluations.* Beverly Hills: Sage, 1979, pp. 71–102.

Bentler, P.M., and J.A. Woodward. A Head Start reevaluation: Positive effects are not yet demonstrable. *Evaluation Quarterly* 2 (1978): 493–510.

Bohrnstedt, G.W., and E.F. Borgatta (eds.). *Social measurement: Current issues.* Beverly Hills: Sage, 1981.

Bohrnstedt, G.W., and T.M. Carter. Robustness in regression analysis. In H. Costner (ed.), *Sociological methodology: 1971.* San Francisco: Jossey-Bass, 1971, pp. 118–46.

Boruch, R.F. On common contentions about randomized experiments. In G.V. Glass (ed.), *Evaluation Studies Review Annual,* 1976.

Boruch, R.F., and H. Gomez. Measuring impact: Power theory in social program evaluation. In L.E. Datta and R. Perloff (eds.), *Improving evaluations.* Beverly Hills: Sage, 1979, pp. 139–70.

Boruch, R.F., A.J. McSweeny, and J. Soderstrom. Bibliography: Illustrative randomized field experiment. *Evaluation Quarterly* 2 (1978): 655–95.

Boruch, R.F., and L. Wolins. Quasi-experimental design: Further explorations. *Proceedings of the American Statistical Association: Social Statistics Section.* Washington, D.C.: ASA, 1969, pp. 327–32.

Boruch, R.F., P.M. Wortman, and D.S. Cordray (eds.). *Re-analyzing program evaluations: Policies and practices for secondary analysis of social and educational programs.* San Francisco: Jossey-Bass, 1981.

Box, G.E.P. Use and abuse of regression. *Technometrics* 8 (1966): 625–29.

Bynner, J.M., P.M. O'Malley, and J.G. Bachman. Self-esteem and delinquency revisited. *Journal of Youth and Adolescence* 10(6), (1981): 407–41.

Campbell, D.T., and R.F. Boruch. Making the case for randomized assignment to treatments by considering the alternatives: Six ways in which quasi-experimental evaluations in compensatory education tend to underestimate effects. In C.A. Bennett and A. Lumsdaine (eds.), *Evaluation and experiment.* New York: Academic Press, 1975.

Campbell, D.T., and J.C. Stanley. *Experimental and quasi-experimental designs for research.* Chicago: Rand McNally, 1966.

Carmines, E.G., and J.P. McIver. Analyzing models with unobserved variables: Analysis of covariance structures. In G.W. Bohrnstedt and E.F. Borgatta (eds.), *Social measurement: Current issues.* Beverly Hills: Sage, 1981, pp. 65–116.

Cohen, J. *Statistical power analysis for the behavioral sciences.* New York: Academic Press, 1968.

Coleman, J.S., T. Hoffer, and S. Kilgore. *High school achievement: Public, Catholic, and private schools compared.* New York: Basic Books, 1982.

Corcoran, M. Sex differences in measurement error in status attainment models. In

G.W. Bohrenstedt and E.F. Borgatta (eds.), *Social measurement: Current issues.* Beverly Hills: Sage, 1981, pp. 209–28.

Cronbach, L.J., D.M. Rogosa, R.D. Floden, and G.G. Price. Analysis of covariance: Angel of salvation, or temptress and deluder? An occasional paper, Stanford Evaluation Consortium, Stanford University, Stanford, Calif., February 1976.

Cuttance, P.F. Covariance structure modelling of reliability and differential response in educational data. Reference No. 8206. Centre for Educational Sociology, University of Edinburgh, Edinburgh, Scotland, 1982.

Duncan, O.D. *Introduction to structural equation models.* New York: Academic Press, 1975.

Duncan, O.D. Unmeasured variables in linear models for panel analysis. In H.L. Costner (ed.), *Sociological methodology: 1972.* San Francisco: Jossey-Bass, 1972, pp. 36–82.

Goldberger, A.S. Maximum likelihood estimation of regression containing unobservable independent variables. *International Economic Review* 13 (1972): 1–15.

Goldberger, A.S. Structural equation models; An overview. In A.S. Goldberger and O.D. Duncan (eds.), *Structural equation models in the social sciences.* New York: Seminar Press, 1973, pp. 131–52.

Goldberger, A.S. Selection bias in evaluating treatment effects: Some formal illustrations. Discussion Papers, #213–72, Madison: Institute for Research on Poverty, University of Wisconsin, April 1972.

Gorsuch, R.F. *Factor analysis.* Philadelphia: Saunders, 1974.

Hilton, C. Causal inference analysis: A seductive process. *Administrative Science Quarterly* (March 1972): 44–54.

Issawi, C. (translator and editor). *An Arab philosophy of history: Selections from the prologemna of Ibn Khaldun of Tunis.* London: John Murray, 1950.

Jacklin, C.J. Methodological issues in the study of sex-related differences. *Developmental Review* 1 (1981): 266–73.

Jöreskog, K. (ed. Jay Magidson). *Advances in factor analysis and structural equation models.* Cambridge: Abt Books, 1979.

Jöreskog, K.G. Structural equation models in the social sciences: Specification, estimation, and testing. In P.R. Krishnaiah (ed.), *Applications of statistics.* Amsterdam: North-Holland, 1977, pp. 265–88.

Jöreskog, K.G. A general method for estimating linear structural equation system. In A.S. Goldberger and O.D. Duncan (eds.), *Structural equation models in the social sciences.* New York: Seminar Press, 1973, pp. 85–112.

Jöreskog, K.G., and D. Sorbom. Statistical models and methods for analysis of longitudinal data. In D.J. Aigner and A. Goldberger (eds.), *Latent variables in socioeconomic models.* Amsterdam: North-Holland, 1977.

Jöreskog, K.G., and D. Sorbom. Statistical models and methods for test-retest situations. In D. DeGruijter and L. vanderKamp (eds.), *Advances in psychological and educational measurement.* New York: Wiley, 1976, pp. 136–57.

Jurik, N. Women ex-offenders in TARP experiment. Appendix C of P.H. Rossi, R.A. Berk, and K.J. Lenihan, *Money, work, and crime.* New York: Academic Press, 1980, pp. 319–34.

Kenny, D.A. *Correlation and causality.* New York: Wiley (Interscience), 1979.

Klein, S. (ed.). Sex equity in education: NIE sponsored projects and publications. Washington, D.C.: NIE, 1980.

Kmenta, J. *Elements of econometrics.* New York: Macmillan, 1971.
Laeamer, E.E. *Specification searches: Ad hoc inference with nonexperimental data.* New York: Wiley, 1978.
Lawley, D.N., and A.E. Maxwell. Regression and factor analysis. *Biometrika* 60(2), (1973): 331–38.
Linn, R.L., and C.E. Werts. Analysis implications of the choice of a structural model in the nonequivalent control group design. *Psychological Bulletin* 84 (1977): 229–34.
Lomax, R.G. Causal modelling of educational phenomena. (Presented at the System Development Corporation Seminar on Modelling: 1981). Department of Education: University of Illinois at Chicago Circle, 1982.
Lord, F.M. Large sample covariance analysis when the control variable is fallible. *Journal of the American Statistical Association* 55 (1960): 307–21.
Lord, F.M., and M. Novick. *Statistical theories of mental test scores.* Reading, Mass.: Addison-Wesley, 1968.
Magidson, J. (ed.) *Advances in factor analysis and structural equation models.* Cambridge: Abt Books, 1979.
Magidson, J. Reply to Bentler and Woodward: The .05 significance level is not all powerful. *Evaluation Quarterly* 2(3), (1978): 511–20.
Magidson, J. Toward a causal model approach for adjusting preexisting differences in the nonequivalent control group situation: An alternative to ANCOVA. *Evaluation Quarterly* 1 (1977): 399–420.
Magidson, J., and D. Sorbom. Adjusting for confounding effects in quasi-experiments. *Proceedings of the American Statistical Association: 1980.* Washington, D.C.: ASA, 1980, pp. 370–75.
Mare, R.D., and W.M. Mason. Children's reports of parental socioeconomic status: A multiple group measurement model. In G.W. Bohrnstedt and E.F. Borgatta (eds.), *Social measurement: Current issues.* Beverly Hills: Sage, 1981, pp. 187–208.
Mason, K.O., J.L. Czajka, and S. Arber. Change in U.S. women's sex role attitudes: 1964–1974. *American Sociological Review* 41 (1976): 573–96.
Miller, A.D. Logic of causal analysis: From experimental to nonexperimental designs. Chap. 15 of H. Blalock (ed.), *Causal models in the social sciences.* Chicago: Aldine, 1973, pp. 273–94.
Mood, A.M., and F.A. Graybill. *Introduction to the theory of statistics.* New York: McGraw-Hill, 1963.
Mulaik, S.A. *The foundations of factor analysis.* New York: McGraw-Hill, 1972.
Muthen, B. Contributions to factor analysis of dichotomous variables. *Psychometrika* 43 (1977): 551–60.
Muthen, B., and B. Dahlqvist. Latent analysis of dichotomous indicators. User's guide. Manual for a FORTRAN computer program. University of Uppsala, Department of Statistics, Uppsala, Sweden, 1980.
Nesselroade, J.R., and P.B. Baltes (eds.), *Longitudinal research in the study of behavior and development.* New York: Academic Press, 1979.
Novick, M. Data analysis in the absence of randomization. In R.F. Boruch, P.M. Wortman, and D.S. Cordray, (eds.), *Reanalyzing program evaluations: Policies and practices for secondary analysis of social and educational programs.* San Francisco: Jossey-Bass, 1981, pp. 144–62.

Overall, J.E., and J.A. Woodward. Nonrandom assignment and the analysis of covariance. *Psychological Bulletin* 84 (1977): 588–94.
Peng, S.S., J.A. Owings, and W.B. Fetters. Effective schools: What are their attributes? Presented at the Annual Meeting of the American Psychological Association, Washington, D.C., 1982.
Porter, A.C. The effects of using fallible variables in the analysis of covariance. Ph.D. dissertation, University of Wisconsin, Madison, 1967.
Riecken, H.W., R.F. Boruch, D.T. Campbell, N. Kaplan, T.K. Glennan, J.W. Pratt, A. Rees, and W. Williams. *Social Experimentation.* New York: Seminar Press, 1974.
Rindskopf, D. Structural equation models in analysis of nonexperimental data. In R.F. Boruch, P.M. Wortman, and D.S. Cordray (eds.), *Reanalyzing program evaluations: Policies and practices for secondary analysis in social and educational programs.* San Francisco: Jossey-Bass, 1981, pp. 163–93.
Robbins, P.K., and R.W. West. Labor supply response to the Seattle and Denver income maintenance experiments. Menlo Park, Cal.: SRI International, 1981.
Rogosa, D. Causal models in longitudinal research: Rationale, formulation, and interpretation. In J.R. Nesselroade and P.B. Baltes (eds.), *Longitudinal research in the study of behavior and development.* New York: Academic Press, 1979, pp. 263–302.
Rossi, P.H., R.A. Berk, and K.J. Lenihan. *Money, work, and crime: Experimental* New York: Academic Press, 1980.
Rubin, D.B. Estimating causal effects of treatments and randomized and nonrandomized studies. *Journal of Educational Psychology* 66 (1974): 688–701.
Rubin, D.B. Assignment and treatments on the basis of a covariate. ETS Research Bulletin 76-9, Princeton, N.J., Educational Testing Service, 1976.
Rubin, D.B., and D. Thayer. EM algorithms for ML factor analysis. *Psychometrika* 47(1), (1982): 69–76.
Sorbom, D. An alternative to the methodology for analysis of covariance. *Psychometrika* 43 (1978).
Specht, D.A., and D.A. Warren. Comparing causal models. In D.A. Heise (ed.), *Sociological methodology: 1976.* San Francisco: Jossey-Bass, 1976, pp. 46–82.
Stewart, A.J., M.B. Lykes, and M. LaFrance. Educated women's career patterns: Separating social and development changes. *Journal of Social Issues* 38(1), (1982): 97–118.
Stroud, T.W.F. Comparing regressions when measurement error variances are known. *Psychometrika* 39(1), (1974): 53–67.
Werts, C.E., and R.L. Linn. Analyzing school effects: How to use the same data to support different hypotheses. *American Educational Research Journal* 6 (1969): 439–47.
Wiley, D.E. The identification problem for structural equation models with unmeasured variables. In A.S. Goldberger and O.D. Duncan (eds.), *Structural equation models in the social sciences.* New York: Seminar Press, 1973, pp. 69–83.
Wolins, L. *Research mistakes in the social and behavioral sciences.* Ames, Iowa: Iowa State University Press, 1982.

PART VI

CONCLUSION

14

Conclusion

*Barbara L. Richardson
and
Jeana Wirtenberg*

It is the aim of this volume to address the special needs of investigators working on the sensitive questions of sex roles and social change. Our authors' suggestions are intended to help equip researchers with the most useful analytic strategies available. The recommendations reviewed and summarized here provide helpful methodological tools, along with precautions about putting them to use. With increased understanding and appreciation for the techniques of research—conceptualization, methods and design, sampling, measurement, analysis and inference—our findings should have more social utility and impact.

One common theme of this volume is the recognition of the role that values play in shaping all aspects of a research inquiry. Interpretation and judgment are viewed here as inherent in the scientific measurement process. The questions we choose to ask and the meanings we attach to our data are always influenced by our personal definitions of scientific adequacy. Most investigators working on questions of gender and social change know that the field emerged from controversies surrounding conflicts of value and attributions of biased assumptions and interpretations. For this reason, we are especially sensitive to recognizing and reconciling our personal, political and professional values in our own work.

Professional subjectivity, while inevitable, continues to raise questions about its appropriate place in scientific investigation. Most of our authors argue that we have a professional obligation to be conscious of our biases. This volume examines many of the systematic biases surrounding the study of sex roles and social change and proposes methods for reducing the problem.

We conclude, however, that simply being conscious of our own and others' values is not enough. Making our biases explicit is merely a first step. Questions of interpretation and judgment cannot be resolved by simply refining our instruments or statistical analyses. Rather, researchers are urged to expand their repertoire of approaches and draw on multiple methodologies in their investigations.

Parlee (1981) has suggested some useful guidelines in this regard. These include formulating research questions in such a way that they are directed toward an understanding of processes and mechanisms rather than an application of labels; studying value-laden topics from more than one perspective; bearing in mind the practical significance of our research findings for our subjects and the populations they represent. Such pragmatic suggestions take on renewed significance at a time when many of our research findings are introduced as court evidence, reinterpreted in the popular press, and used as guidelines for implementing social policy.

Throughout social science history, there has been a perennial fascination with the possibility of universal laws of behavior. Yet, because of the equally strong persistence of change in the human condition, such truths are generally illusory, and show little resilience across time, place, and historical moment. This is particularly true during historical periods such as the one we are now experiencing (circa 1983), which is characterized by rapid shifts of opinion, and strongly conflicting ideologies.

Within this volume, we start from the premise that scientific endeavor is always taking place within one among many possible paradigms. While some paradigms periodically hold more dominance in the field than others, no one seems likely to hold sway without significant competition. The authors of this volume reflect this view in their frequent references to the importance of examining issues from a variety of perspectives. Similarly, there is a need to be sensitive to the range of standards which should receive consideration when establishing validity for the generalizability of our measures. The criteria we choose to use as evidence of validity show changes with each generation of researchers. Our criteria for validity shift in response to the social definitions of objectivity and fairness current at a particular time. Likewise, relationships and correlations that held true in one population may show different patterns with the passage of time.

The problems of establishing reliability and validity are not unique to sex-role research or the study of social change. Many of the issues we have identified—the lack of adequate or consistent construct definition, lack of adequate reliability, and lack of demonstrated validity—are common to other areas of the social sciences. There is, however, a growing consciousness of the importance of addressing these issues if we are to advance our models by building on each other's data. Rather than calling for new instruments, most of our authors are asking instead for more detailed reporting of reliability and validity and descriptions of methods more useful for integrative reviews of the literature.

There is a recurrent tension between those who advocate building systematically on the work of the past and others, more eager to move further in substantially new theoretical and methodological directions. For example, one pragmatic argument for restraint in the construction of new scales, is that they are time-consuming, costly, and more critically, may actually slow the process of consolidating, analyzing, and interpeting the data already available. Some reemphasize the importance of rooting our analysis in theory which has been grounded in concepts already proven valid through repeated testing in a specific context. Others advocate broadening the range of settings, sometimes phrasing this suggestion as a call for "ecological validity" or "authenticity."

Among sex-role researchers, there is evidence of a growing interest in studies outside of the experimental laboratory, and movement towards a closer examination of real-life behavior in naturalistic settings. There is also evidence of a growing interest and awareness of interdisciplinary findings and approaches within the field. We believe that the widespread national interest in women's studies programs across the country has contributed to the facility with which students and scholars are learning to borrow more freely across the disciplines. Research within both traditional and emerging paradigms is showing the benefits of this new integration. Also contributing to this integration are ideas and constructs drawn from political movements outside of academia, like the women's movement, civil rights, and the peace movement. This kind of expansion is also a useful form of building upon the past. It clearly enriches us to add to our scientific vocabularies. But, we will also be challenging our best technical skills to make the analyses necessary to allow us to make meaningful comparisons across our many terms and methods. This volume is intended to help us address such a challenge.

CONTEXTUAL AND CONCEPTUAL ISSUES

We can clearly benefit from new theories and the measures derived from them. Gilligan's experience (Chapter 2) in expanding a model of moral development provides one such example. She sees an undue emphasis on linear ordering of development in our educational and social system. Gilligan's work demonstrates the value of exploring developmental issues in broader populations than those usually selected by experimental psychologists. In her own work, Gilligan (1977, 1982) moved away from research using young males, to studies of mature adult subjects from a range of backgrounds. Her approach highlights lines of development currently obscured by traditional research designs or inadequately measured by our available constructs. Her research style invites us to explore the place of values in our designs, measures, and theories.

Even as Gilligan questions the "invariant and universal" sequence of moral development, Richardson and Kaufman (Chapter 3) question the linear models of career trajectories used to describe the achieving person in American society. The most popular theories of achievement in both psychology and sociology neglect the more dynamic aspects of this lifelong process. The static designs and traditional instruments used in classical achievement research underestimate the influence of gender roles on variables key to predicting career success. In their review of the early achievement research, Richardson and Kaufman find that the emphasis on trait theory and personality models places too much importance on psychic and motivational factors for both men and women. At the same time, they also tend to neglect the institutional obstacles present in daily social encounters. Social structural forces such as occupational segregation and interpersonal patterns of sex discrimination need to be considered in any efforts to understand sex differences in achievement.

In both the areas of achievement and moral development, the most popular models rely on operational definitions, scales, and measures based on the patterns of men's lives. Single sex (i.e., male) studies continue to be the norm in the status attainment literature of sociology. Consequently, the methodological issues arising from the available research on female subjects have not been fully explored. The growth of special sections of sex role researchers within the professions has helped to provide a forum for examining the mounting empirical evidence on the importance of gender as a mediating variable.

There is also a continuing need to be aware of the problems of bias emerging from this renewed interest in sex differences. Jacklin's article (Chapter 6) addresses some of the common problems of interpretation and analysis she found in her review of the sex-difference literature in psychology. She observes that when both sexes are included in a sample there is a tendency to overemphasize the magnitude of the difference. In her own survey of the evidence, Jacklin found that the two sexes tend to fall in overlapping bell curves on most variables. But, they are often described in research reports in a way that ignores or minimizes the commonalities between them. There is also a frequent failure to fully acknowledge or account for within-sex variation. Nevertheless, the belief in dichotomized sex differences persists, even when empirical documentation is weak or decidedly mixed.

What repeatedly emerges from the analyses in this volume is a recognition of the methodological difficulties inherent in operationalizing any theoretical approach. Consequently, our authors emphasize the need for repeated scrutiny of our conscious and unconscious human biases in pursuit of scientific "truth." A vigorous feminist critique has emerged across the social sciences, in the wake of groundbreaking reexaminations of traditional literatures like that offered by Maccoby and Jacklin (1974) in *The Psychology of Sex Differences*. The trend continues to be toward a diversity of philosophical and methodological approaches. There also appears to be a shared recognition of the difficulties such diversity can hold for communication among even the most highly motivated researchers. Consequently, there is support for the clarification of terms and constructs popularly used in analyzing sex role and social change issues. These theoretical and methodological distinctions are critical checks on the accuracy of our shared understandings of the daily research enterprise. These sorts of discussions also make up the backbone of our many lively professional panels and internal scholarly debates in the journals.

RESEARCH METHODS

The authors, reviewing the current issues in research methodologies, emphasize the importance of choosing our techniques in relation to our questions. They remind us that it is we, rather than our measurement tools, who introduce values and bias into the process. For this reason, they generally advocate the use of multiple methodologies within the same research project. Despite the cost of time and complexity, triangulation or converging operations have considerable advantages over reliance on a single technique. We realize that there is more involved than a philosophical orientation toward experimentation and interest in developing and applying a range of new techniques. Clearly, the availability of the basic financial resources necessary for such multiple measurement approaches is critical. It is important for researchers to consider the cost-benefit value of these approaches from their own best scientific perspectives before weighing in the pragmatic costs as well.

Triangulated designs, combining quantitative and qualitative techniques, are becoming increasingly popular in sex role research. Wallston's paper (Chapter 4) provides the most cogent argument for analyzing information gathered from a variety of perspectives. For example, they give us a better chance of reducing systematic biases and uncovering subtle or unanticipated relationships. When using a single methodological approach, we might inadvertently neglect to measure the most crucial variable. Another appeal of the triangulation approach is that it may help blur the distinction between qualitative and quantitative analysis. Wallston argues that when using converging operations it is important to place equal value on the methods used, rather than allowing one to be "window dressing" for the other.

There has been a history of debate in the social sciences on the relative merits of qualitative and quantitative inquiry, or "hard" and "soft" science (Cook and Campbell 1979). Wallston observes that the calls for more qualitative research approaches during this past decade have come from many circles. However, she finds the dichotomy overdrawn and suggests that the distinctions between these two perspectives might better be conceptualized as two ends of a continuum.

Wallston emphasizes that no research approach is inherently biased. Rather, our methods seem most constructively viewed as tools for answering questions. By building on the unique advantages of various methods we are more likely to create something that is both new and especially sensitive to the subject of our inquiries. While ecological and ethnographic designs clearly value a subjective phenomenological approach, survey techniques can also assess experience from the perspective of the actor. Wallston encourages investigators to avoid restricting themselves to narrow guidelines specifying where and when to use a method. Rather, she encourages the sifting through of methods while refining the goals of the investigation.

This type of open consideration of the potentialities of a variety of approaches should allow for a better fit of the method to the questions. Most professionals need encouragement to resist the temptation to slip into research approaches they find familiar and comfortable because of habit and early professional training. These suggestions for improving methods and design are consistent with those made by our authors writing on sampling, measurement, and analysis. There is strong encouragement for researchers to expand their repertoire of methods and techniques.

Bagenstos and Millsap's helpful discussion (Chapter 5) of the use of evaluation research techniques in women's studies illustrates a methodological approach that should be of special interest to those interested in the development of social policy and change. Evaluation research helps to inform the direction of social change by identifying both the intended and unintended consequences of social programs. In direct contrast to research designs seeking to avoid dealing with subjective judgments, evaluation research specifically aims to build on the goals and aspirations of its subjects and target research audience. It is explicitly interested in assigning value and worth to various measurable outcomes. It capitalizes on the involvement and awareness of those with the greatest stake in the program under study. Evaluation research is process oriented and builds on multiple measures and perspectives. Within this general framework there are still a variety of approaches to program evaluation, each with a different purpose, audience, and methodology.

The challenge of working with an evaluation model is one which growing numbers of researchers are taking up. Program directors are interested because of its advantages for staff and its potential for addressing user needs—such as morale and productivity. The criteria used in measuring success and failure are generally dynamic and responsive to shifts in the particular social situation being evaluated. Beyond the field of women's studies, the range of application of evaluation techniques is enormous. Evaluation research is especially well suited to social change issues. Because evaluations ordinarily take place in an explicitly political context researchers need to anticipate the anxieties and pressures that will arise concerning the use to which findings will be put.

In contrast to the settings and questions of evaluation research, much of the sex-role literature surveyed by Carol Nagy Jacklin (Chapter 6) takes place in an experimental laboratory with young children or college students. Surveying the patterns of inquiry over several decades, Jacklin feels we have overly restricted our topics to studying a narrow range of differences between males and females. She argues that with fewer variables confounded with sex, gender will account for smaller percentages of variance. She observes that "paradoxically, the better the sex-related research, the less useful sex is as an explanatory variable." Thus, "in the best controlled sex-related research, sex may account for no variance at all." Jacklin hopes this will force researchers to stop focusing upon trying to explain the "trivially small amounts of variance accounted for by group differences, and start trying to explain the vast variance between individuals within the groups." We join her in feeling that there are many more interesting ways in which the life experiences of males and females can be studied.

Several modest changes in expectations for reporting and publishing results might help to reduce the undue emphasis on group differences. One is to provide some measure of the size and amount of variance represented by statistical differences within and between groups. This type of detailed information on statistical significance (or lack of it) should be provided for the entire sample. Jacklin also focuses our attention on the need for more regular reporting of nondifferences or what Rosenthal refers to as the "file drawer problem." She is describing the familiar research difficulty of retrieving negative results and sorting out nonreplications from true tests for group differences. These are both methodological and policy questions which can be addressed directly by editors and others in the field responsible for establishing standards for publications and presentations at meetings.

Many of the issues Jacklin identifies are essentially methodological errors which need to be addressed by researchers themselves in the design and analysis of their own work. These include:

- confusion of within-sex differences with between-sex differences
- confusion of sex of stimuli effects with sex of subject effects
- interaction of experimenter effects with sex of subject effects
- disregard of systematic differences in self-reports
- reliance on a number of variables confounded with sex which make comparisons of sex difficult

These sorts of basic methodological concerns should by now have entered into the standard illustrations of bias and error provided in graduate level statistics courses in addition to the more specialized reviews provided by women's studies courses.

SAMPLING AND MEASUREMENT

One persistent issue is the criteria used in the selection of the research groups being compared, i.e., the choice of sample. Once made, this decision strongly restricts the range of explanations we can bring to our findings. For it is our sample, which once drawn, restricts the boundaries of our inference. To cite one example, research on the impact of maternal employment carried out during the 1950s, made generalizations to all working women from samples for which there were few, if any, controls on socioeconomic status, age, or even husband's presence. Consequently, many of the reported correlates with employment were actually more closely related to family income or class. This competing explanation was not given serious consideration until later in the decade. Most of the concerns identified in this section are heavily influenced by the impact of cultural stereotypes guiding the researcher in the selection of topics and hypotheses. Through an expanded awareness of the complexity and variability of the groups being studied, experimenters should better appreciate the need for refining their measures, and generating alternative hypotheses.

Historically, women and minorities have been neglected in social science, most literally, by their absence from the research discussion entirely. A most immediate concern for women's studies scholars has been the recovery of long neglected history and the introduction of female subjects into traditional social change theories. This has called for new attention to the problems of sampling and ensuring representative coverage of a wider population of subjects than has ordinarily been the case. Before turning to questions of measurement, social change researchers need to be alert to procedures for ensuring a good sample. In the fourth section of our book our authors addressed many of these critical issues in sampling and measurement.

Charol Shakeshaft and David Gardner (in Chapter 7) provide a useful set of guidelines for selecting a sample. They advise weighing the project's theoretical goals in relation to basic practicality, measureability, and economy. Each factor calls for separate consideration in designing a sample. If there are special subgroups of interest, for instance, it is important to plan appropriate strategies for selecting a representative and sizable enough group, despite the problems there may be in locating them. The critical methodological challenge is to ensure the generalizability of the sample to the population in all of its parts.

Shakeshaft and Gardner provide a collection of practical methodological techniques for improving a sample's quality. In general, they advocate using the largest sample possible, while bearing in mind that size alone should never be the only consideration. Though there are many practical problems confronting researchers on limited budgets or with elusive subjects, the investment of time and money to ensure an adequate sample is the first basis for meeting most other criteria. While there will be many occasions in which small exploratory samples are useful for clinical and descriptive analysis, probability sampling still remains the accepted approach for generalization and inference in social science.

The commonly found weaknesses in sampling designs identified by Shakeshaft and Gardner all relate to problems that jeopardize the generalizability of the sample back to the original population. Researchers should be alert to the following: (1) noncoverage of the population by the sample; (2) the use of accidental or volunteer samples; (3) inappropriate sample size; and (4) nonresponse by a large portion of the sample. Poor sampling can jeopardize the credibility all investigators want to provide for their data.

Carole Beere's excellent technical review (Chapter 8) of the development and validation of "old" and "new" measures identifies some persistent problems in the area of measurement. She concentrates on two of the methodological concerns which have been examined throughout this volume: reliability and validity. Interrater reliability is of special concern for researchers attempting to establish whether differences are due to genuine differences between subjects or errors in the procedures used in coding. This issue was also raised in critiques of the stability of the fear-of-success construct across social groups.

The issues and problems in establishing measurement reliability and validity are not unique to sex role research. We share in common many of the problems of other fields—the lack of adequate or consistent construct definition, lack of adequate reliability, lack of demonstrated validity. There is a growing commitment to address these problems, as shown in the many special issues of journals and sessions at professional meetings, devoted to exploring methodological problems and developing research guidelines (Beere 1979; Gage 1975; Tikunoff and Ward 1977; Wolins 1982).

The chapters (8 and 9) by Beere and Vaughter identify some reasonable guidelines for constructing our instruments and measures. Given the high visibility and media attention associated with much contemporary research, our subjects are often quite aware of what the right answers are. Beere warns that the potential for "faking" and the impact of social desirability is a research hazard that should always be kept in mind.

Several authors urge the use of behavioral correlates as a criterion in developing a strongly predictive attitude measure. But, just as a single item is generally not used as a measure of attitude, a single behavioral observation should preferably not be used as a measure of behavior. Rather, multiple measures should be constructed and combined to form an index. Beere recommends that if this is not possible, then at the very least, the investigator should use repeated measures of the single act behavioral measures.

There is no doubt that today's researchers face difficulties in developing measures which can keep up with changing cultural attitudes and behaviors and remain subtle enough to get honest responses to complex, emotionally sensitive questions (Bentler and Speckart 1981). Popular magazines and newspapers even publish articles and offer self-help quizzes using many of our favorite measurement items. Thus, our measures, which may have been reliable at any one point in time, may quickly become outdated because of their content or their familiarity. When making comparisons across new populations, we need to be especially aware of the range of unmeasured factors which may be contributing to the differences we encounter in our data.

Visibility and dissemination increase communication among today's researchers, but also fan the problem of appropriate usage of our measurement tools. Unfortunately, borrowing measures for purposes other than those they were originally intended for is an all too common practice. Beere warns that it is a frequent, but inexcusable, error for a researcher to modify an existing measure and presume that the reliability and validity of the modified measure is equivalent to that of the original measure. Androgyny, for example, is a concept that has been measured by a potpourri of measures designed originally for purposes ranging from clinical diagnosis of mental health to correlates of job satisfaction. Even as our data analysis needs to reflect our original questions, so also must our measures be valid for our particular research purpose.

This may be the time for sex roles and social change researchers to concentrate more of their energies on refining available measures and instruments than they have previously. Several authors have noted the difficulties in drawing comparisons across studies in which our measures are insufficiently validated. Both in this section, and the next, there is a concern that in our rapidly developing field, our abilities to draw generalizations may be hampered by inattention to methodological considerations. Psychometric refinements will also be useful when they are tied back to theoretical models. For it is through the understanding of the concepts we are attempting to measure, and their hypothesized relations to each other, that we establish priorities in our measurement agenda. Reesa M. Vaughter writes "... we need theoretical models to specify which attitudes we want to measure, which behaviors we want to monitor or predict, and how these variables are mediated or linked together" (Chapter 9).

To move beyond bits of description to explanation and prediction it is helpful to have more broadly developed models of social behavior. Such a model is very useful in identifying the domains which may be the most difficult to measure because of their cultural sensitivity. There are always conscious and unconscious expressions of ideology underpinning the attitude-behavior relationship. Developers of psychometric scales need to be aware of changes in the social climate shaping the validity and reliability of responses over time. In general, attitudes seem to be more sensitive to change than behaviors. For this reason, we join several other authors in encouraging the concurrent development of behavioral measures which circumvent or minimize many of the problems associated with attitude scales used alone. In studies of teaching and instruction, for instance, it is now recognized as methodologically sound to include behavioral observations along with attitudinal measures. There seems to be a convergence of opinion that diagnostic profiles of attitudes and behaviors may yield more accurate assessments and more definitive recommendations for social policy. We join the other authors in this volume in encouraging more creative uses of combined behavioral and attitudinal indicators to strengthen the validity and sensitivity of our measures.

There is a fundamental complementarity among the strategies recommended for each stage of the research process dealt with in this volume. They generally reemphasize the importance of examining the procedures and criteria we use in selecting our data analysis techniques and relating them back to their context and the fundamental research question. In the section on analysis and inference that follows, special attention is given to the importance of researchers documenting their own experiences in enough frank detail for others to learn from.

ANALYSIS AND INFERENCE

In the last section of our book, dealing with analysis and inference, our authors encourage us to accept the fact that research is generally complicated and messy at some stage of the analysis. After the data are collected, the researcher begins the first stage of description and statistical analysis. This stage rarely provides a clean or clear picture of what is happening in the data. Rosenthal (Chapter 10) argues that we ought to share our problems, with this aspect of research, more openly with each other. She writes that since "social researchers, like magicians, never publicly reveal all their secrets," and "editors impose severe space limitations," or authors commonly "publish their work in little dribbles to maximize the number of publications," we are deprived of the full discussion of the process that went into generating the final reported results.

Four strong recommendations emerge from Rosenthal's chapter. The first is to preplan the analysis stage. Second, consider a range of analysis strategies. Third, learn to use complex statistical techniques when they suit your research questions. Fourth, describe your procedures in sufficient detail for others to follow and evaluate. These fundamental guidelines should be useful to the field as well as to the individual researcher.

Rosenthal spells out the basic procedures for preparing data analysis plans. She reminds the investigator to design methods in response to the original questions posed. Other suggestions include: (1) developing research questions and data analysis plans concurrently and interactively; (2) exploring the data fully to learn its structure and its limitations before applying any multivariate statistical technique; (3) trying more than one statistical technique; and (4) working with secondary analyses to either reformulate hypotheses to fit existing indicators or develop new indicators from existing data and supplement with new data.

Often, the most valuable insights a researcher can share are the surprises and unanticipated problems encountered in the analysis stage. This sort of information, along with basic documentation of procedures, is critical material for researchers building on each other's work in an area. This need is well described in Jackson's guidelines (Chapter 11) for synthesizing knowledge through integrative reviews. He emphasizes the importance of systematically exploring the reasons for differences in results as well as the consistent patterns. Speculating on why systematic analyses of the correlates of varying findings are not done more often, he wryly suggests that it may be "because the reviewers find so many differences among studies that they despair of being able to find systematic relations..." Another reason may be simple confusion in the methodologies used to generate the results being compared.

Integrative reviews are an especially popular format for presenting results in our field. Despite their popularity, few guidelines exist for formulating and presenting such syntheses. Jackson's article usefully lays out such a groundwork and conceptualizes the basic tasks involved in this approach: (1) selecting the questions or hypotheses for the review; (2) sampling the research studies that are to be reviewed; (3) representing the characteristics of the studies and their findings; (4) analyzing the findings; (5) interpreting the results; and (6) reporting the review. Each step of this process calls for a systematic consideration by the researcher of the possible biases being introduced. Jackson emphasizes that an especially important task for the author of such an overview is the identification of critical issues for future research.

Overreliance on secondary sources is one issue of particular concern to several authors, and one that is also relevant to social change research. There is often a temptation to accept the summary observations of earlier authors reviewing previous research. Particularly in a field like sex roles, in which there is a wide range of opinion, changing measurement, assumptions and indicators, it is important to go back to the original sources. As has been documented by several authors, stereotypical assumptions and values concerning masculinity and femininity can easily influence interpretations of researchers' data and bias the outcomes reported in published results.

In addition to going back to original sources, Patricia Campbell (Chapter 12) stresses the hazards of simply overlooking literature related to whole sets of variables because they seem irrelevant to the topic. The use of socioeconomic status, for instance, as an independent variable may have a different pattern of predictive validity for males and females depending on the issue being studied. The findings for different age or ethnic groups may be important for developing a sampling strategy. If a search of the literature neglects studies done with class as the independent variable, a critical hypothesis may be lost. Such sources of bias can be potential sources of invalidity in an otherwise well-planned research design and analysis plan. Overreliance on early work in a field can limit perspectives on appropriate topics for research. This appears to be less of a problem for sex-role researchers than in many other areas of the social sciences because of their generally critical interpretation of much of the preceding literature.

Campbell's comprehensive review of the impact of societal biases on research methods includes a detailed review of several other hazards of relying uncritically on secondary sources. When data are reported selectively, they tend to exaggerate sex differences rather than similarities. This pattern reinforces the same tendency observed in the construction of our designs and measures as well. Another area that is a concern with secondary sources is the inaccurate attribution of causality. Campbell illustrates this point with a discussion of race and sex—variables which cannot be manipulated or randomly assigned to subjects. They may be related to a dependent variable but cannot be treated as an independent variable causing something to change. Other related attributes may instead be accounting for observed differences. Differences in children's play may be caused by boys' and girls' attire, language, stereotypes of the children of each other or bias on the part of the observer. Sex and race may be associated with clearly defined patterns but they should not be used as explanations of cause. It is often instructive to examine the findings of cited studies for inappropriate types of inferences.

Robert Boruch (Chapter 13) further specifies the kinds of information we need for advancing beyond the results of simple hypothesis testing toward a better understanding of the causal relationships operating in our data. He argues that structural models are a fine vehicle for orderly examination of small sets of causal arrangements. They are useful for examining the fit between theory, measurement, and data. The approach encourages researchers to be explicit in laying out the problem and developing verifiable characterizations of the model and data being considered. The technique requires explicit statements about causal influences among variables and generally involves large samples and careful testing (where possible) of competing models. In exchange, structural models permit the researcher to formally test and make probabilistic statements about how well a system of causal models fits the data, tests competing systems of models, and deals with unobservable variables and measurement error.

Research approaches like structural modeling hold promise for the sex roles field at a time in which there is a need for greater clarity in the dialogue involving growing numbers of researchers. Because the phenomenon under study is itself dynamic, the many discrepancies in our findings may be a result of genuine change as well as measurement error. Variability across generations may be due to shifting attitudes as well as revised instruments.

Because of the increasing political, conceptual, and methodological challenges to our inferences and conclusions in the area of sex roles and social change, it is critical to use the best tools available for reducing uncertainty about where we have been, where we are now, and what the possibilities are for shaping a better future.

REFERENCES

Bart, P. Psychotherapy, sexism, and social control: A review of *Women and Madness*. In *Society,* 1973.

Beere, C. *Women and women's issues.* New York: Jossey-Bass, 1979.

Bentler, P.M., and C. Speckart. Attitudes "cause" behavior: A structural analysis. *Journal of Personality and Social Psychology* 40 (1981): 226–38.

Bronfenbrenner, U. Toward an experimental ecology of human development. *American Psychologist* 32 (1977): 513–31.

Campbell, D.T. Recommendations for APA test standards regarding construct, trait, or discriminant validity. *American Psychologist* 15 (1960): 546–53.

Cook, T.D., and D.T. Campbell. *Quasi-experimentation: Design and analysis issues for field settings.* Chicago: Rand McNally, 1979.

Gage, N.L. (ed.). *Research methodology.* National Conference on Studies on Teaching. Washington, D.C.: U.S. Department of Health, Education, and Welfare, 1975.

Gilligan, C. Woman's place in man's life cycle. *Harvard Education Review* 49(4) (1977):431–46.

Maccoby, E., and C. Jacklin. *The psychology of sex differences.* Stanford: Stanford University Press, 1974.

Parlee, M. *Issues of construct validity in sex roles and social change.* (NIE commissioned paper under contract NIE-P-81-0077.) Washington, D.C.: National Institute of Education, 1981.

Tikunoff, J., and B. Ward (eds.). Exploring qualitative and quantitative research methodologies in education. *Anthropology and Education* 7(2)(1977).

Wolins, L. *Research methods in the social and behavioral sciences.* Ames: Iowa State University Press, 1982.

Index

Ability 169–71
Accidental sampling 104–5, 107–8
Achievement: attribution 37–39; correlation with ability, aspirations, and expectations 169–71; expectancy-value model for 39, 44; family and work variables and 236–37; and motivation 34–35; reconceptualization of 7–8, 254; research on 33–48, 206–8, 232–33
Adjective Check List 117n
Affirmative action programs 148
Aggression in children, television and 234–36
American Educational Research Association 209
American Psychological Association 39, 209
American Sociological Association 209
The Analysis of Cross-Classified Categorical Data 165
Analysis of Nominal Data 166
Analysis of sex role and social changes 12–14, 151–248, 261–64
Analyzing Multivariate Data 165
Analyzing Social Data 156
Androgyny: definitions of 121, 126; future study of 126–27; as measured in sex role scales 118–21, 125
Anorexics 57
Applied Multivariate Analysis and Experimental Design 158, 165
Archival research 59, 63, 67
Area sampling 107
Aspirations 169–71
Assertiveness and women's studies programs 87–88

Assertiveness-training 57
Attitude Interest Analysis Test 116
Attitude scales 44
Attitudes: and behaviors 11, 139–48, 261; theoretical considerations about 145–48
Attitudes Toward Women Scale (AWS) 140, 143, 144, 145
Attitudinal measures 139–48
Attribution theory 37–39

Bagenstos, Naida Tushnet 9, 77
Bayesian statistics 82
Beere, Carole 10, 113, 259
Behavior settings 64
Behavioral measures: appropriateness of 11–12; and attitudes 139–48; and sex role scales 125; simulated 131
Behavioral validity 144–45
Behaviors: and attitudes 11, 139–48, 261; theoretical considerations about 145–48
Bem Sex Role Inventory (BSRI): criticisms of 120–25; described 117–27; for gender identity measurement 140–41, 145; scoring of 119–20; short form of 118, 123, 124
Bias: and achievement 8, 41; and conclusions 7, 13, 208–9; defined 13, 197; in developmental theory 27–31; in ethnography 60; impact of on research methods, 197–209; and measurement 13, 206–8; nonresponse 109–11; and "objective" research 197–98; in observational research 13, 62; toward positive findings 93–95, 199; and research design 201–3;

266 • SEX ROLE RESEARCH

and sampling 203-6, 242; sexual 199-201, 206; and topic selection 13, 198-201; in true experiments 55; and validity 201-2, 263
Bipolar nature of the sexes 117, 122
Bonhoeffer, D. 31
Boruch, Robert 12-13, 215, 263
Bridgman, Percy 5

Campbell, Patricia 12-13, 197, 263
Canonical correlation analysis 161-63
Case study designs 57, 109, 158
Category selection 61, 63, 66
Causal models: applications of 224-27; assumptions of 161-63; defined 13-14, 216-17; examples of 224-27; importance of 215-44; and other approaches 239-43; problems with 228-33; purpose of 13-14, 216-17, 243-44; role of theory in 221-22, 228-29, 236-37, 243, 263; and statistical analysis 186, 217-23
Causality in sex role research analysis 12-14
Ceiling and floor effects 231
Choice as measurement issue 42-43
Clinical interventions, studies of 57
Clinical observations and structural models 216
Cluster sampling 103-5
Coding reliability 187, 193
Committee on the Status of Women in Sociology 201, 209
Complex data analysis 12, 153-72, 260
Connection versus separation in development theory 28-31
Construct validity: and achievement research 38; defined 115; in research design 52; and self-reports 38; and sex difference research 38; in sex role research 132, 259
Consultants 78-79, 82, 89
Content analysis 63
Content validity 114-15, 129
Contextual and conceptual issues in sex role research 7-8, 12, 15-48, 131, 153, 253-55
Control groups 54-56, 85-86, 185
Correlational studies 57-58, 67
Covariance analysis 238, 240-42
Criterion-related validity 115, 132
Cross-lagged panel correlation 234-36
Cultural stereotyping and achievement research 37

Data analysis: complex 12, 153-72, 260; for ethnology 60; and researcher bias 13; and sampling techniques 62; and theory 166-72
Data analysis plan 12, 154-58, 262
Data base 93, 97-98
Data transformations 155-56
Decision-theoretic approach 82, 89
Demographic trends and sex role change 3
Development concepts 17-31, 253 (*See also* Moral development)
Difference (*See* Sex differences)
Difference method of scoring 119-20
Dualistic nature of the sexes 117, 122
Duncan Socioeconomic Index (SEI) 157

Ecological psychology 64
Ecological research 63-64, 66, 256
Ecological validity 253
Educational Resources Center (ERIC) 86
Egalitarian attitudes 142-45
Einstein's Space and Van Gogh's Sky: Physical Reality and Beyond 5
Equivalence of measures 114
Erikson, E. 22, 31, 206
Estimating procedures (sampling) 110
Ethnographic research 58-60, 66, 256
Evaluation: critique of in women's studies 86-88; defined 77-78; determining technical adequacy of 90; development of 78-80; mystique of 78-80; perceived as a threat 79-80; reporting results of 89-90; research designs 85-86; types of 81-86; use of consultants

in 78–79, 82, 89; uses of in women's studies 80–81, 256–57
Evaluation research: designs 85–86; reporting results of 89–90; use of consultants in 78–79, 82, 89; in women's studies 9, 77–90, 256–57
Expectancy-value model of achievement 39, 44
Expectations 169–71
Experimental design in evaluation of women's studies 86
"Experimenter effects" 55, 93, 97, 257
Experiments (See True experiments and Quasi-experiments)
External validity: in integrated reviews 183; in research design 52–53, 64

Face validity 115, 132
Factor analysis: of sex role scales 122, 124; and statistical analysis 161–63, 243
Fakeability: and meta-analysis 185; of sex stereotype measures 130–32, 259; of sex role scales 124–25
Fear of success: construct 39–40, 259; literature on 8; study of 4, 34, 97, 133
Feinberg, Stephen 165
Female achievement (See also Achievement): research into 33–44; and status attainment 41–44
Female development 7, 17–31 (See also Moral development and Moral judgment)
Femininity: future study of 126–27; measurement of 116–27; nature of 117, 121–22, 126, 140–41
Feminism: defined 84; and expression of sexist attitudes 147; and methodology 52–53; and social science research 33–34, 40; and women's studies 87–88
Feminist attitudes 142–45
Feminist scholarship 9, 40, 157
Feminists and evaluations of women's studies 84–85

Field/laboratory distinction 52, 55
"File drawer problem" 95
Freud, Sigmund 18, 19
F-tests 155, 160, 185

Gallup polls, sampling problems 107, 205–6
Gardner, David 10, 103, 258
Gender identity: measurement 139–48; and sex biased behavior 11, 141–42; and sex typed behavior 11, 141
Gender roles as intervening variables 39, 42
General linear model 161–65
Generalizability of sample 103–11, 159, 258
Gilligan, Carol 7, 17, 254
Glass, Gene 175, 185–88, 193
Goal-free evaluation 82–83
Gough Femininity Scale 116, 122
Great Society 80
Green, Paul 165
Guttentag, Marcia 82, 89

Head Start 80, 227, 238
Hierarchies versus networks 26–31
Heise, David 165
Historical research 63, 67
History as threat to validity 55–58, 183
Human development, concepts of 17–31 (See also Moral development)
Hunter, Jack 193
Hypothetical constructs 6

Identity and self-esteem 35–36
Impact objectives 84
Individual differences versus sex differences 93, 98, 257
Inferences: problems with 37–39; from restricted samples 6; in sex role research 12–14, 151–248, 261–64
Instrumentation 57, 58
Integrative reviews: data collection for 176; defined 13, 173; difficulties in doing 173–74; and interpretation

188–89, 194; methodological problems with 179–80, 182, 187; and primary studies 180–88, 193–94; and question selection 176–78, 191; reasons for 13, 173–74, 262; reporting of 189–90, 194–95; and sampling 178–80, 191–93; tasks of 176–95, 262; validity of 181–83, 187
Internal analysis 226–27
Internal consistency (homogeneity) of measures 114, 118–19, 122, 131
Internal validity 52–58, 183, 185, 188
Internships in women's studies programs 87
Interpretation of research 7–8
Interrater reliability of measures 114, 259
Interviews 25, 59, 62–63, 67
IQ and sex differences 98, 207
It Scale for Children 127–28

Jacklin, Carol Nagy 9–10, 93, 257
Jackson, Gregg 12–13, 173

Kaufman, Debra 7–8, 33, 254
Kerlinger, Fred 165
King, Martin Luther 30–31
Kohlberg, L. 19–26, 30–31

Ladner, Joyce 36–37, 39
Leshan, Lawrence 5
Levinson, D. 29, 206
Log linear analysis 164–65, 168
Log odds analysis 161, 164
Longitudinal studies 57–58, 67, 109

Mail surveys 109–10
Mann-Whitney U 185
Margenau, Henry 5
Masculinity: future study of 126–27; measurement of 116–27; nature of 117, 121–22, 126, 140–42
Mathematics achievement and anxiety 217–19
Maturation: assessment of 56–57; as threat to validity 55–58, 183

Maturity 17–31 (*See also* Moral development and Moral judgment)
Measurement: and researcher bias 13, 206–8; of sex role attitudes/behaviors 11; of sex roles and social change 10–13, 101–50, 258–61; theory 224–26
Measures: assumptions of gender identity 117; problems within a changing society 113–33; scoring issues 119–20
Median split method of scoring 119–20
Meta-analysis 175, 185–88
Methodological issues: in attitude/behavior research 11, 139–48; in evaluation of women's studies 78, 85, 90; in female achievement studies 33–44, 254; in sex related differences 93–98, 257–58; in sex role research 9
Methodology, advances in 5, 33–34
Michigan's Panel Study of Income Dynamics 225
Microethnography 59
Millsap, Mary Ann 9, 77
MMPI 116
Moral development: measurement of 24–27; research on 19–24; sex differences in 19–31; theories of 19–20
Moral judgment: and self-descriptions 27–29; research on 19–24
Morality, concept of 18–19
Motivation and achievement 34–35
Multiple Classification Analysis (MCA) 168–69
Multiple correlation 159
Multiple methods/perspective, integration of 6, 60, 64, 252, 256
Multiple-partial correlation 160–61
Multiple Regression in Behavioral Research 165
Multivariate analysis of covariance 159–60
Multivariate contingency-table analysis 164
Multivariate statistical techniques of sex

roles and social change 154–55, 158–60, 165

Namboodiri, N. 165
National Fertility Survey 157
National Institute of Education 11
National Longitudinal Surveys of Labor Market Experience 158
National Science Foundation's Women in Science Program 83
Naturalistic observation 64
Need-achievement 34–35, 39–40
Networks versus hierarchies 26–31
Noncoverage of population by the sample 105–7
Nonequivalent control groups 55–56
Nonindependence 232–33
Nonprobability sampling 104
Nonrandomized experiments 227
Nonresponse bias 63, 104, 106, 109–11

Objectives: and research designs 85; types of 84; use in evaluation research 80–85, 87, 88, 90
Objectives-based evaluation 83–86
Observational surveys 227
Observational techniques 61–62, 67, 109
Ordinary least squares regression 239–40

Participant observation 59
Path analysis 161, 163–64, 170, 234–36
Personal Attributes Questionnaire (PAQ): criticisms of 120–25; described 117–27; for gender identity measurement 140; scoring of 119–20; short form of 118
Piaget, J. 19, 29, 165
Platt, Marjorie 4
Political issues in evaluation of women's studies 78, 88–90
Politically motivated research 5, 9
Politz-Simmons weighing method (sampling) 110
Post-only design 85
Pretests 55–57, 241
Predictive validity 44

Pre-post design 85
Posttests 55–57, 241
PRF ANDRO: criticisms of 120–25; described 117–27; scoring of 119–20
Primary sources: in integrative reviews 178, 180–88, 193–94, 262–63; methodological problems of 179–80, 182, 187
Probability sampling 103–5, 259
Proceedings of the National Bureau of Economic Research 242
Process objectives 84
Professional judgment as mode of evaluation 81–82, 88
Project WELD 87, 90
Projective measures 44
Prospective studies (*See* Longitudinal studies)
Provus's discrepancy evaluation 82
Psychology, changing methodological approaches in 33–34, 44, 254
The Psychology of Sex Differences 255
Public Use Samples 158

Qualitative measures: and feminist scholarship 9; versus quantitative 6, 65, 67, 255–56
Qualitative research 58–60, 65, 67
Quality of Employment Surveys 158
Quantitative analysis 64–65, 67
Quantitative measures versus qualitative 6, 65, 67, 255–56
Quasi-experiments: and causal analysis 241, 244; defined 55, 57, 66; in evaluation of women's studies 86, 90; and meta-analysis 183, 186; and sex differences 56–57, 66; types of 55–57
Questionnaire (*See* Interview)
Q-sort 66

Racism and sexism 36–37, 133, 209
Random assignment 54, 66, 241
Random sampling 103–5
Randomized field experiments 226–27, 242–43

Rawls, John 31
Reactivity 60, 62
Reduction strategies 60
Regression analysis: and causal analysis 232–33; and multivariate statistical analysis 159–60, 163; of sex role scales 120
Relationships, construction of and morality 18–19
Reliability (*See also* individual types of reliability): in category selection 61; changes in 232, 252–53, 261; in gender related studies 113–33, 259; in historical research 63; importance of 113; types of 114
Replacement procedures (sampling) 110–11
Replicability 60, 159
Representative design 64
Research assumptions and interpretations 7
Research designs: and bias 201–3; comparisons of 60–61; dichotomies in 65–66; and multiple views 34, 38–39; and objectives 85, 90; and research questions 64, 255; and research techniques 52, 61, 64; and statistical analysis 52; types of 54–61
Research methods: impact of societal bias on 197–209; overview of 51–68; in sex role research 8–9, 49–100, 255–58
Research questions: and research techniques 64, 255; and statistical analysis 153–54, 158
Research techniques: and research designs 52, 61, 64; and research questions 64, 255; types of 61–64
Researcher values: influence on other elements 8, 13; recognition of 6, 9, 13, 251–52, 254
Reynolds, H.T. 166
Richardson, Barbara 3, 7–8, 33, 251, 254, 267–68
Rosenthal, Evelyn 12–13, 153, 261–62

Sample designs 103–5
Sample selection 105
Sample size 54, 93–94, 108–9, 231
Sampling: and bias 203–6; in integrative reviews 178–80, 191–93; issues and problems in 103–11; representative, and validity 44; and researcher bias 13; in sex role research 10–12, 101–50, 258–61; strategies 4, 62, 258–59
Schmidt, Frank 193
Scholastic Achievement Test 169
Scholastic Aptitude Test 206, 208
Seasons of a Man's Life 206
Secondary analysis: and data analysis 155–56, 158; for integrative reviews 175; in locating specialized populations 107; utility of 4–5
Self-confidence and women's studies programs 87–88
Self-description and moral judgments 27–29
Self-esteem: and achievement 34, 37, 142–43; and identity 35–37; and sex roles 11
Self-report measures: reliability and validity of 38, 44, 63; in sex differences research 93, 97, 257
Semantic differential scale 129
Separation versus connection in development theory 28–31
Sex bias in research 199–201 (*See also* Bias)
Sex-biased behaviors: and attitudes toward social roles of women and men 11, 143–45; defined 140
Sex differences: in children 94, 96; concept of 9–10, 93–94; confusion of within and between 93, 95–96, 254, 257; evidence of in psychological research 18–19; genetic causes 93, 96–97; versus individual differences 93, 98, 257; in intellectual performance 94, 96, 98, 107–8, 202, 254; methodological issues in 93–98,

202–3, 206–8, 257–58; and moral development 19–31; and sex similarities 95, 199, 262
Sex role changes and demographic changes 3
Sex role research: and racial prejudice studies 133; and statistical analysis 153–72
Sex role scales: adult 10–11, 115–27; children's 127–28; criticisms of 120–25; future use of 126–27; newer 117–28; older 116–17; and other measures 125, 133; scoring 119–20; and terminology 127
Sex Role Stereotype Questionnaire 129
Sex roles, measurement of 115–28
Sex roles and social change: analysis of and inferences about 151–248, 261–64; contextual and conceptual issues in the study of 7–8, 15–48, 253–55; in the 1970s 3–6; research methods in the study of 49–100, 255–58; sampling and measurement in the study of 101–50, 258–61; statistical analysis in 153–72
Sex similarities 95, 199, 263
Sex stereotypes: degree of by grade level 166–67; measurement of 128–33; in measures 122–23, 127, 130; and sexism 143
Sex-typed behaviors: and attitudes toward social roles of women and men 11, 142–43; defined 140; and social policy change 147–48
Sex typing 119–20, 128–29
Sexism: definition of 147; intellectual 157; measures of 140; model for 146–47; and racism 36–37, 133, 209
Sexist behavior/attitudes (*See* sex-biased behavior)
Shakeshaft, Charol 10, 103, 258
Significance versus size 93–94, 108–9
Single sex samples 204–5, 254
Single subject designs 57 (*See also* Case studies)

Situational variables 132–33
Social changes (*See* Sex roles and social change)
Social desirability 130–32, 147, 259
Social science research on women 33–34
Societal bias (*See* Bias)
Sociological Methodology 165
Sociology, changing methodological approaches in 33–34, 41–44, 254
Sociopolitical context and theory 8
Sourcebook of Measures of Women's Educational Equity 133
Spearman's rank-order correlation 185
Specialized populations 107
Stability of measures 114, 131
Statistical analysis: and causal relations 186; interdependence of with research questions 153–54, 158; of large number of variables 158–66; and research design 52; and sample size 109; in sex roles and social change 153–72, 261–62
Statistical models 217–23, 239–43
Statistical power 231
Statistical validity 52
Status attainment and female achievement 41–44
Stereotypes (sexual); in achievement research 35–38, 44; and racial stereotypes 36–37; and social policy change 147–48; types of 140
Stewart, Abigail 4
Stimuli versus subject effects 93, 97, 257
Stratified sampling 103–5
Strong Vocational Interest 43
Structural equations/models: applications of 224–27; defined 13–14, 216–17; examples of 217–21; importance of 215–44; problems with 228–33; purpose of 13–14, 216–19, 243–44
Studying Women in a Changing World 4
Substitution procedures (sampling) 110
Survey (*See* Interview)
Systematic sampling 103–5

Telephone surveys 106–7
Television and aggression in children 234–36
Terman Genius Study 98, 108
Test-retest reliability 118, 119, 241
Thematic Apperception Test (TAT) 34–35, 97
theoretical models, need for 145–48
Theory: and causal models 221–22, 228–29, 236–37, 243, 263; construction and category selection 61; and data analysis 166–72; and research techniques 238, 253
Time-series designs 57
Timing as a measurement issue 42–43
Topic selection and researcher bias 13, 198–201, 258
Trait theory 34
Triangulation 65, 67, 255
True experiments: defined 54–55, 66; and meta-analysis 183, 186; and validity 54
True score theory 224–25, 238
t score 119, 185

Unintended consequences 83, 90
Univariate tests 184
University of Massachusetts 83

Vaillant, G. 29
Validity (*See also* individual types of validity): and bias 201–2; in category selection 61; changes in 232, 252–53, 261; in gender-related studies 113–33, 259; in historical research 63; importance of 113; of integrated reviews 181–83, 187; types of 114–15
Value issues in evaluation of women's studies 78, 88–90
Value-laden research 5, 198
Value recognition in researchers 6, 9, 13, 251–52, 254
Vaughter, Reesa 11, 139, 259–60
Vocational interest inventories and sexual bias 207–8
Volunteer samples 107–8

Wallston, Barbara 8–9, 51
Weigel, Russell 11–12
Wirtenberg, Jeana 3, 251, 267
Women's liberation, attitudes about 142, 144
Women's studies: definition of 77; effects of on research 253; evaluation issues in 77–90; and feminism/feminists 84–85, 87–88; and personal skills development 87–88
Women's Studies: Evaluation Handbook 86
Women and Women's Issues: A Handbook of Tests and Measures 133

Zill, Lloyd 92

About the Editors

BARBARA L. RICHARDSON is Research Associate at the National Institute of Education where she monitors and sponsors research in the areas of teaching and instruction, staff development, social development, and educational equity. Her interest in methods of studying social change, and their place in feminist scholarship, reflects an ongoing involvement with women's studies research in the social sciences.

Dr. Richardson has a Bachelor of Arts *(cum laude)* from Harvard University in English history and literature and a Master of Arts degree from Columbia University in psychology and higher education. She completed her Ph.D. in social psychology at Cornell University and went on to serve on the faculty there in the Department of Human Development and Family Studies. She has directed a range of international research projects concerning the impact of maternal employment on family interaction in locales including New Zealand, Turkey, England, and rural Appalachia. Since the 1960s she has assisted in the founding and development of women's studies programs and professional caucuses.

Dr. Richardson is recognized for her leadership efforts on behalf of older women and publishes in the area of sex equity and education. Most recently she coauthored with Debra Kaufman, *Achievement and Women: Challenging the Assumptions* (The Free Press, 1982), an interdisciplinary synthesis and critique of the achievement literature.

JEANA WIRTENBERG is Research Associate at the National Institute of Education, where she is responsible for carrying out a broad range of management responsibilities in the largest research program of the U.S. Department of Education. The chapters in this book were developed from conference papers and commissioned papers, sponsored by the Social Processes/Women's Research Team, which Dr. Wirtenberg headed from 1979 through 1982. This team formulated, conducted, and evaluated research activities related to processes of socialization and social interaction affecting the educational and life achievement of women and girls. Before joining NIE, Dr. Wirtenberg was a social science analyst at the U.S. Commission on Civil Rights, where she conducted studies on the portrayal of minorities and females in textbooks, and developed a resource guide to fair textbooks.

Dr. Wirtenberg has a Ph.D. from U.C.L.A. in developmental psychology, with extensive background in social psychology and measurement and statistics. Her dissertation, "Expanding Girls' Occupational Potential," won first prize in the Social Issues Dissertation Award competition from the Society for the Psychological Study of Social Issues. She received her Bachelor of Science degree in mathematics from The City University of New York, graduating *magna cum laude* and Phi Beta Kappa. She has published and presented extensively in the fields of psychology of women, sex equity in education, and alternative educational futures. Most recently, she was coeditor with Sandra Tangri of "Women and the Future," a special issue of the *Psychology of Women Quarterly* (Fall 1981).